Baking Second Chances

"In *Baking Second Chances*, Ann Haut continues her husband's family memoir which began with *Listen to Your Bread*. The author's writing style brought back memories of stories told around my own family's table, and just like a good slice of sourdough rye smeared with butter, I was unable to put down this book. Entertaining and poignant, *Baking Second Chances* is an engaging and nostalgic delight that satisfies with each turn of the page."

—MARTIN J. BRUNNER, professor of culinary and pastry arts, Sandhills Community College

"*Baking Second Chances* throws open a welcoming door and invites you into the heart of a family by way of their journey from make-do lean-to bakeshop to the commercially successful Haut's Cookie Shoppe. Haut takes her cues from Icky's cookie creations, baking a narrative that is subtle, familial, and warm —a narrative in which hardship is overcome by grit and grace and a generous Christian faith provides sustenance throughout. A delicious read."

—CRYSTAL HARDIN, author of *Prophetic Preaching: The Hope or the Curse of the Church*

"In *Baking Second Chances*, Icky Haut struggles to grow from a small-town cookie baker into the owner of a major business. But for him, baking is more than a job or even a profession; it is a calling, a vocation. As a Lutheran pastor and theologian, I am grateful that the author has woven throughout the narrative a well-grounded understanding of vocation. And as a reader who craves good stories, I sure enjoyed Ann Haut's book. It's great entertainment with a serious core."

—WOLFGANG D. HERZ-LANE, Lord of Life Lutheran Church

"*Baking Second Chances* is a winsome, history-based story that transported me back to Olean, NY, where my mother Jean Bauer was involved with Icky's Cookies in its formative years. I was barely in elementary school at that time, so until reading this book, I was unaware of the extent of her contributions. What I do remember is slipping into the kitchen with the son of the bakery's owner to sample delicious sugar cookies as they cooled on tray racks. Thanks to author Ann Haut for filling in blank spots and stimulating warm memories of years gone by!"

—JOHN A. BAUER, pastor emeritus, St. Luke's Lutheran Church

Baking Second Chances

ANN HAUT

RESOURCE *Publications* • Eugene, Oregon

BAKING SECOND CHANCES

Copyright © 2024 Ann Haut. All rights reserved. Except for brief quotations in critical publications or reviews, no part of this book may be reproduced in any manner without prior written permission from the publisher. Write: Permissions, Wipf and Stock Publishers, 199 W. 8th Ave., Suite 3, Eugene, OR 97401.

Resource Publications
An Imprint of Wipf and Stock Publishers
199 W. 8th Ave., Suite 3
Eugene, OR 97401

www.wipfandstock.com

PAPERBACK ISBN: 979-8-3852-1987-2
HARDCOVER ISBN: 979-8-3852-1988-9
EBOOK ISBN: 979-8-3852-1989-6

05/06/24

New Revised Standard Version Bible, copyright 1989, Division of Christian Education of the National Council of the Churches of Christ in the United States of America. Used by permission. All rights reserved.

For Mark.
Thanks be to God for you.

Contents

	Acknowledgments	ix
	Prologue: The Secret	1
1	In the Still of the Night	3
2	Take My Life	9
3	Batter Up!	13
4	What Will People Think?	22
5	Setting Boundaries	29
6	Sharing Secrets	35
7	Superheroes	44
8	Getting a Grip	47
9	Unexpected Blessings	54
10	From How Many to How Much	60
11	One for the Money	69
12	Two for the Road	72
13	A Sweet Ride	78
14	Shifting Gears	84
15	Divine Inspiration	90
16	Caring for the Flock	98
17	Smoking	104
18	Getting Out of a Jam Jam	109
19	Digging In	117
20	Work Hard, Play Hard	122
21	The Icing on the Cake	125
22	Too Much Salt	129
23	The Devil in the Details	134
24	Just Making Conversation	143

25	Can't Read Your Mind	149
26	Out of Nowhere	154
27	Expert Opinions	162
28	On the Floor and Out the Door	167
29	Chemical Reactions	172
30	First Fruits	181
31	Raucous and Rowdy	186
32	Now the Heat's On	193
33	Biscuit and Cracker Baker	196
34	Breaking the Law	203
35	Moose Men or Cookie Men?	210
36	Stopgap	220
37	Getting Trashed	225
38	Fumes	229
39	From Every Direction at Once	233
40	Stoked	238
41	Nobody's Leaving and Nobody's Getting Fired	244
42	Getting Grilled	249
43	Hitting the Roof	259
44	Toasted	263
	Author's Note	269

Acknowledgments

Baking Second Chances is the story of how baker Edward A. ("Icky") Haut and his wife Millie started Haut's Cookie Shoppe in Olean, New York. The idea for the book originated with family memories, and is supported by newspaper articles, corporate newsletters, business correspondence, photographs, guestbooks, and even a tall stack of gift cards which accompanied bouquets from the bakery's grand opening celebration. All of these materials were stored in boxes by Mary Lou (Haut) Bingham, the founders' daughter, and a huge debt of gratitude is owed to her for safeguarding them over the last half century. She and her husband Bill also read and critiqued the manuscript, and offered suggestions to nuance the final version of the story.

Conducting research for this book was a labor of love—which is to say that as people who knew the Haut family responded to questions, I felt the love and respect that accompanied memories they shared. The now-grown children of The Rev. Frank and Jean Bauer—John A. Bauer, Mary Salgado, and Anne Blais—recalled details about their parents' lifelong friendship with Icky and Millie Haut. Bertie Heinz shared sweet recollections on how her husband John began his career at Haut's Cookie Shoppe, and later became a baked goods distributor for Icky's Cookies®. Sharon Godfrey talked about how her grandfather Frank Neiler not only ran the bakery's jam department; he also helped formulate recipes. And insights into how Sid Shane's legal expertise protected the business side of the bakery were provided by his son, attorney Mike Shane.

Authors Linda Braswell (*Quest for Respect*) of Southern Pines, North Carolina, and Gail Bellamy (*Cleveland Food Memories*) of Cleveland Heights, Ohio, read unpolished pages of an early draft. Each of them provided honest feedback, delivered with the sort of gentleness that builds trust. I treasure their friendship.

When a later version of the manuscript was ready for reading, I looked to long-time friend and writer Cathy Petryshyn of Columbus, Ohio, whose ability to see the big picture is always balanced by keen attention to detail. She also has a delightful sense of humor, and is a real pleasure to work with.

The Rev. Dr. Wolfgang Herz-Lane has always inspired us with the insights he brings to Reformation Sunday sermons, so I was especially grateful for his willingness to suggest German expressions that position the story in its cultural milieu. I look forward to building on the friendship that this work initiated.

Martin Brunner's lifetime of commercial baking experience gave me confidence that the pastry claims made in this story are accurate. I was amazed that he devoted so much personal energy into checking and double-checking the manuscript, even calling a chemist friend to confirm a section that gave him pause. A simple "thank you" doesn't say how grateful I am for his support.

While I was writing and editing *Baking Second Chances*, I enjoyed speaking to a number of book clubs whose members were reading *Listen to Your Bread*, the book which precedes this one, and tells how Icky Haut apprenticed as a bread baker in 1930s and '40s. Readers' reactions to that work helped me understand what people are interested in knowing about commercial baking. Special thanks is owed to members of the Pinehurst and Southern Pines Writers' Group, Constant Readers Book Club, Turning Leaves Book Club, Book Club West, Belle Meade Book Club, Women of Seven Lakes, and the Lamb of God Bookworms—and especially the people who generously arranged those engagements, among them, Irina Heisey, Jean Lawrence, Joan Matula, and Donna Glover.

I am also grateful to personal cheerleaders who keep in touch when I hole up in my office for too long, who send lovely notes as soon as Haut's Cookie Shoppe books roll off the printers, who recommend the book on the "Olean… Memories Back In Time" Facebook page, and who put "Read It!" post-a-notes on book covers in the community library: Michelle and Bernie Capron, Marlys Cartwright, Carla Cohen, Bob and Emma Connelly, Pam Cyr, Richard and Sue Dell'Acqua, Phil and Vicki Garber, Charles Millender and Pat Harwood, Sharon Payne, Beau and Layla Papania, Mark Ramseth, Joanne Scheuerman, Lisa Sheridan, Dan and Christel Shumate, David and Diana Smith, Sally Starr, Janet Stolle, David Sullivan, Gerry and Sharon Tryhane, and Angela Webb.

Thanks also is owed to Wipf and Stock Publishers' Managing Editor Matt Wimer for seeing merit in this story, and for his patience in guiding it through the publishing process; to Shannon Carter for cover design; to Savanah N. Landerholm for typesetting, and to Joe Delahanty for marketing expertise.

Biblical references are taken from NRSV Bibles, to whom thanks is owed for the use of their work. See http://nrsvbibles.org for more information about their contributions to the Christian conversation.

Researching the history of Haut's Cookie Shoppe began in 2014 when Mark Haut and I married. As we celebrate our tenth anniversary this year, I am delighted to say that stories about how this man grew up in a cookie bakery never get old. Thanks to you, Mark, for inviting me in to your family, for always answering my questions, and for your love. You are a blessing.

Prologue: The Secret

"We agreed we wouldn't tell anyone—not yet," Herta protested, her index finger pressed over her lips.

"—because you didn't want your Ma to know until it's all settled," Roy insisted. "But things have changed. Now your brother . . ."

"He'll do what he wants—just like always," she disagreed. Besides, she believed she'd stomached more than her share of their difficulty: being employed by a sibling, giving up their privacy to move in with her parents—not to mention sneaking around. Worst of all, she wasn't accustomed to failure, and failure was what she felt Roy and she brought back home with them.

Her husband would dispute that last one. He didn't think they'd had any choice but to abandon their bakeshop when they escaped. And where else could they go? Working in Icky's bakery was a godsend, and helping them save enough money to get their lives back on track. So, he'd argue, returning to Olean wasn't failure; it was dealing with life's ups and downs. Someday they'd turn it all around, and then . . .

"Let's wait to see what he does, hm?" Herta contested.

"Nope, nope, nope, this has gone too far to keep to ourselves now," Roy stared straight at her, hard.

She knew that look. He wasn't going to budge.

"Fine," she said with calm precision. "Tell him—but only him."

He left their tiny bedroom and tromped down the stairs, two treads at a time, before she could call him back. Then, nodding respectfully to his mother-in-law, he grabbed his jacket from a hook behind the back door, and went outside. A cold autumn wind had kicked up; its chill braced him for the reaction he expected from his brother-in-law.

Ma Haut watched Roy cross the lawn, enter the house next door, and head down the stairs. *The deed is done, then,* she thought to herself. *Icky's not going to like this.*

And neither did she.

1

In the Still of the Night

THE SACRED TRANQUILITY CLOAKING their slumber was pierced by a tiny metal hammer madly striking the alarm clock's twin bells. Icky's neck and shoulders immediately jolted upright as if shocked by an electrical current. He shot out a hand to silence the brutal banging beast, and the evil clock settled into a metronomic tick-tick-tick-tick: not a beating heart, but a countdown. Numbers encircling its expressionless face jeered: three-thirty.

His wife rose first and, rebuffing the alarm's rude offense, lifted herself from beneath their patchwork quilt. She despised being ripped from sleep before the ragged edge of darkness disappeared in the morning sky. But the time had come. Eyes shut, she tiptoed to the bathroom.

"You're next," she whispered when she returned from her shower.

He gave her a single no-nonsense nod, and stretched both arms over his head. I guess I asked for this, he admitted a minute later as he splashed cold water on his face. He threw on clothes from the day before, slipped down the hall, and quietly stepped from his wife's kitchen into the new make-do lean-to bakeshop they'd attached to the back of their Quonset hut home. The eight-by-thirty-foot addition provided just enough room to accommodate the larger equipment they needed to fulfill their first open-end purchase order. He hoped they wouldn't operate in temporary quarters for long—maybe a couple of years, or so. By then he hoped they'd be able to put up a more substantial building.

Millie measured grounds for their morning coffee and set out mugs while Icky preheated the new Blodgette deck oven, mixed the first batch of cookie dough, and moved it to the cutting station. The beaters whirred around the start of a second batch as he dashed back into the hut for a quick shower and a fresh pair of baker's whites. They slipped past one another in the doorway, and she gently mouthed, "Coffee in five."

"First batch on the table," he patted her arm affectionately. They both were grateful, so *very* grateful, for this work.

At exactly four o'clock, Icky's sister and her husband arrived, each of them blinking back the harsh bluish glare of fluorescent lights. Millie was already rolling dough, and they nodded silent greetings.

Roy checked to see that the oven was heating correctly: three hundred ninety degrees—the exact right temperature for large, soft, sugar cookies. Radiant heat would soon warm their workspace, so Herta tossed her sweater onto a hook behind the door, and took her place in production. Following Millie's lead, she sectioned off a hunk of dough and began rolling.

Work is buzzing ahead even without caffeine, Roy noted as he cracked fourteen eggs into a large pitcher that already contained two quarts of buttermilk and vanilla.

"Whose bright idea was it to start this bakery?" he feigned the role of a grumpy inquisitor as Icky returned with four heavy, white mugs, their large handles threaded through his fingers.

"Yours—and eventually, mine, too," he answered as he handed the first mug to his brother-in-law.

"Yep, yep, yep, guilty as charged," Roy admitted. Nearly two decades earlier when he was Icky's first supervisor, he predicted the guy was destined to run his own operation. Icky blew the idea off. He was happy enough just to have a job during the Great Depression, and had no intention of leaving—not then, not ever.

"I thought you'd pitch that clock through the window this morning," Herta looked at her husband as she took a moment to sip coffee.

"It deserves whatever it gets at this hour," Roy defended.

"Downright uncivilized," Icky concurred. "I wanted to do the same with ours."

Four o'clock was an unfortunate start time, but as they all knew, most bakers prefer first shift instead of sweating next to ovens in the afternoon heat. Besides, rising before dawn wasn't new to any of them. Both men worked at Bolles Bakery during the first half of their careers, which meant their wives were also familiar with bakery schedules. When Roy quit Bolles, Herta helped him run his own shop. Icky was out Bolles's door, too—although as it turned out, not of his own accord. Now the four of them were together again.

The bakeshop wasn't a major operation—and bread baking was out of the question; Icky would never steal business from his former employer. Cookie production, however, was an entirely different market and free for the taking. Or earning, Pa would correct him, and Icky was doing that.

"Looks like we've got orders for seven hundred twelve-counts," Roy glanced over the day's production sheet. Preparing a work schedule for a four-person operation might have seemed unnecessary to anyone else, but both men knew the importance of managing efficiencies.

"Right," Icky agreed as he moved the girls' first trays of cut dough toward the Blodgette. "That's twenty-eight batches—one every fifteen minutes."

"Yep, yep, yep," Roy noted. "Friday's orders are always bigger."

"Guys get paid today, so grocery carts get filled," Icky pulled on the oven's three wide doors until they yawned open. The hungry maws panted hot air into the room, begging to be fed.

"Stores want enough product for Saturday sales, too," he continued as he shoved in the trays, shut the doors, and set the timer: seven minutes. Millie heard the squeaking complaints of wooden porch steps next door as her father-in-law carried down his bicycle.

"I hear Pa leaving for work, so Ma is up," she said. "Time for me to check on the kids."

She slipped back into the Quonset hut to make sure thirteen-year-old Mary Lou was dressing for school. Mark, who was ten years younger, would need help tugging on his corduroy pants and tying his Buster Brown shoes before he dashed across the dewy lawn to spend the morning with his grandmother. Ma Haut appreciated a regular schedule, and would have the boy's rye bread and coffee drowning in canned milk ready when he pounded through the back door. Millie would have liked order in her days, too, but bakery demands meant her household no longer got the attention she felt it deserved.

"What's the chance you can make deliveries for the next week or so?" Icky asked Roy. "I'd like to increase orders from local accounts before expanding outside of town, and afternoon is the best time to catch store managers."

"I guess I could handle 'em, but I'd have to clean up before heading out," he said, and then paused. Settling his hands on his hips, he asked, "How much growth are you aiming for?"

"As much as possible," Icky answered. "I've been calculating potential output, and the Blodgette can bake five thousand packages per shift. Today we're doing only seven hundred, so the oven is working at 14 percent capacity."

"But seven hundred twelve-counts is the maximum productivity of your four-person crew," Roy pointed out. "*We* can't work any faster."

"Friday is the only day we're running at that pace," Icky countered. "I'm hoping to stretch sales on the other days."

"How do you figure that?"

"By increasing orders Monday through Thursday," Icky insisted—not that he thought they'd been slacking off.

"Don't forget: You gotta' figure for seven hours, not eight," Roy cautioned, returning to the mixer.

"I did," Icky reported, "with one hour at the end to cool, package, box, and load the last batches."

Roy nodded. They'd managed capacity and staffing at Bolles on a similar schedule.

"After Olean, where are you opening accounts?" He wouldn't argue with his brother-in-law, but he did think the guy was running hot—just like always. When Icky was at the top of his game at Bolles, he controlled an entire bakery floor: both product and people. Now he was building instincts for the market, too. He read trade reports on what housewives were buying, listened to his vendors, and urged grocery store managers to give his cookies regular shelf space.

"I'd like to start selling in Salamanca," Icky answered, aware that the burden of making deliveries usually fell on his own shoulders. Once in a while Roy worked a double shift and got behind the wheel—like the day the old oven went kaput and Icky needed to stay back to try to fix it. But that was an emergency, not a regular occurrence.

"Salamanca is a thirty-minute drive," Roy cracked two eggs at a time into the pitcher, "and round trip, that's an extra hour on the road."

"Yeah, but worth it if I open up more than one account." He lifted a hundred-pound sack of flour onto his shoulder, hauled it across the shop, set it next to the bench mixer, and tore it open with the practiced ease that came from years of line baking experience. "Anyway, if you're willing, I'm hoping you can make deliveries this afternoon, and maybe a couple of times next week. You can clean up while Millie finishes packaging, and then be out the door on time."

"Okay, but you're going to need additional production staff if you grow these accounts too much," Roy advised.

"I hear you," Icky confirmed.

"Should I pick up inventory on the way back? We got enough sugar for Monday, but that's it."

"Good idea," Icky thanked him. "That'll lighten the job next week when we get fresh eggs."

Millie returned as another batch of product was pulled from the oven, and noticed the aroma of pure vanilla filling the bakeshop; its calming scent always restored her spirit. She sectioned off a hunk of dough, flattened it with the palm of her hand, and began figuring the pace Herta and she needed to keep. Icky said seven hundred packages, so she multiplied seven by twelve in her head and added zeros: eighty-four hundred cookies.

She picked up the large steel rolling pin.

So divided by two, Herta and I each need to put out . . . roll, roll, roll . . . forty-two hundred cookies. She picked up her cookie cutter, . . . cut, cut, cut . . . divided by seven hours, that's six hundred an hour, . . . cut, cut, cut . . . which is about ten cookies per minute, though that doesn't include time to roll the dough. Also, . . . cut, cut, cut . . . we need to account for time lost when I have to dash into the Quonset hut to answer the phone.

She transferred cut cookies onto a baking sheet, moved it aside, set out a second tray, and removed the last hunk of dough from the bowl. . . . roll, roll, roll . . . And we sure don't want to lose orders, even though Herta gets stuck with doing all the cutting when I have to grab the phone. But I'm also stuck at the end of our shift with more cookies to package by myself, so everybody does more of something. I wish we'd thought to move the telephone line out here when we built this temporary bakeshop. . . . roll, roll, roll . . .

She picked up her cutter.

Thank goodness Herta can be depended on to scrub the mixer, bowls, and hand tools. . . . cut, cut, cut . . . While she's sanitizing, I'll package the last batches, box up each customer's product, and affix delivery labels. . . . cut, cut, cut . . . That shouldn't take more than an hour.

Her thoughts wandered to organizing housework.

Maybe I can slip into the hut to toss a load of laundry into the washer when the guys take a seven-minute break; they never stop longer than one run of product going through the oven.

But if I can do that, the whites will be washed by noon, and I can hang everything up on the clothesline as soon as the truck leaves.

She slid full trays to the table next to the oven so the men could switch baked cookies for raw batches when the timer rang. Then she hauled another thirty-inch bowl of dough to the cutting station, sectioned out a hunk, and picked up her rolling pin.

Since Roy is making deliveries, . . . roll, roll, roll . . . Icky might get home from sales calls in time for dinner with the kids for a change. Before we sit down, I'll bring in the last basket of laundry from the clothesline, and maybe grab a few minutes to iron everybody's clothes for church on Sunday. . . . roll, roll, roll . . .

She thought she had a workable plan for the day.

2

Take My Life

"Many of you probably have seen the new television program called *What's My Line?* hosted by John Charles Daly," began the Reverend Frank Bauer. Bauer's posture—shoulders back, chest out, stomach in, chin up, plus his dark well-groomed mustache and wavy hair parted neatly on the right side—suggested a military bearing. But his eyes were warm and generous, belying any assumption that his preaching might be rigid. Even so, a message that began with a TV program was unusual. Teenagers raised an eyebrow with a small amount of interest, while grandparents stiffened their necks.

Good, I've got their attention, he thought to himself as he prayed his message would reflect the Gospel.

"Daly's personal history is quite interesting," Pastor Bauer continued. "When he was eleven, his family left Johannesburg, South Africa, where his father was a geologist, and returned to Massachusetts. There, he eventually attended Boston College to study journalism, and in due time, became a White House correspondent for CBS. Perhaps you remember his voice; he was the newsman who told our nation that Japan attacked Pearl Harbor."

He saw small nods in the congregation. Everyone knew exactly where they were when they heard that chilling newscast. It probably still echoed in some of his members' ears, and likely became woven into the fabric of many of their families' stories.

"As a war correspondent in 1943, Daly reported on battles under General George Patton's command in Italy. When the war ended, his career shifted to hosting an educational program which is now called *You*

Were There with Walter Cronkite. This fall, Daly moved over to a new program called *What's My Line?* In case you haven't seen it, let me just say that four panelists ask yes-and-no questions as they try to identify a guest's occupation.

"Daly's gifts are many: listening, interpreting, reporting, educating, and most recently, entertaining. So, the question for each of us gathered here this morning is 'What's *your* line?'"

Icky's thoughts wandered as he suppressed a yawn. He'd seen Daly's show on Ma and Pa's television, and imagined yes/no questions that Arlene Francis, Bennet Cerf, Dorothy Kilgallen, and Steve Allen might ask: "Do you work a nine-to-five job?" "Does your work require physical strength?" "Do you make a product?" "Would any of us on this panel be likely to purchase that product?"

He silently inhaled through his nose to suppress a second yawn as he stretched back his shoulders, and forced himself to pay attention to the sermon.

"What I'm asking us to ponder is this: What does being 'called' look like in our daily lives?" Pastor Bauer continued.

"Our epistle today says that 'there are varieties of gifts'—that is, we each have different talents or skills, and that 'to each is given the manifestation of the Spirit for the common good'.

"This reference to 'the common good' means that God expects us to use our various talents not only to meet our own needs, but also to meet the needs of our neighbors. Indeed, it is through all of our gifts that God cares for the world. So, let's consider that.

"For me, three questions come to mind. First, what is each of us good at? Secondly, who needs our skills? And thirdly, how does sharing our gifts with others impact our own lives?

"Let's not skim too quickly over that last one," he continued, "for as I've already said, the gifts that God blesses us with are the ways in which the Lord's work is accomplished.

"So, what is that work?

"Love.

"God loves this world. And by this, I mean the whole needy world. God loves all of it.

"It is significant, I think, that today's epistle reading comes right before Paul's discussion on love, for in I Corinthians, chapter 13, he says that love is God's greatest gift! Love is God's *way*. This is not an *idea* about love. No, this is love *lived out*. Some background may be useful here. Paul is speaking to Greeks living in Corinth. He probably can see that they don't know whether or not he's worth listening to, but that doesn't stop him. He's got news! God, he says, loves *them!*

"Think about that: Paul is not limiting God's love to the people of Israel. He's saying that the God of Israel loves people who look different, who eat different foods, who share a different culture and history—just like here in Olean, where some parts of town are German, some are Swedish, some are Irish, some are Polish, some are Italian, and so on. *All are loved!*

"And we also should hear gladness in Paul's voice, for his letter declares, '*Each* of us is blessed with *gifts*!' Today, factory workers provide skills needed by manufacturers, and contribute to our nation's growing economy: that's sharing God's love. Teachers educate our children, and in so doing, contribute to their futures: that's sharing God's love. Farmers till the soil and care for cows, bringing our food and our milk: that, too, is sharing God's love.

"In all of our endeavors, we are 'called' when we share our gifts to meet the needs of our neighbors—here in Olean, across the ocean in Johannesburg, and everywhere in between—for in so doing, we too are touched by God's love. And in so doing, we reflect God's glory. That's what it means to be 'called'. Let it be so. Amen."

Organ music repeating the hymn of the day, "Take My Life, That I May Be," rose softly at the end of the service as everyone stood to leave. Ma Haut's thoughts shifted to the pork roast she was braising in a slow oven at home; she wanted to return to her kitchen as quickly as possible. Pa and she were expecting the Reverend and Mrs. Bauer to join their family for dinner.

As they shuffled up the aisle toward the door, knots of friends and neighbors paused for a moment to greet one another. Ma spotted John Heinz with his parents, and could see joy in their faces.

"*Danke dem Herrn*," Ma thanked the Lord prayerfully in her heart: their boy was safely home from the Korean War.

Mrs. Heinz caught her gaze.

"Your son is home, *ja?*" Ma said kindly.

"Yes, he is, praise be to God," Mrs. Heinz acknowledged God's grace in returning their son. "Now he needs a job."

"*Ja*," Ma Haut agreed, adding that the pastor's sermon was certainly timely.

"And your son Idkä is busy with his new bakery, I see," Mrs. Heinz noted Icky's venture. After all, wasn't it polite to redirect the conversation to Ma's family?

"*Ja, Dankeschön*," Ma acknowledged the generous mention of Icky's work, adding, "And good work we also hope for your son."

They wished one another well as they reached the door, with the Heinz family greeting their pastor first. Pa and Ma were next in line, and thanked him for his sermon, adding that they were looking forward to seeing his family at Sunday dinner in about an hour.

Icky, Millie, Mary Lou, and Mark were only a few steps behind.

"Business must be good," Frank said personably as they approached. The Reverend Bauer and his wife were close friends with the younger Hauts, so while Pa and Ma addressed their pastor formally with his title, the two younger couples were on a first-name basis. "I hear that you put an addition onto your Quonset hut last week!"

"We did!" Icky said. "We got our first major account: Loblaws grocery store, so we needed space for a larger oven!"

"Growth is clumsy, though," Millie nodded at their youngest child, who was fidgeting. "Like having twin toddlers."

"You'll have to tell us all about it at dinner," Frank acknowledged to allow them to deal with their children and move along. "Jean and I will see you there shortly."

3

Batter Up!

The Bauers piled out of their sensible black two-door Ford sedan—the appropriate choice for a pastor and his family—just as Icky, Millie, Mary Lou, and Mark emerged from their Quonset hut to walk next door to Pa and Ma's house.

"Right on time!" Icky said.

"We'd never turn down an invitation to your mother's Sunday dinner," Frank called back with a smile as wide as heaven's gate. Then, turning toward Icky and Millie's hut, he added, "Your bakeshop went up quick!"

"In just one week—but it's only temporary," Icky noted. "Want a nickel tour?"

"Take Mark and the Bauer kids to Grandma's house," Millie instructed Mary Lou. "We'll be right there."

The four adults entered the bakeshop; the door was never locked. None of the houses in their neighborhood were.

"Wow!" Frank compared the wider workspace to Millie's compact Quonset hut kitchen. "This gives you a lot more elbow room!"

"We needed it to accommodate this new Blodgette," Icky pulled down its doors. "It's a three-deck oven that lets us bake more product in less time."

Both Frank and Jean leaned in to inspect.

"I see why this wouldn't fit in your hut kitchen," she said. "It's as big as a baby crib!"

"It also gets really hot! We couldn't install something like that near a little boy who's reaching up to grab every knob and handle," Millie added.

"That would be impossible," Jean agreed. Frank and she had a boy and girl, too, their eldest well past the age when he needed constant attention. Their daughter was Mark's age, so she was ready to spend time with a babysitter.

"And this is one big mixer!" Frank noticed.

"It handles up to twenty-five pounds of dough at a time," Icky confirmed proudly.

"I bet you're enjoying your new space," Frank said.

"We are, though it came with unintended consequences," Millie started toward the door. "From way out here, I can't reach the phone."

"Every time it rings, she dashes into the hut to grab it," Icky explained.

"Toddler practice: I move quick," she smiled.

"—because morning calls are usually cookie sales," Icky explained.

"But when I step away from production, Herta has to pick up the pace," she added.

"Solving that problem is on my to-do list," he assured her.

Of course, Millie would support his efforts. Herta and Roy would, too—and that wasn't just idle talk. Pa and Ma reared their children to look out for one another. If one was genuinely in need, the rest were expected to step up. This time it was mutual; his sister and brother-in-law needed his help as much as he needed theirs.

"As I recall, convincing Roy and Herta to move back to Olean was your mother's doing," Frank said.

"Ma's letters told them how busy we were," Icky opened the door for everyone to walk out.

"And living on the island was becoming dangerous," Millie said. "They said Cuba is accusing the United States of interfering in its politics and economy."

"Their government blames us for their gambling and racketeering troubles, too," Icky added. Of course, no one needed to say anything about Olean's connections to underworld crime; nearly everyone knew somebody whose life was touched by it, one way or another.

"Ma didn't want them on the front lines of a revolution," Millie concluded.

"I can understand her concern, but revolutions don't generally happen all at once," Frank said. "Usually, some faction tries to create a schism first, to shift a nation's beliefs and laws."

"Thank goodness that couldn't happen in the U.S.," Icky said.

"I don't know about that. People don't often realize what's happening—not for a very long time," Frank said.

"Well, Ma smells trouble brewing in Cuba," Millie said. "Somehow she's sure of it."

"So Roy and Herta came home," Icky added, "and we're lucky they did."

In point of fact, he didn't know how he would have filled orders from a large account like Loblaws without their support—and not only because of Roy's knowledge and muscle. His brother-in-law also had his back, and that helped relieve some of the pressure he felt from risking everything to start a bakery.

"What made them move to Cuba in the first place?" Frank asked. "Hemingway?"

"His books sure make island life sound enticing," Icky agreed, "but Herta and he moved south when they were first married. I think they were just dreaming big."

"Weather was a reason, too," Millie remembered. "Herta's letters always mentioned tropical breezes."

"Ah, yes. I read an interview Hemingway gave to a literary magazine after finishing *For Whom the Bell Tolls*—which he actually wrote in Cuba—and he mentioned the trade winds. I don't suppose Roy ever met him?" he mused as they crossed the lawn together.

"Hemingway? His wife wandered into their bakery once in a while," Icky said. "They sold pastries to her, but I think that was the extent of their contact."

"I bet you're glad to be working with a guy who brings so much experience," Frank noted.

"I am," Icky confirmed. "In fact, way back when I was just an apprentice, he was my first boss—so he knows what I know, and what I still have to learn."

"Such as?"

"Leavenings, for one thing," Icky said.

"Okay, I'm no baker, but I know about leavening from the Bible. I like to think of it as something that 'enlivens,'" Frank interjected.

"Right!" Icky agreed, "especially in bread; yeast grows and gives dough its rise. But cookie dough gets its rise from baking soda and baking powder—which are actually chemicals. Managing the pace of those reactions helps control the production schedule—and that's important since we expect to expand our accounts."

"You sound sure of that!" Frank smiled.

"Our Pillsbury rep says grocery market trends are showing a 40 percent increase in demand for commercial baked goods. We're hoping to tap into it."

"Then why put up a temporary bakeshop?" Frank nodded toward the lean-to. He knew they moved into the Quonset hut only until they could get back on their feet, but building onto the old barracks suggested a longer commitment.

"We couldn't fill Loblaw's purchase order without a larger oven, that's all," Icky explained. "We're saving up to build something more substantial."

"Last week, Icky approved architectural drawings for a commercial bakery," Millie added.

"And a ranch house with business offices in the basement will go up after that." Pointing to the corner lot, he added, "Pa sold us that section of his yard. The new house will face N. Fourteenth Street, and the bakery will face Sullivan—where a garage usually is sited."

"You must be excited about all this," Jean said to Millie.

"I am when I can stop long enough to think," she answered. "I usually just try to get through each day, one crazy minute at a time."

"She's doing everything," Icky said. "Rolling and cutting dough, packaging product, boxing orders, handling customer calls, keeping records . . . anything that needs to be done."

Millie shrugged and smiled indulgently. She'd never expected to be gainfully employed, not that she was now. No, any income she might be earning remained in the business. Besides, what she needed wasn't pay; it was a day off. Even a peaceful afternoon would be good. Or a solid night's sleep.

"What if . . ." Jean looked at her husband speculatively as they reached Pa and Ma's porch. "What if you had help handling the phones, and maybe doing some paperwork, too?"

Frank nodded agreeably toward his wife.

"Since our kids are old enough to stay with a sitter part of the day, Jean has been looking for a job," he said.

"Just part-time," she stipulated. "I'm really good at organizing people and projects."

Icky and Millie looked toward one another. He immediately thought hiring Jean was a good idea, and yes, the bakery could afford it since girls were paid less than men. But was office support the next employee they needed to add? He'd been planning to hire production staff. That's what he told Roy, too.

"We didn't mean to butt in," Frank hesitated.

"No, it's not that at all," Icky reassured him. "We appreciate the offer."

"Yes," Millie concurred. "It's really thoughtful of you."

"Can you give us a couple of days to think about how that could work?" Icky asked. He and Millie always talked over business decisions in private.

"Of course," Jean smiled.

"Right now," Frank climbed the back porch steps, "I smell your Ma's pork roast!"

#

Ma's pork shoulder was roasted to perfection, and its aroma filled the house with deliciousness.

"Two leaves today," Pa said as he lengthened the kitchen table.

"*Ja*, a big group we got," Ma answered, "so on your tool chest we sit the two boys."

Pa's big wooden chest was considered a dinnertime place of honor among the boys in the family. Pa kept it locked, so they knew its contents must be valuable: all his tools, which he loaned out only one at a time (and expected to be returned in perfect condition); plus hose parts, screws of various sizes, glue, extra-large rubber bands, string, tape, and strange bits and pieces of anything he needed for repairing the house, car, and bikes. Nothing was wasted. Mark would have liked to investigate it, but nobody got more than a glimpse when Pa slid off the lock, grabbed what he needed, and then slammed down the lid with a hard bang. That peek was fascinating, though—and another reason why the chest was reserved only for boys at Sunday dinner. No girls allowed.

Roy and Herta heard the children tumble through the back door, and hurried downstairs to gather them around the table. Their parents arrived five minutes later, and the blessing was said before Pa passed a bountiful platter. Ma always lead the dinner conversation, seeking issues that would invite polite discussion, contribute to proper digestion, and offer life lessons for the children to follow. This time, since the Reverend Bauer was from New York City, she also chose a topic she thought he would enjoy.

"The newspaper says that the Giants baseball team fired a shot so loud that everywhere in the world the people hear it," she began.

"What a game!" Pastor Bauer immediately picked up the ball.

"Yep, yep, yep," Roy stepped to the plate. "Bobby Thomson hits a hot bat, that's for sure!"

"So what is this loud shooting noise?" Ma asked. It was an honest question. Moving to the U.S. from Germany meant Pa and she didn't always understand American expressions.

"Thomson's bat blasted the ball so hard that it made a cracking sound, like when a gun fires off a bullet," Icky caught the question. "That's why they said it was a 'shot heard around the world.'"

"So, this sound is about the bat hitting the ball?" Pa confirmed.

"Yep, yep, yep," Roy ran with it. "And with that play, Thomson won the game for Brooklyn."

"And brought home the National League pennant for the Giants," Icky added.

"—which was a surprise since they were thirteen games behind the Dodgers in August. They were way back in league standings," Roy reinforced.

"And not even expected to be in the playoffs," Icky continued.

"Right! And then they *resurrected* themselves from the dust to clinch the pennant," Pastor Bauer came out of left field.

Jean decided to play relief batter and rescue everyone from feeling that her husband was going to grab all the bases and haul them off to the pulpit.

"He views everything through the Bible," she said, "—even baseball stories. You get used to it."

"I see where you go with this," Ma allowed. She wasn't sure if resurrection language was allowed in discussing baseball, but if their pastor said it, and his wife smiled, she thought it might be okay.

"Now we see who wins the World Series," Pa moved the conversation along. "Joe DiMaggio and the Yankees: tough to beat they will be."

"Yep, it's been a good year for baseball," Roy said.

"What about the Amateur Baseball League?" Pastor Bauer asked. "Don't they play across the street in Marcus Park?"

"It's my favorite place to watch the games," Pa said.

"But none of you play?" Pastor Bauer pursued.

"Nope, not me," Roy sat back, looking at Herta. "I'm too busy with chores."

"Same here," Icky agreed. "I've been working in a bakery since I was thirteen years old."

"Thirteen or fourteen: this is when boys start learning their trades in Germany," Pa held firm, "and served you well, the work did. Today, a new *Mittelstand* you run." That's what Pa called the bakery: a small- to medium-sized business, just large enough to support their family.

"With some help from everyone at this table," Icky agreed. He'd admit, though, that he would have enjoyed playing baseball. Being on a team would have been more fun than sweeping floors and sanitizing equipment at Bolles. Back then, he always felt like he was racing from home to school, from school to work, and then trying to stay awake long enough to do homework over a reheated meal. He never forgot how grueling those years were, and decided that one day his son would have time to play ball with his pals, if that was what he wanted.

#

After dessert, the Bauers took their children home, and Pa, Roy, and Icky walked Mark across the street to Marcus Park. Corky Cornell was tossing a ball to his son, Tommy, and the men thought their boys could run off some steam together.

Millie and Herta helped Ma wash the dinner dishes.

"That was a tasty meal, Ma," Herta picked up a dish towel. "Your plum pie is the best in the church."

"*Ja*, I steal some of the tree's fruit before Pa starts the wine making," she admitted.

Herta nodded knowingly. "And your pork roast was perfect," she added.

"Yes, the fat was extra crispy," Millie concurred. "I could hear it crackling in the oven. How do you do that?"

"All morning the pork roasts in a slow oven," Ma began. "Then, home from church we come, and up to the highest temperature goes the heat."

"For how long?" Millie asked.

"On the high heat: four hundred fifty degrees Fahrenheit for twenty minutes," she answered. "Blistered and puffy the fat should be when out of the oven we take the pork."

"It was delicious," Herta emphasized. "And baseball invited everyone into the conversation."

"Everyone together, and a good time we made," Ma said, adding, "The new bakeshop also they see, *ja*?"

"Frank and Jean seemed impressed," Millie answered. "But when Icky showed them the oven, they peered in so intently that I thought they might fall in!"

"Like Hansel and Gretel?" Herta recognized the reference to Grimm's fairy tales.

"Never would you shove in the pastor and his wife!" Ma followed her daughter's lead. She could make a little joke, privately, just among the women in the family.

The three of them shared a conspiratorial grin.

"Especially not now," Millie added, "since Jean might work for the bakery!"

"Re-e-ally?" Herta inquired slowly. Icky promised production help, but she hadn't expected him to find a candidate in two days!

But then she saw Ma's furrowed eyebrows and pursed lips, the combination of which intimated restrained disapproval.

Millie saw it, too, and decided she ought to explain.

"We didn't ask for help. She offered."

"She likes baking?" Herta lifted the last plate from the dish drainer.

"No, office work. She'd answer phones, take orders, do paperwork—just part-time," Millie speculated. "She's been exploring employment options."

"Mrs. Bauer has a job!" Ma bristled without turning away from scrubbing the roasting pan. Her elbow jabbed the air behind her with the energy of a jack hammer. "She is our organist, and head of all the women's work: the Ladies' Aid Society, the spring tea, the kitchen. That is how the church is run!"

Ma was sure other women in their congregation would agree.

"But . . . what if Jean wants to pursue something on her own?" Millie countered. Most women stepped back from factory jobs when their husbands returned from the war, but a few remained in respectable women's work like teaching and nursing. Secretarial and office administration jobs were now available, too, as employers redirected operations from wartime needs to opportunities in the booming American economy. Certainly, Jean could apply for those openings, especially since she wasn't seeking a position that rightfully belonged to a man.

"Even if the work is meant for a woman, taking advantage of her willingness to help: that Icky cannot do," Ma struggled to curb the tension in her voice.

"Icky would pay her," Millie defended, adding, "and Frank nodded in agreement."

Ma's jaw dropped. First, television is preached from the pulpit, then the Good Book is used to explain baseball, and now the pastor's wife wants her own pay? No! The world was spinning out of control!

And worse: Icky's bakery could be in the middle of it. What would people think!

"It's not decided yet," Millie finally added.

"Good!" Ma's voice snapped like a crisp sheet pinned to a clothesline and fighting against the wind. Maybe a way out of this debacle could be found before everyone learned what her son and daughter-in-law were planning.

4

What Will People Think?

"Jean's offer to handle phones for the bakery was a surprise," Icky said as he slid into bed.

"It would be a huge help, but I'm not sure Ma will approve," Millie revealed.

"Ma?" he asked as he propped his head on his elbow.

"I mentioned Jean's offer when we were doing dishes, and I wish I hadn't."

"Why not? Wives have been allowed to work outside the home since World War II. Even Alma worked in a munitions factory."

"Your little sister taking a man's job during the war isn't the same as luring the pastor's wife away from the church," Millie explained.

"Luring?" Icky repeated. "She offered! Besides, this is just office work."

But Millie understood that although a man would be slapped on the back for using his grit, a woman could expect some finger-wagging for showing some gumption—especially if she was the pastor's wife.

"Ma seems to think we'd be stealing Jean from the congregation."

Icky heaved an obvious intentional sigh.

"Well, before we debate Ma's worries, what do you think?" he shifted. He'd learned that married life was happier when he included Millie on large decisions, even though that meant giving her time to consider options and weigh outcomes. But on this question, she didn't hesitate.

"We need the help, and Mary Lou can babysit her kids after school, so I think it's a great fit for everyone," she said. "Or, I did before I spilled the beans to Ma."

"Well, since you think hiring Jean is a good idea, and I think it's a good idea, and Frank and she seem to agree, then that's how it's going to be."

"Oka-ay," she stretched out her response. "But you get to tell Ma."

He knew she was right, but maybe he'd bring it up with Pa first, after double-checking with Frank to be sure he really was comfortable with Jean's offer.

#

At the end of his Monday delivery run, Icky drove the bakery truck past the church and saw the light on in their pastor's office. He'd been thinking about Ma's concern over hiring Jean: that the bakery would be taking advantage of her good nature.

"Are you sure this is okay?" he asked Frank. "Ma thinks pastors' wives are too busy with church duties to take outside jobs, even part-time."

"Congregations sometimes assume that when they call a pastor that they should bestow upon his wife the honor of leading women's organizations and running events," Frank generously framed unrealistic expectations. "And in the past that may have been how churches functioned."

"But not now?" Icky asked.

"Jean enjoys church activities, but her spirit is hungry for opportunities to serve God in ways unrelated to my work," he explained.

Icky didn't say anything.

"She isn't expected to limit her gifts to making my life easier," he clarified.

"But if she's helping you, aren't you both working toward the same goal?"

"Which is what?"

"Well, um, serving the church," Icky echoed Ma's assumption.

"We all serve the church—including you," Frank corrected, "each in our own ways. Jean is *able* to manage parish activities; by that, I mean she has the skills. And we *need* skills like hers. But ability and need are only two ways to discern our true vocations."

"What else is there?"

"Joy! Jean knows the Lord wants her life to be so filled with *joy* that she genuinely reflects God's glory—God's love!—in all she says and does. That's why she spoke up. Something about the opportunity to manage a bakery office filled her heart."

"And that's what she's 'called' to?" Icky doubted. "Office work?"

"It's like this, Icky: Our deepest calling is to grow into our most authentic or genuine selves, whether or not that conforms to someone else's idea of who we're supposed to be," Frank defended gently. "She feels this position provides that opportunity."

"I hope Ma understands," Icky said, "because when I get home, I get to tell her we're making an offer to Jean."

Frank nodded. He understood how difficult that conversation might be, but he'd seen Mrs. Haut come to terms with other situations she found difficult.

"Shall I tell Jean to call you then?"

"Let's have her call Millie," Icky suggested. "They're friends, and Millie will like being the one to welcome her."

#

Much to Ma's chagrin, Pa and Icky rearranged the hut's living room to accommodate a file cabinet, chair, and small desk near the telephone so Jean could begin her new job.

"Wellbeing and security for the family: these things your mother protects," Pa said as the two men lifted the sofa and moved it across the room.

"Yeah," Icky said, "I remember her worrying about Herta and Roy in Cuba."

"And your brother's decision to serve with the Marines during World War II: this also was difficult, especially with the injuries he suffered fighting Japan," Pa added.

"Ma studied for the American citizenship exam when that happened," Icky remembered.

"More history there was to that decision than you know," Pa intimated.

Icky looked at his father to see whether or not he intended to say more. His parents were resolutely private, and he and his siblings knew that the story of their ancestry was a conflicted inheritance. This time, though, the situation with the pastor's wife caused such disruption that Pa thought Icky ought to know why.

"To the New World Ma came when she was young: this you know," he selected as few details as were necessary. "What you do not know is that it was so soon after her mother died. Her father remarried quickly, and the woman he chose did not want his children—so devoted they were to their own mother."

"How awful for them," Icky shoved an arm chair into its new spot.

"Hard-hearted was the new wife," Pa condemned her.

Icky paused to consider what that must have been like for children who'd just lost their mother.

"How could Ma's father choose a stranger over his own flesh and blood?" The question was rhetorical; no answer was thinkable.

"*Ja*, their mother they lost, and then, so it seemed to the children, their father, too," Pa unplugged a lamp. "At first, the woman tried marrying off the daughters just to have them out of her house."

"Her house? They'd moved in with her?"

"No, the wife moved in," Pa said, "but the roost is ruled by the woman, and she wanted out of it any connection to their mother. So, to make the peace, Ma's father made arrangements through their church for his eldest daughter—your ma—to take work in America."

"All alone?" Icky was shocked.

"All alone," Pa confirmed. Then, refusing to leave the experience wholly without merit, he added, "But she learned to stand on her own two feet, and this is good."

"What was Ma's work?" Icky asked the easier question.

"She was a nanny," Pa said. "She didn't speak the English, so she studied newspapers and taught herself."

That made sense, Icky responded with a nod. Ma was devoted to *The Olean Times-Herald*.

"What about her sister?"

"Ma saved all she could, and two years later, she paid for her to take the boat. Glad to leave she was, too! They said their father's second wife was as hard as a carved out pumpkin, with dark and hollow eyes. Her glaring face: this the children could not bear," Pa revealed.

That one little bit of the family's history could explain why Ma's sister could be so difficult, Icky realized. She suffered longer under the woman's scorn.

"And also, their father thought that living in this country would be safer," Pa added, almost absent-mindedly.

"Safer?"

"*Ja*, being tolerated is not the same as being safe," he alluded to another reason behind Ma's stubborn attachment to her heavily starched principles. "So, Ma has her reasons to fuss."

"How old was she when she left Germany?" Icky asked as he settled into a chair to see how the living room felt with the addition of office furniture. Pa dropped onto the sofa for a moment, too.

"Middle to later teens probably."

Icky was silent. He never would send Mary Lou away, especially to the other side of the world and without an adult to protect her. The realization that his mother suffered such rejection was chilling, and he shook his head over all she endured.

"Poor Ma," Icky finally said.

Silence lingered as Pa watched him absorb the inadequacy of words. German folktales of a wicked step-mother forcing a child out of the home were real to her.

"The suffering that comes when the world turns its back: this she knows," Pa explained.

"Is that why she send blankets and warm clothes to her cousins every winter?"

"Germany lost the war. Even if the Free World does not understand their misery, Ma does not let her family suffer a cold shoulder. The gifts are comfort as much as warmth." Returning to the point of his disclosure, he added, "Also, it's why hiring the pastor's wife is a worry to her. She does not want to cause division in the church or see friends turn against us."

Icky nodded.

"And she likes to be right," Pa concluded.

Icky felt the truth in that observation. Ma was right about most things. If she didn't know an answer to a question, she looked it up, even if she had to wait until the weekend when Pa and she could find time to go to the library. The entire family knew better than to disagree with her assertions, too, because Ma would quote her sources.

"The job is only part-time," Icky defended, "and since Mary Lou will watch her kids after school, it's perfect for Jean."

"Give to your mother some time," Pa said. "A strong woman she is, and will soften when no harsh judgment on the family falls."

"I hope so," Icky said, "because Jean will be here at eight o'clock tomorrow."

#

Millie looked up from rolling dough when Roy and Herta came in the next morning. She hoped their faces would reveal what had gone on in her in-laws' house once Ma knew they'd hired Jean. But Herta wouldn't share family unpleasantness unless forced to defend someone.

Besides, hadn't Millie been the one to initiate discord by blurting out Jean's offer? That didn't sit well either.

Roy, however, cracked a small half-smile toward Millie. He'd give Icky a run down, if asked.

"How's the weather?" Icky inquired broadly as he came in with four mugs of coffee.

"Definitely a chill in the air," Roy answered. "No storm on the horizon, though."

"Not yet," Herta cautioned. "But keep your slicker nearby, just in case something pops up, hm?"

Whenever Herta said "hm?" she wasn't asking a question; she was insisting.

Millie set down her mug, and picked up her rolling pin again. She wanted to work ahead of her production goals so she could spend a few minutes settling Jean into her job when she arrived.

"These things have a way of fizzling out," Roy insisted as he poured a pitcher of eggs, vanilla, and buttermilk into the creamed sugar. "How many are we baking today?"

"Six hundred fifty twelve-counts," Icky said.

"Your Olean sales calls must have gone well," Roy noted. "Wednesday orders usually top out at five hundred dozen."

"Not anymore," Icky said. "Stores are running low midweek, so they were willing to stock up. And yes, we'll be baking this many packages every Wednesday; they all signed new purchase orders," he anticipated Roy's next question.

"Yep, yep, yep, that's how to do it," he agreed.

"Next week we'll need to bake samples for sales calls, if you can make deliveries again."

Roy looked at Herta. Her face held secret thoughts, but she nodded once, slowly, her head tilted at an angle.

"That should be okay," Roy said. "But when you sell more, we bake more. Soon we'll need help in production."

"I hear you," Icky said.

"I don't think you do," Roy contended. Herta and he faced the same problem with their own small bakery, so they knew first-hand how growth spurts could cause production problems. "If any of these Olean stores increase their orders, which they could do . . ."

"They could," Icky interrupted, "but that's why I went to see them last week. I think I know what they need now, so I feel okay about heading out to Salamanca."

Roy didn't respond. He knew Icky always worked his numbers and made plans, so he'd wait to see what would unfold.

"I'm aiming for at least two long-term purchase orders; that'll make delivering out there cost-effective," Icky explained. "Then, when we've got enough income to support increased payroll, we'll hire production help."

"Now you're talking," Roy said. "I'll cover you for now. But if this goes on too long or gets too big to handle, we gotta' talk."

5

Setting Boundaries

"What were you girls giggling about?" Millie asked as Mary Lou hung up the telephone.

"Nothing," her daughter answered vaguely. "Just the movie we saw last weekend."

"What movie?" Millie pressed.

"*Too Young to Kiss*," Mary Lou unsuccessfully restrained giggles.

"You're right: you are too young," her mother agreed.

"Not me," Mary Lou protested. "Peggy's older sister, Bertie. She took the girls to the Palace Theater last week, and when they came out, they bumped into some guy who was one of their older brother's friends. He just got home from Korea."

"Korea?"

"He was in the Army," she shrugged.

"Oh, yes," Millie said. "That must have been John Heinz."

"I don't know," Mary Lou answered.

"So why did that make you giggle?"

"Bertie was wearing a plaid skirt and saddle shoes, so she looked like she was still in school. The guy patted her on the head—because Bertie is only about five feet tall—and he asked what grade she's in," Mary Lou smirked. "So, Bertie sassed him with something like, 'I'll have you know that I've graduated, and I'm working!' Anyway, now he's calling her house and leaving messages with her mother. Peggy thinks he wants to take her out. On a date!"

"So?" Millie urged.

"So the movie was called *Too Young to Kiss*, and he thought she was just a kid, so . . . get it?"

Millie paused to consider how to respond to a young teenager's idea of what was funny.

"I think we should talk about the films you girls are seeing," she diverted.

"I'm earning my own money to pay for movie tickets, so I should be allowed to choose for myself," Mary Lou disagreed.

"And we're your employer. You wouldn't want your income cut off, would you?"

Mary Lou understood the dire consequences arising out of losing a job, and decided not to argue. But she also wouldn't volunteer any more details on the shows she and her girlfriends wanted to see.

#

"I'll help package the last batch, hm?" Herta suggested at the end of her shift. "Roy will be ready to load the truck in a couple of minutes."

"Thanks," Millie answered, alert to her sister-in-law's unusual offer. Something must be on her mind, and if so, it was best to get it sorted out before Ma heard about it.

"I'm sorry if you felt burdened today," she ventured. "I know I got behind when I went in to help Jean total new orders and rewrite tomorrow's production sheet."

For days, she'd been expecting Herta to react to their decision to add administrative staff instead of increasing the production crew. She probably felt Icky went back on his word.

"Learning takes time," she allowed. "And she works hard."

"Yes, she's a quick study," Millie sought common ground. "She's making all the delivery box labels, too. That gets the truck on the road on time."

"Being organized helps the work flow," Herta asserted with rule-like authority.

Millie felt icy air pass between them.

"It sure does," she refused to shiver. "The way Jean handles customers' last-minute orders lets me continue to cut dough."

"I hope so," Herta insisted, "because last week Icky increased sales with Olean stores, and now he's bringing in new business from Salamanca. I know he thinks production can be increased, but we didn't move back up north to work double shifts, hm? By noon, Roy is exhausted, so giving him the deliveries is going to wear him thin."

And there it was: the motive behind Herta's offer to help pack boxes.

"Do you miss running your own bakery?" Millie chose a conciliatory tone.

"We do," Herta refused to admit that she certainly did prefer being her own boss. "But family is family, and for now, we're happy to help."

Millie suspected that "happy" was an overstatement.

"I also don't want Roy to get into an accident," Herta pressed her point. "When he gets home from delivering product, it's all he can do to eat a bit of dinner before falling into bed. Then we're up again at three-thirty in the morning. I'm just worried for him, hm?"

"Here's the label for that last box going to Richardson's corner store," Jean entered the bakeshop. "I thought you'd need it."

"Thanks, Jean," Millie turned her attention. "You're right. We do need it."

"And I wrote the store name on the delivery manifest, too," she handed it over. "That way, Roy won't be doubling back at the end of his run."

"See?" Millie said to Herta as she slanted an eye in Jean's direction, "Already, she's ahead of the game."

"I'm just trying to help," Jean smiled and returned to the desk.

"Thanks for telling me what you're going through," Millie said to Herta when they were alone again. "We do rely on Roy and you, and your efforts are more than either of us could have imagined."

"Well, like I said, family is family, so Roy and I are happy to help, as . . ."

Silence fell from her unfinished sentence like flour dust drifting through sunlight. Millie looked up and waited for her to continue.

"As?"

"As you already know, hm?" Herta decided. She pulled back from saying something like "as much as you need" or "as much as we can." No, she wanted to establish boundaries, not set false expectations. Not that she was stingy. No, she meant only to stand up for her husband's best interests.

"I do know," Millie veiled her annoyance. She also knew that Icky was paying both of them at the top of the industry standard—plus overtime, of course, which he would have done even if the Fair Labor Standards Act hadn't required it. And if she wanted to press the point, she could argue that the extra pay was helping Herta and Roy recover the financial loss they incurred when they left behind everything in Cuba.

Also, Millie silently steamed, while they were paid a wage, she never took a penny from the bakery. No, like most wives, she counted on her husband to provide any money she might need. Choosing her words carefully, she said, "I know Roy and you are doing more than anyone has a right to expect. And we . . . respect your willingness to step up."

"I think we're finished here now," Herta closed the last package of cookies.

Even if it weren't the last one, Millie was prepared to thank her sister-in-law for staying to help, and add that she could handle the rest by herself.

As Herta walked to Pa and Ma's house, she considered whether or not her remarks would be taken seriously. Sharing ill feelings was a luxury she couldn't afford—not since Roy and she were living under her parents' roof. Certainly, she was grateful for the family's goodwill. But while she didn't want to cause trouble, Roy needed someone to stand up for him.

Besides, Millie was doing the same for Icky. She was sure of it.

#

Millie waved good-bye to Roy as he pulled out of the driveway with the deliveries, and quickly shifted her attention from the bakery to her household—a transition as abrupt as leaving the alluring scent of vanilla for the astringency of bleach. She decided a whiff of fresh air would help, so she grabbed a basket of laundry and called Mark to play outside while she hung sheets on the clothesline. Quiet mornings with his grandma meant the boy would be ready for some rambunctious fun with Buko, the family boxer.

Mark and his dog tumbled and practiced free falls in the grass while Millie reached up on her tiptoes to drape linens over the line and secure them with wooden pins to keep the wind from stealing them away. When they all were hung, she dropped the remaining clothespins into her basket, and turned to tell Mark to follow her indoors. But the kid was nowhere to be seen.

"Mark!" Millie called out. "Buko! Mark!"

Maybe he went indoors for a cookie. Wasn't he was always trying to share food with the dog?

But neither of them were in the bakeshop.

She ran quickly through the entire length of the Quonset hut, calling out their names.

Silence.

"Mark!" she shouted as she returned to the outside. Maybe he went next door to see his grandma again. Or crossed the street to Marcus Park—with those railroad tracks on the other side! Left or right: which way should she run?

Then she saw, padding steadily along the cinders at the edge of Sullivan Street and turning left onto N. Fifteenth Street, a dog and a fair-haired child, afternoon's bright sunshine encircling the boy's head like a halo.

"Mark!"

No response.

"Buko, stop!"

The dog turned toward her voice. Finally, the kid did, too.

She ran top speed all the way, yelling, "Mark Haut, you stay right there! Don't move!"

She was gasping from the bottom of her lungs when she grabbed his arm, and bent over to put her face close to his and look him directly in his eyes. For a brief moment she considered: Did she want to protect him? Or strangle him?

"Hi," he said innocently. "Want to come with us?"

"Where do you think you're going?" she asked as she tipped her head back to catch her breath.

"To find Tommy," he answered.

"You don't know where he lives," she challenged.

"Uh-huh, I do," he disagreed.

"Where?"

"That way," he pointed. "I saw his daddy take him home from the park."

That was after Sunday dinner with the Bauers, she reminded herself.

"Which house?" she asked gently.

"I don't know," he said, "but I can find him. Buko can help."

Millie released a measured, shaky breath.

"Let's get a biscuit for Buko first," she led Mark home. She'd have a long talk with Icky about the wandering child.

#

"Buko isn't the only one to take off," Millie reported at the end of the day. "You've got to do something, and a fence isn't enough. That kid will climb over it."

Icky knew she was right, so after he finished weekend maintenance in the bakery, he asked Pa for parts from his big tool chest, and made a harness strong enough for a three-year-old. Millie leashed it to the clothesline, and left Mark in the yard while she watched from inside the bakeshop to see what the boy would do. First he tested the length of its run, back and forth, back and forth, across the lawn.

"C'mon, Johnny Ralph," he yelled, holding out a hand. Millie didn't know who Johnny Ralph was, but the kid seemed happy. Finally, he coaxed Buko into one of their boxing matches.

"How can you do that to your son!" Ma exclaimed. She saw the boy from her window, too, and went looking for Icky.

"Millie and I got chores to do, and he won't stay put," Icky said. "Besides, he has the whole yard to play in."

"Never would I tether you in a harness," she countered, boldly.

"Never would I have defied your order to stay put!" he defended.

He wouldn't have either. No one ignored Ma's orders. She was . . . Ma!

"I will watch him," she suggested in an appeasing tone of voice. In truth, she intended her words as an offer to help, not a mandate. Besides, the boy needed to develop some sense of *selbständigkeit*, for without self-reliance, how would he walk himself to school when that time came?

"You do enough, Ma, watching him every morning," Icky acknowledged. "We thank you for that. But in the afternoon and on the weekend, he is our responsibility."

And that was the end of it. Ma knew that when Icky made up his mind, there was no changing it. He'd been like that all his life. Just like his father.

Stubbornness must run in that side of the family, she thought to herself, unaware of the possibility that Icky could just as easily have inherited the trait from her.

6

Sharing Secrets

AFTER THEIR EVENING PRAYERS, Jean asked Frank if she could talk about something she heard at the bakeshop. She didn't want to cross lines, but she also thought the two of them might be able to help solve a problem.

"I don't think they intended me to hear," she admitted, "so I don't know whether or not I can share what they were saying."

"If it's something that concerns you, I'll hold it in confidence," he promised her. "First, though, let me ask if everyone is okay. And for your sake, is Mrs. Haut upset about you working at the bakery?"

"I don't know how Mrs. Haut feels, but Millie is happy, so I hope everything is okay," she answered. Then looking into her husband's eyes for guidance, she hinted, "What I wanted to talk with you about is how hard they're working."

"I'm listening," he encouraged her.

She paused, considering how to start.

"Roy and Herta start baking with Icky and Millie at about four in the morning. Then Icky makes sales calls, while Roy makes deliveries," she began. "Herta told Millie she's worried that Roy is putting himself at risk, driving so many hours after baking all morning.

"Mixing dough is exhausting," Jean continued. "They're lifting hundred-pound sacks of flour and sugar, and running equipment. And with batches going in and out of the oven every seven minutes, well, the heat is oppressive. I don't know how they do it."

Frank acknowledged her concern with small nods.

"After eight hours of physical labor, both men are on the road until evening, so it's like they're pulling double shifts," she reinforced her point.

"And how did you think we'd be involved in solving this problem?" Frank asked. "I know you don't expect me to mix dough or drive a truck."

"No, but maybe you know someone who is looking for a job. Didn't you say John Heinz came in to see you yesterday?"

Frank smiled, and leaned back in his chair.

"You, Mrs. Bauer, are an amazing woman," he recognized his wife's ability to connect people. "I'll talk to Icky."

"Really? Does that mean you agree with me: that hiring John could be good for both of them?"

"I have no way of knowing," Frank said, "but I think we should pray on it. Would you like to begin, or shall I?"

#

"Before you add stores in Salamanca to our accounts, I need to share a conversation I had with Herta," Millie decided to tell Icky. Evenings had evolved into a quiet time for talking out business challenges, and she thought she'd simmered this one on a back burner long enough to cook it down to the essence of her concerns.

"What is it?" he said casually. Roy was up front about work problems, so he assumed Herta's questions, if there were any, were being addressed, too.

"She made a point to stay late to talk to me," Millie said, aware that Icky would find that unusual. Like Icky, Herta was *pünktlich* in both her arrivals and her departures, a habit their parents instilled, and which he interpreted as what was probably intended: never make people wait, and never over-stay an invitation.

"So?" he urged.

"She said that . . . ," Millie paused. Should she repeat Herta's words, or just digest them to her main points? "She said Roy and she didn't move back to Olean to work double shifts. And she's worried about him getting into an accident while making deliveries because he's worn out from baking all morning."

Icky pulled a pack of Camel cigarettes from his shirt pocket, tapped one on the table and thoughtfully lit it. He recalled Roy glancing at Herta before agreeing to deliver product. And she'd nodded, but slowly, maybe delaying agreement.

Millie removed a Winston cigarette from its package, and picked up a Zippo lighter, but Icky held out his hand. She gave it up, and he snapped open the lid against its tiny hinge, ran his thumb across the rasp to light her cigarette, and then clicked it shut. It was a small gesture, like opening a car door.

"Roy gets to the point, but Herta hints," she slowly released a mouthful of smoke.

Icky nodded.

"I saw it, too," he tapped ashes into a shared ashtray.

"She got me wondering whether or not we ought to be growing our accounts this fast," Millie revealed. "What if we fail?"

"What's all this about?" Icky asked. He hadn't expected Millie to doubt the direction he was taking with the bakery.

"We've never run a business before," she pointed out. "Roy and Herta have done it, and their advice helps, but they gave up everything to escape Cuba. Now they have nothing to show for all their hard work.

"I don't want us to end up like that," she continued before drawing on her cigarette. Then, speaking through a cloud of smoke, she added, "and I sure don't want to hire people, even in production, if our bakery won't survive."

Icky pulled in a long drag and held it as he considered Millie's concern. Until now, she'd never wavered in her support.

He released the smoke from his cigarette in one long breath.

"So, this is about becoming an employer?"

"This is worrying about people who would depend on us for their livelihoods," she chose a magnanimous response. "We've never had that responsibility before, and I didn't realize how it would feel until it became clear that we need to add crew if the business is to grow.

"And also," she finally revealed her underlying concern, "I don't know how much we ought to count on Roy and Herta. Don't you wonder why they're helping us when they could be starting their own business again?"

She wasn't concerned that they'd open a competing bakery; they'd never do that. In truth, though, she didn't feel comfortable working with her sister-in-law, not the way she would have liked. Ever since Roy and she returned to Olean, Herta seemed torn, balancing the pain of losing their storefront bakery against the tendency to wear an air of superiority. Or maybe it was always there: the know-it-all eldest daughter who'd grown up looking out for four siblings. Perhaps that take-charge attitude simply overflowed into other parts of her life.

Or perhaps even more to the point, Millie was bothered by the fact that since returning to her parents' home, Herta had Ma's constant ear, while she was only the daughter-in-law. She brooded over feeling unintentionally relegated to the role of an outsider: a member of the family in name, but not by blood. It wasn't true, of course. Ma would never abide exclusion. Still, concern over the natural closeness of mother and daughter had an unsettling effect on Millie, and try as she might, she couldn't shake it.

"I don't question their motives," Icky answered easily. "Ma wanted Herta and Roy out of Cuba, we needed help, and they needed jobs. It's all working out."

"Well, with only four of us, we're sunk if they quit," Millie suggested the warning she felt Herta was mixing into the bowl. "We're in a tight spot until we can be sure that they're committed to sticking around."

"What would 'committed' mean?" Icky asked. "We never planned to add partners."

"Should we?" Millie snubbed out her cigarette like she had a grudge against it.

"No!" he said firmly. "We can't put a price on all we've invested and all we've risked."

She nodded, though she'd also admit that with two children, they'd had little choice. They needed to put food on the table and a roof over their heads.

"We've got two years of research, planning, recipe development, market testing, vendor negotiations, account management," he listed start-up costs, in part to support his position, and in part to weigh the value of the business.

"Sleepless nights," Millie added, aware that Icky didn't rest well.

"We've still got those," he admitted to raw exhaustion. "And the truth is, we'll probably have them for as long as we operate a bakery."

Millie grimaced at Icky's easy acceptance of allowing work to rule his life. He let that happen when he worked for Mace Bolles, too, and that hadn't turned out so well.

He took a short drag from his cigarette. The hot smoke released thoughts he'd been carrying, too.

"And I don't want the added burden of having my decisions second-guessed." He was thinking of Roy's reservations about increasing orders from Olean's stores, and then his caution about the extra work that would arise from new accounts in Salamanca. If it were up to his brother-in-law, the bakeshop would hire and train new production crew first; Icky knew that was what he'd been pushing for. And the bakery's savings account could cover payroll for a short time while they brought on new staff. But those funds were designated for construction. If Millie and he were to build, they shouldn't divert their reserves to daily operations.

"Don't get me wrong. I value Roy's experience, and I trust his advice," Icky added.

"He's also the one guy I go to when I want to toss around ideas or solve problems. But those problems are mine—or rather, *ours*—because this is *our* business. I don't want to change that."

Millie nodded again, bolstered by Icky's determination to retain sole ownership.

"I agree," she said, "but Herta makes me wonder if a partnership question is going to come up, sooner or later. And also, maybe she's right to tell us when she's unhappy."

"About?"

"Well, she's indirect, so I'm not sure," Millie nursed her grievances, "but you know how she likes to be in charge, so I don't think we should underestimate her."

"That's for sure." He knew he could count on his older sister's loyalty, but Herta also required acknowledgement for her contributions.

He sighed.

"I want to increase orders," he looked intentionally at his wife. "And there's no reason not to. The numbers show we can put out more product with existing staff."

"We can, but do we want to run that hard all day, every day?" Millie asked.

"For now, yes, we do," Icky confirmed. "We need to keep growing so we can pay cash for everything. And we do need to pay cash, because like you said, this is a new business. The banks won't give us the best loan rates, if they give us a loan at all."

"Are we in trouble?"

"No," he said immediately. "In fact, we're right on track. Funds for the architect's fee and the building are covered, and we're socking away money for equipment. But on the negative side, the truck has a lot of hard miles on it. Something unexpected could come up, too, so we need to keep building our account."

Millie nodded as he pulled in a final drag.

"I think Roy understands that production isn't running full out," Icky decided.

"But close to it," Millie warned. "Remember how he said Olean orders have us working near capacity on Fridays? Wednesday's production will be at capacity soon, too."

"*Almost* to capacity," he corrected. "And I still say that he's aware of what I'm doing, and he's okay with it. But to your point, I can make sure he knows that Salamanca stores will be offered product only on Tuesdays and Thursdays. Then we're controlling production."

"How about capping that increase, so Herta can grow into it, too," Millie suggested, "because with more orders, I'll need extra time at the end of my shift to do packaging—which means she'll get stuck cutting dough by herself."

"Right," he agreed.

"And one more thing," Millie knew Icky realized this, but she felt better suggesting it, "mention that you're restricting Salamanca increases—keeping them to midweek—to be respectful of all the work your sister is doing."

Because, Millie told herself, Herta's irritation bristles like static coming from a radio when a station isn't properly tuned in.

#

As Icky drove to Salamanca, he organized a plan for approaching new accounts. Calling on Olean stores had been easy because Millie and Ma were regular customers, so managers knew his family. They didn't have personal contacts in Salamanca, though, so the cookies would have to sell themselves.

His first stop was Food Town. He parked the old Studebaker in the middle of the lot, and grabbed two packages. "This," he said with bold hope as he approached the door, "is all I need to close a sale."

He saw his reflection in the plate glass window and wondered whether or not he should have worn a suit. Too late to change clothes now, he decided as he entered and began to look for the baked goods aisle. Lined up at eye level were all the usual offerings: Sunshine's Hydrox sandwich cookies, Crispo assorted biscuits, and Nabisco Fig Newton cakes—which was the only soft cookie, so the store could offer another variety. He'd point that out. Then he'd report strong sales of his cookies in Olean.

"We're ready to deliver on Tuesdays and Thursdays," Icky suggested when he met with the store manager.

"Only one variety?" he asked.

"They're the best sugar cookie on the shelves," Icky countered with enthusiasm. "And to your point, we're about to introduce a couple of new recipes. Maybe you'd like to be a test market?"

"If they're as good as this one, bring some around," he said. "We can see how they do."

"Great!" Icky agreed.

"Let's start by featuring your sugar cookies next to the home-baked product, both days," he pointed to a table in the middle of the aisle.

Icky would have preferred dedicated shelf space with signage, but any new business was good, and the manager had agreed to an ongoing commitment. "I'll pick up a purchase order tomorrow with your first delivery," he set the terms. "We'll front the cost for the first two weeks. Then, when you see how well they're selling, we'll look for a check each Tuesday."

As Icky walked out to the parking lot, he was already planning his next call. One more account, he told himself, and the cost of delivering a half hour away is covered.

#

"So, I thought 'one down, one to go,'" he reported to Millie that evening, "because we need two stores to cover delivery costs."

"Right," she recalled.

"After I closed a small order from Leonard's Grocery, I still had time left, so I decided to call on one more."

"And?"

"The manager in the third store already knew about Icky's Cookies. When I told him we were delivering in Salamanca, he signed a purchase order on the spot!"

"Three new customers in one day!" Millie said enthusiastically.

"Two are smaller stores, but we're delivering only twice a week," he said.

"Wise move," she noted.

"It was your idea!"

"So we can control production," she pointed out. "How much did they order?"

"Altogether, eighty," he said.

"Thirty more than you planned," Millie said. "Herta is going to notice that."

"But we'll be no busier than on Wednesdays," he emphasized. "And Monday production is still below capacity."

"Not by much," Millie debated.

"We're just making the best use of existing resources. It's standard practice."

"I know you're right," she allowed, partly because he was, and partly because it was a wife's duty to encourage her hard-working husband. "Just be sure you smooth it over when you tell them."

"I'll talk with Roy in the morning," he assured her.

"Herta, too," she added, "because we can't lose their help."

"Right. And it won't be long before we hire crew for production." Then, to catch up on her day, he asked, "How's everything else?"

"Two boxes arrived," she answered. "One smells like cinnamon. The other is heavy and covered in arrows with 'This Side Up' stickers. Jean stored both with the inventory."

"Good! I ordered three cinnamon varieties to try in a new spice cookie. One of the Salamanca accounts agreed to be a test store, so I want to finish formulating that recipe soon."

"And the second box?"

"Probably a new product called Numoline."

"Nu-what?"

"Numoline," he repeated. "Three syllables, *New*-mo-leen—just like Olean is pronounced *Oh*-lee-ann. It's invert sugar syrup, and supposed to mix easier than granulated. I want to try it in our sugar cookie recipe."

"Is everything okay with the kids?" he changed the conversation again.

"Mary Lou spent the afternoon with her girlfriends after the Bauer kids went home. And I think Mark has an imaginary pal," she answered.

"How do you know that?"

"When I set the table for lunch, he told me to put out an extra plate for Johnny Ralph."

"Johnny Ralph?"

"He didn't introduce us," she said, "but he told me—somewhat brashly, too—'You can't see him.'"

"What did you do?"

"I set out another plate, and swept my empty hand across the table to put an invisible peanut butter sandwich on Johnny Ralph's plate, too."

"So the 'three' of you had lunch together?"

"I guess so," Millie said. "Afterward, I asked him if his friend likes peanut butter, and he nodded. Then he announced they were going outside to look for toads, so I buckled him up in his harness, connected it to the clothesline, and told him to stay near the sandbox."

"No harness for Johnny Ralph?" Icky asked.

"Oh! I didn't think of that," Millie admitted. "When I came in, I just let Buko out the door to join him—or rather, to join *them*."

"I never had imaginary friends," Icky said.

"You had three sisters and a brother," Millie pointed out. "Ma didn't need any extras."

"Then maybe setting another place for Johnny Ralph is okay," Icky agreed. If the kid wanted a brother, an imaginary one was going to have to be enough.

7

Superheroes

"Come and get it," Icky delivered four mugs of hot coffee. Steam lifted off each one, adding the beans' nutty, caramelized aroma to the scent of freshly baked cookies coming out of the oven.

"You're full of energy," Herta accepted a mug.

Roy set a hundred-pound bag of flour next to the mixer, and grabbed one, too. "Thanks," he said. "I need it after yesterday's deliveries. How did your calls go in Salamanca?"

"Good news, bad news, good news," Icky answered. "Good news: We got three new accounts, each of them twice a week. Bad news: We need to increase production on Tuesdays and Thursdays. Good news: I'm following your advice and hiring some production help."

"Yep, yep, yep," Roy said, relieved. "That's what you gotta' do."

"And we thank you for that," Herta agreed. "This bakery's growth is going to wear out your big sister over here, hm? And Roy..."

"...can handle it," her husband waved his hand. He could speak for himself if he had to, which he didn't.

"I know," Icky said, grateful for Roy's intervention. "And we thank you—both of you—for stepping up. We couldn't take on additional business without your help."

"Yep, well, you're working as hard as we are," Roy said. "And we know it's tougher at the top. Millie and you also got the weight of making it or breaking it."

"We do want to make it, but without breaking you along the way," Icky played with his brother-in-law's remark. "So, if you can handle splitting deliveries until we get more crew hired, I'll take Tuesday,

Thursday and Friday; those are longer runs with Salamanca's orders. I know Wednesday's orders are full on, but Monday's are the lightest. And it won't be for long."

Millie noticed Herta nod once toward Roy. Icky saw her, too.

"Okay," Roy said. "Let's give that a try."

#

"I thought Roy was making deliveries," Jean said as she brought labels to the bakeshop.

"He does when Icky is on sales calls or if there's an emergency," Millie answered as she continued packing boxes. "And for a while, Roy will make Monday and Wednesday deliveries."

"Icky's meetings in Salamanca must have gone well, then," Jean said, adding, "I can fold the box lids for you."

"Thanks," Millie shifted to the next order. "And yes, the calls went well—almost too well. Tuesday and Thursday production will be as busy as on Wednesdays and Fridays."

"Whew!" Jean smoothed her hand over a label.

"And thanks for adding those store names to the delivery manifest," Millie added.

"You're welcome," Jean said. "I don't know how you manage inventory, but I might be able to help with that, too."

"Let's ask Icky," Millie suggested.

"I'm also looking at the supply of boxes. You've got space to store a lot more, and buying in quantity cuts costs. That's what we do at church."

"What's that?" Frank asked as he came in the door. "You said 'at church.'"

"Hi!" Jean greeted her husband.

"You two look busy!" he noted.

"We're boxing the last packages so Icky can get on the road," Jean said, adding, "Tuesdays are one of *his* three delivery days."

"He'll be right out," Millie offered. "He's showering so he's presentable again."

"He does that?"

"Yummy-tasting product can't come from a sweaty-smelling baker," she explained.

"Here," Frank took a carton from his wife, "let me grab that for you."

"Put it on top of the other one," she said, "by the door."

"New pastor duties?" Icky came in with the delivery manifest.

"Why not?" Frank said. "You look busy!"

Icky picked up three cartons of cookies and backed himself out the door to load the truck. Frank picked up two and followed him. Outside, next to the truck, he'd have a chance to talk to Icky about John Heinz.

"Whoa!" Frank noted as he set them down. "These are heavier than I expected!"

Icky placed his fists on his hips in a Superman pose, and said, "Muscles!"

"No kidding!" Frank agreed. "After baking all morning, I'm surprised you have energy to make deliveries, but I guess that's what it means to work as hard as one of America's favorite comic book superheroes: 'Faster than a speeding bullet . . .'"

"'More powerful than a locomotive,'" Icky finished the theme. "We signed three new accounts, so the bakeshop is busy at both ends."

"Just like church," Frank said. "New families join, and we need more Sunday school teachers."

"That's how it goes," Icky opened the bakery door and grabbed three more cartons.

Frank followed with two more. As they reached the back of the truck, he added, "If you're interested in hiring a driver, I might have someone for you."

Icky hadn't considered adding a delivery man. Frank's suggestion made sense, though. Just as hiring Jean relieved Millie from office administration, hiring someone to deliver product would relieve both Roy and him from being on the road at the end of the day.

But the guy would have to be reliable. Fresh, home-baked flavor differentiated their product from national brands.

"Who do you have in mind?" Icky asked.

"Do you know John Heinz?"

"Heinz?" Icky repeated. "Yeah, I think so. His parents are friends of Pa and Ma."

"Right," Frank said. "John just got out of the Army, and I think he's looking for work."

"John Heinz," Icky repeated the name. An Army veteran would be strong enough to handle heavy boxes. "I'd have to talk to Millie. We agreed to hire more people, but she's looking for help with production."

"Well, if you decide to go in this direction, let me know," Frank said. "I'd be glad to put you together."

8

Getting a Grip

"Roy!" Icky pulled the truck up at the end of his delivery run. "Got a minute?"

"What do you need?" Roy yelled back from the driveway at Pa Haut's house. Grease from his car engine dotted his forehead and arms.

"Advice," Icky answered. "Frank Bauer stopped by today when he picked up Jean. He said a guy in our congregation—John Heinz—asked if he's heard of any job openings, and Frank wondered whether or not we need a delivery man."

"Do you know this Heinz guy?" Roy and Herta had been out of the country so long that they'd lost touch with some of the families in their church. This Heinz guy probably was ten or eleven when they left.

"He just got home from serving in Korea. I saw his family talking with Pa and Ma a couple of weeks ago," Icky answered. "He seemed personable, and should make a good impression with our customers."

"Then what are you waiting for?" Roy challenged.

"Like you said, we need to hire in production first," Icky explained.

Roy paused.

"How much business did Salamanca bring in?"

"Enough to raise production on two days to near capacity—which we needed to do . . ."

"And it'll go even higher when product sells out—which it will," Roy crossed his arms in front of his chest. "Then they'll ask for delivery on Fridays, too."

"Yeah. I'm thinking we're in the crosshairs between adding another employee and keeping up with orders," Icky explained.

"Facing the reality of what you can't do—and recognizing what you can't do *yet*—is part of growing," Roy said.

"So?" Icky pressed.

"So, I know you like to calculate capacity, and so on, but, Icky, you gotta' use a gentle grip on those figures when opportunity comes along."

"Which is why I've been growing the customer base," Icky explained.

"Then meet that growth head on," Roy said.

Icky mimicked Roy's stance then, crossing his arms in front of his chest, as if it would help him follow his brother-in-law's argument.

"Good help is always hard to find," Roy continued, "so if you like this guy, hire him."

"Even though that means not hiring production crew?" Icky challenged. "Because hiring a driver will divert money from bringing on the crew we've been talking about."

"Not necessarily," Roy challenged. "You're ready to offer another product, right?"

"Right," Icky agreed. Actually, he'd been developing two new recipes. "A box of cinnamon samples just came in."

"Yep, yep, yep," Roy said. "I smelled it in inventory."

"And if the recipe for the new cookie comes out as well as I'm hoping, I'll have samples for Ma and you to taste test after dinner on Sunday."

"That's your answer then," Roy said. "Stores won't stop ordering sugar cookies when you offer a second variety; they'll buy *both*. And the same thing will happen again when you introduce a third, *so* . . . ," he held up his thumb to indicate a first step, "grow your customer base—just like you did in Salamanca."

Then, raising his index finger he continued, "grow your product line with that second cookie, and . . . ," Roy added his middle finger to the first two, "get us some relief in the bakeshop so you don't wear out your sister. Or me."

Icky's eyebrow stretched up into a question mark.

"Do all three?" he verified.

"All four," Roy insisted by stabbing the air toward the ground. "Hire that guy to deliver product."

Icky seemed to be calculating again.

"Why not?" Roy challenged. "You said yourself that you've got the oven capacity."

"The oven doesn't increase costs; it's paid for," Icky said. "Adding to the crew . . . "

"—will be covered when you add another product. Like I said, a second cookie immediately doubles sales," Roy interrupted. "And a third will triple demand."

Icky didn't say anything.

"Think about it!" Roy persisted adamantly.

Icky remembered how blunt Roy could be when they worked together at Bolles—a straightforward attitude that meant the guy had no hidden agendas.

"You . . . you're right. Orders *are* going to double."

"Which you won't be able to bake without adding to the crew, so-o-o . . . "

"I get it," Icky finally agreed. "Thanks, Roy."

"So, when are you gonna' see this Heinz fellow?" he asked.

"Frank said he'd put us together on Sunday," Icky said.

"Good," Roy nodded with relief. "Make the offer. I'm done doing deliveries."

#

"I smell cookies," Millie peeked into the bakeshop at dawn on Saturday. The oven made the lean-to warmer than the Quonset hut at that hour, and she was glad to crack open the door between the two kitchens. "I didn't hear you get up."

"Try this," Icky handed her a cookie. He usually wore just a white t-shirt with his white baker's pants, but with the chill of the wee hours, he'd added his baker's jacket. It was buttoned only halfway, and combined with his wild, uncombed hair, he looked like a mad scientist who'd been up half the night. "I wanted to work with a new ingredient."

She bit off an experiment-sized taste.

"Mm-*hmm*," she emphasized. "It's definitely our sugar cookie, but richer somehow. What did you do?"

"I substituted that," he nodded at the container of Numoline, "for some of the sugar."

"This is the stuff that came in that heavy box?"

"Right. A trade magazine said it mixes faster than granulated sugar—and it does," he said. "But it made the dough sweeter, too, so I've been adjusting our formula to correct the ratio. You're tasting the latest version."

Millie sampled another bite.

"Part granulated sugar, part Numo-syrup?"

"Numoline. What do you think?"

"This batch has the right balance," she said. "But the vanilla is also more intense."

"Do you like it?"

"I do!" she agreed. "But I always like extra vanilla, so you probably should ask Roy and Ma about flavor."

She rolled a nibble around inside her mouth, and added, "And I don't quite know how to describe it, but this cookie seems softer."

"Yeah," he agreed. "Sometimes I like cookies with a sandy finish, but in a sugar cookie, I prefer this."

"They brown up nicely, too," Millie flipped over a couple that were cooling on the racks.

"Shiny bottoms!" Icky recalled the first time he told her about checking the underside of a cookie to determine doneness.

"So what's next?" she smiled.

"I'm not sure. I don't like to alter the product we've been building our reputation on."

"But if it's better . . . ," she considered.

"Right," he agreed. "And half of our product line will be based on this basic formula, so now is the time to make adjustments."

"Is that risky?"

"Probably some risk," he removed another batch from the oven. "Not everybody likes the same thing."

Millie studied the half-eaten cookie in her hand.

"Before finalizing it, I need to scale the recipe to learn whether or not the syrup maintains consistency in larger quantities," he continued. "Then I'll price it out."

"You didn't compute cost first?" Millie challenged. Icky didn't like to consider alternatives that drove up a product's shelf price.

"I didn't know how much Numoline we'd use until the recipe was re-formulated. That's what I was working on when you came out."

"Sorry for interrupting," she said, honestly.

"It's okay," he answered. "I want to know what you think. Once I scale and cost out the recipe, and then double-check the bake time to be sure the production schedule isn't thrown off, we'll know whether or not we can keep the price at thirty-five cents a dozen."

"Absolutely!" Millie advocated for wives' household budgets. "Don't increase the price!"

"I know," he allowed.

"Are you planning to solve this today?"

"This morning! Oven and mixer maintenance need to get done this afternoon." Of course, he'd rather just develop recipes. And the cinnamon samples were calling him.

"I'll leave you to your work," she slipped out, but she didn't think he heard her.

#

After supper, Icky returned to the bakeshop. All day, he'd been thinking about his new cookie. It's warmest notes would come from cinnamon—but which variety: Indonesian, Ceylon, or Saigon? He'd purchased all three, hoping one would differentiate his product from others on grocery store shelves.

He tore into the box, lined up the three samples, and gently slit open the first bag. He'd seen shoppers choose baked goods based on smell, so he leaned over to inhale, deeply. After a few seconds, he raised his head to hold the scent and capture words to define its dominant characteristics.

"Indonesian: sweet, strong."

He turned over a fresh sheet of paper in his spiral-topped notepad, and wrote it down.

Next, he opened the bag labelled Ceylon cinnamon. Again, he leaned down and inhaled. "Ceylon: subtle, maybe floral, or . . . citrus? Probably an apple pie cinnamon."

He made a note.

Finally, he sampled the Saigon cinnamon. Its heavy, exotic fragrance swirled around and entered his nostrils enticingly. He wrote "robust" and "lingering," and then added "a hot spice."

He poured small amounts of each variety onto sheets of waxed paper, and examined their physical properties. The Indonesian cinnamon was light brown and powdery; the Ceylon was dark with a rough texture, and the Saigon was reddish-brown and almost oily.

He'd already mixed a small batch of dough: lard and sugar, then fresh eggs, dark molasses, and sour milk. He followed with scarce amounts of ginger, allspice, and cloves. Flour, bread crumbs, salt, and baking soda were stirred in last, as he never liked to mix the flour too hard or too long; overbeating made cookies tough.

He separated the dough into three portions, and mixed a different variety of cinnamon into each with his bare hands. He wanted to feel it between his fingers, and study how the spice was mixing in. The Saigon cinnamon spread more evenly than the other two, and he guessed that its oiliness might be contributing to the way it clung to the flour and crumbs.

"Now, this is what I've been looking for," he pronounced with satisfaction. He rolled the dough to one-eighth-inch thickness, cut circles to fill three cookie trays—one for each of the cinnamon varieties—and slid them into the oven. Perspiration beaded up on his forehead as the temperature in the bakeshop rose, so he stepped outside to cool off. As he leaned against the door frame, he gazed up at ancient stars dusting the sky: twinkling sugar, he decided, with cloud silhouettes made of flour. Is that what God thought of as the Lord created the heavens?

And if Roy is right, in a couple of weeks we'll be baking as many cookies as there are stars in the sky: from eight hundred dozen a day to twenty-four hundred dozen. That's going to complicate getting enough inventory at the moment when we need it. With one truck, it'll complicate deliveries, too.

The oven's buzzer went off, and he returned to the bakeshop. He tugged on oven mitts, removed hot sheets from the oven, and slid the cookies onto cooling racks. After church, he'd ask Ma and Roy for evaluations.

He washed the mixer and beaters, sanitized the bakeshop, and quietly slipped through the door into the hut's kitchen. The lights were turned down, and Millie was propped up in a wooden chair like a small flour sack. She should have gone to bed. Instead, she'd decided to sit—just for a few minutes—to take in a quiet moment and warm her hands on a cup of hot coffee.

It had gone cold. She didn't want to drink it anyway, not at that late hour.

Icky watched her lean forward, put her elbow on the table, and rest her chin on the palm of her hand. Her face was blank and unfocused, the eyeless stare of exhaustion.

"You look tired," he finally whispered.

She lifted her head.

"What do you expect? We've been up since 'o-dark-thirty,'" she yawned, covering her mouth with the back of her hand, "and it's the weekend."

She'd spent half the day on housework, and the other half cleaning up mud dragged in by Mark and Buko, who got themselves into a mess while investigating puddles. Thankfully, Mary Lou washed the dishes after dinner, so Millie could get the dirty kid bathed and tucked into bed. She was only a few pages into *Frog Went A-Courtin'* before he was out for the night.

"Finally!" she'd said to herself as she tiptoed out of the children's bedroom. The only remaining task had been ironing, and she'd finished it just before Icky came in.

"Did you decide which cinnamon you like?" she asked.

"We'll test it tomorrow," he said.

"You worked on two products today, plus all the equipment maintenance," she noted. "You've got to be bushed."

"Comes with the job," he answered. "Besides, the Numoline and the cinnamon arrived at the same time, so I had no choice."

She could only nod.

"C'mon, Millie," he held out his hand. Her curls were as disordered as a dust mop. He loved that easy look on her.

"We both need a few winks. Tomorrow comes mighty fast."

"Are you still planning to talk with John Heinz after church?" she asked as she shoved her chair under the kitchen table.

"Absolutely," he confirmed.

"Then, I'm going to sleep like a baby."

9

Unexpected Blessings

BERTIE BLINKED HER EYES widely.

"John Heinz called for *me?*" she asked her mother. John and her older brother played sports together when they were in high school—which was why she took exception when he patted her on the head as everyone emerged from the Palace Theater. All she could think to do in the midst of a crowd of movie-goers was to extricate herself from further humiliation, so she grabbed her sisters and tromped the three of them down the street to the bus stop.

"Are you sure he didn't want Billie?" she asked.

"He's phoned twice," her mother said matter-of-factly. "He's asking you to return his call, but you should wait."

Bertie knew what her mother meant. Despite magazine columns advising readers on the modern maneuverings of 1950s dating etiquette, girls who were wise would still allow fellows to pursue their interests—if that was why John was calling.

"What if Billie tells him that you gave me the message, and I ignored it?" Bertie asked.

"Billie doesn't need to know," her mother suggested. "Then he won't have anything to tell."

Bertie agreed and prepared to wait, but only an hour passed before John called again. Her mother let the phone ring three times before answering, and then handed over the receiver with a small smile.

"Hello, this is Bertie," she said as her mother retreated.

A few minutes later, however, Bertie's mother told her husband that dinner would be a half hour early because their daughter agreed to join John Heinz for a ride at seven o'clock.

"Billie's friend? That John Heinz?" he asked.

"Yes, that John Heinz," she confirmed with interest in her voice.

"This is good then," he smiled.

"*Very* good," she agreed.

Bertie sorted through her closet to find her most grown-up looking dress: a nipped-waist, full-skirted design with a high collar and elbow-length sleeves. Even though John invited her only for a ride in his Packard, she was going to make the most of this little excursion—from curled hair to nylon stockings. And matching two-tone Spectator heels, too. She might be petite, but she wasn't a child, and she wasn't going to give him a single reason to think she wasn't old enough to be worthy of his attention!

Before she left her bedroom, she sprayed a fine mist of perfume in the air and walked through it as it diminished. She didn't want an overpowering scent, but she thought the gentle fragrance of honeysuckle and lily of the valley might linger in his car after he returned her home: a small reminder of their evening together.

#

On Sunday morning, Icky caught sight of John Heinz walking up the block to the church with his parents, and called him aside.

"Welcome back!" he greeted him.

"Thanks," John responded. "It's good to be home."

"Frank—or rather, Pastor Bauer—says you're looking for work," Icky dove right in. "Would you be interested in delivering cookies for our bakeshop?"

"Yes!" John answered immediately. Driving Bertie around town and stopping for a soda was all he could afford the evening before. He'd sure like a way to earn some bucks so he could start seeing her seriously. "When do you need me to start?"

"How about coming in on Tuesday, about eleven-thirty," Icky said. "You can see our operation, help load the truck, and ride along with me. If you like the work, the job is yours starting Wednesday."

"Eleven-thirty is great!" he repeated. "Thanks!"

John slipped into the pew next to his parents, and immediately whispered to his father that the Haut's son—the one with the new bakeshop—just offered him a job.

Mr. Heinz smiled, nodded, turned toward his wife, and whispered the news to her. Her mouth formed a silent "O." Then, leaning forward to look directly at John, she placed the palms of her hands together prayerfully beneath her lips.

He smiled, and nodded back. God is good, he agreed. Very good, indeed.

#

Mrs. Heinz recalled mentioning to Icky's mother that John was looking for a job, so at the end of the service, she made a point to seek her out next to Oak Hill Park, as Pa and Ma Haut always left their car alongside N. Fourth Street.

"Emma! Thank you for telling Icky that John was looking for a job," she said with gladness in her heart. "He talked with him this morning before church!"

"*Nein*," she quickly denied telling Icky about John. "About this I know nothing!"

Mrs. Heinz pulled back her head in disbelief, turned it gently left and right, and smiled.

"First Icky hears Mrs. Bauer's prayer for work," Mrs. Heinz insisted. "Then he learns that John is looking. I think you helped."

Ma's eyes widened and pulled her shoulders back, stunned that Mrs. Heinz knew that the pastor's wife had taken a job at the bakeshop.

But didn't she speak with an approving smile? And she said God was working through them to help Mrs. Bauer, so perhaps other members of the congregation would be inclined similarly, especially since Icky also apparently offered to hire John.

"*Nein, nein!*" Ma insisted again. "I thank you, but I said nothing to Icky."

"As you say," Mrs. Heinz allowed as they parted. But she didn't believe her.

"This job offer to John Heinz is news to you?" Ma asked Pa after a few steps.

"*Ja*," he said. "Yesterday Roy and Icky talk about hiring a driver, but the man they would ask: this I did not know."

Ma stopped in front of their Pontiac to look directly at Pa.

"And you think Mrs. Bauer working for the bakeshop: this also is good?" she pressed. After all, Pa did lend a hand with moving furniture—which was not to suggest that he was complicit in the decision to hire the pastor's wife. Still, he had helped it come about.

He sighed.

"Maybe wives working in jobs outside the home was not allowed when our family was young," Pa recalled. More than half of the states made it illegal for married women to hold jobs during the Great Depression; taking work from legitimate breadwinners would have endangered U.S. family stability. Besides, wasn't the domain of the German woman also consigned to *kinder, küche, kirche*: children, kitchen, church. It all made sense, at the time.

"But," he continued, "maybe today this is not the same." He opened the car door, and helped her into her seat. He could see she was working out a conundrum; her face bore evidence of it.

"This we will ask Icky," she decided as Pa put the key into the ignition and turned over the engine. "He can tell us how he decides to offer to John Heinz a job."

"*Ja*, Ma," Pa said evenly.

"Because taking credit that is not mine: this I do not want," she added.

He nodded. He knew his woman didn't like to accept credit even when she was the one to whom thanks was owed. The Reverend Bauer was speaking of Ma in that sermon about following God's call to do the Lord's work. Of this, Pa was certain.

#

After dinner, Roy set three large plates of Icky's cookie samples in the center of the kitchen table, and invited everyone to try them.

"I'm testing three varieties of cinnamon," Icky said. "Which do you like best?"

"What is this cookie called?" Millie asked.

"I don't know yet," Icky said. "You're in charge of naming."

"Okay, then what's in it?" she persisted, taking a bite.

"Like I said: cinnamon and a few other ingredients," he said.

"I taste molasses. And this one," she pointed to her favorite after tasting all three, "is strongest."

"That's the Saigon cinnamon," Icky said.

"Cinnamons are different?" Pa asked.

"Right," Icky answered, "in color, smell and texture. And I like the Saigon cinnamon, too."

"What's better about it?" Roy studied the samples.

"At first, I was looking for an aroma that would attract shoppers. But when I started to work the dough, I saw that the Saigon cinnamon disperses evenly."

"Why is that?" Roy pursued.

"Probably because it's oilier," Icky guessed.

Heads around the table bobbed in acknowledgment of the cinnamon differences as everyone smelled and tasted samples.

"Regardless of the one we choose, we'll be able to switch production from sugar cookies to this variety without changing equipment," Icky added.

"Yep, yep, yep, that's operational efficiency!" Roy noted. "Good move."

"And this new recipe tastes and smells quite different from your sugar cookies, so housewives will want to buy both, hm?" Herta added. "I like it!"

"Which?" Icky urged his sister's opinion.

"Saigon," she said. "Definitely, the Saigon."

"What do you think, Ma?" Icky asked. She hadn't said anything, and she was the family arbiter on everything coming from a kitchen.

"I think hiring John Heinz is good," she answered.

The table went silent. Ma had been quiet during the cookie tasting, so everyone assumed her attention was directed toward choosing her favorite. But no. A bubbling cauldron of both the strength of her faith and the pain of her hard-won convictions, her thoughts were elsewhere.

"John asks you for a job?" she leaned forward with both arms crossed on top of the table. "The same way Mrs. Bauer says she will work for you?"

"No," Icky answered cautiously. "Mrs. Bauer offered to work for the bakeshop because she already was looking for a job. Then, on Tuesday when Pastor Bauer picked her up, he said John was looking for work, and he suggested that if we need a delivery man, he'd put us together.

"And he's not hired yet," he added. "He'll decide after he rides with me this week."

Roy and Herta refused to make eye contact with anyone—not when they lived under the same roof with Pa and Ma, and worked with Icky and Millie.

Ma finally rested against the back of her chair and nodded, satisfied with Icky's easy explanation.

"These jobs you offer after the Reverend Bauer preaches the sermon about the television show," she summed up her thoughts. She'd been tossing back and forth his message on what it means to be "called" to do God's work against what she feared people would say if they found out that their pastor's wife was diverting her time from serving the church to favoring the business of one of its members.

"Yes," Icky said.

"You will tell Mrs. Heinz that the offer you make to her son did not come from me, Idkä," she used his baptismal name—which always called him to attention. "She wants to thank me for it. She can thank the Reverend Bauer!"

"Do you like the new cookie?" he asked.

"*Ja*, sure," she answered. After a moment, she tapped the plate with the Saigon cinnamon and added, "This is the best. You use the dark molasses?"

"Of course," he said. "Light molasses would have been too sweet, and blackstrap is bitter."

"Dark molasses also strengthens the cinnamon," she agreed.

"If John accepts our job offer, he'll start working on Wednesday," Icky confirmed. "I'll tell him to be *sure* his mother knows that Pastor Bauer recommended him."

"I thank you for that," she ended the conversation.

#

"Are you asleep?" Millie asked in the dark.

"Almost," he yawned, his eyes half-closed. "We have to be up in six hours."

"I have a name for your new cookie," she said.

"What?" he responded.

"Keep it simple, so 'Spice Bites.'"

He didn't answer.

"Do you like it?" she whispered.

He snored.

10

From How Many to How Much

"Jean, can you reach Tom Hubbell for me? He's at Pillsbury," Icky asked between mixing batches of dough.

"Do you want me to tell him why you're calling?" she thumbed through the Rolodex.

"We need to increase our flour order," he said.

"Can I do that for you?"

"Next time," he agreed. "This time, I may need to negotiate delivery charges. Let me know when he's on the line."

A few minutes later, Jean called Icky in from the bakeshop.

"Tom!" Icky greeted him. "When will you be in Olean?"

"Hey, Ick! How's business?"

"Good enough that we need to increase our flour order by 20 percent—and then double it next month."

"I can write a new purchase order over the phone," Tom confirmed. "Is the Michigan and Ohio wheat working for you?"

"Super!" Icky said with enthusiasm. "That lower protein blend gives our sugar cookie the softer texture I was looking for."

"Just what you wanted then," Tom penciled a note on a Haut's Cookie Shoppe purchase order.

"What about delivery cost on the larger purchase?" Icky said.

"We'll just load your order onto the back of the same truck going to other accounts in Olean," Tom decided. In fact, Pillsbury delivered to three nearby accounts, all of them bread bakeries, including Roy and Icky's former employer. "That way we can absorb the charge."

"Are you sure you want to do that?" Icky pressed. "I expected to pay."

"Look, we want to be part of your future," Tom said, "and the way I see it, you'll be selling cookies all over the east coast soon. That's when we'll start charging—because then you'll need railcars of flour."

"Whoa! Let's add a few more stores around western New York first," Icky said.

"I'm not talking about individual stores, Icky," Tom clarified. "I'm talking about chains and distributors. They buy from bakeries like yours."

Icky didn't think his bakeshop was anywhere close to putting out enough cookies to meet the demands of a national chain. But construction on the new bakery would start soon, so why not check out what larger buyers might be interested in?

"Can you recommend any contacts?" he asked.

"Sure," Tom agreed. "We can give you a referral, too, but I don't think you'll need it."

#

"Thanks for packing the extra orders so fast today," Icky said when he got home from making deliveries. He fell into a kitchen chair and kicked off his shoes as Millie set a plate of reheated dinner in front of him. "I didn't like leaving you alone with all that last-minute work, but I had to spend time with John."

"Jean helped," she allowed, "and we set aside a couple of packages of cookies for John to take home to his parents."

"He found them with your note reminding him to tell his mother that Frank referred him to us," Icky cut into his dinner.

"What did he decide about the job?"

"He's taking it."

"Good!" she said. "Roy will be glad to hear that!"

"I talked with Hubbell this morning, too," Icky moved on to other topics. "He's increasing our flour order, and still not charging for delivery."

"That's awfully nice," she said, "but I hope it won't get him into trouble."

"I don't think so," Icky assured her. "He says Pillsbury expects us to grow, and they'll charge for delivery when we need a whole truckload—or a full railcar. That's how he put it."

"A railcar full?" Millie repeated. "Where would we store that much flour?"

"We wouldn't, not for long," Icky answered. "We'd bake."

"Even so, who would we sell that much product to?" she challenged.

"Tom thinks I ought to be calling on east coast grocery store chains," Icky told her. "Distributors, too; apparently, they're eager to sign purchase orders with regional bakeries."

"East coast!" she repeated. "That's four hundred miles!"

"I know," he pushed back his half-eaten plate of dinner. "But Tom said the new superhighways let distributors truck in baked goods from all over."

Millie seemed skeptical.

"They re-box them as variety packs, and sell them to smaller chains. Major chains like A&P do the same thing for their stores," he explained.

"We're not big enough for customers that large," Millie challenged.

"Not today," he stood and yawned. "But Tom thinks that soon we could be."

"Then you better hire production staff," she picked up his plate and rinsed it off as he headed off to bed for the night.

#

"What did John decide about the delivery job?" Roy asked the next morning.

"He's starting today," Icky said.

"Salamanca, too?" Roy continued.

"No problem," Icky said. "We drove all the way out there so he could see the entire territory, and he asked why we aren't selling across the state line in Bradford, Pennsylvania."

"I like how he thinks," Roy noted. "What did you tell him?"

"I said I'd open a couple of accounts," Icky answered.

"When?" Roy challenged. More customers meant increased production.

"After we add two people to the crew," Icky assured him. "Millie left an employment ad on Jean's desk with a note asking her to run it in *The Olean Times-Herald*."

"Yep, yep, yep," Roy smiled at his wife. "And make it three people: one to help me, and two to work production with Herta—because with a second cookie, orders will double, and Millie will be too busy in packaging to cut dough."

Herta nodded in agreement.

But Roy's concern wasn't just about production capacity. An uneasy tension was building between his wife and his sister-in-law, even if Icky didn't see the tattered civility they occasionally lapsed into. Separating responsibilities could ease that situation.

Besides, he knew that Icky was developing more cookie recipes, so they'd need the extra hands in production sooner rather than later.

"When did Jean say the ad will appear?" Icky asked Millie to reinforce the point that he was keeping his promise.

"Tomorrow's paper," she answered loudly enough for everyone to hear. "We could have candidates to interview this weekend."

"Do you want to handle that?" Icky asked Roy. "I'm thinking you'd do most of the training."

"Yep, yep, yep," Roy agreed. "And how about hiring an apprentice, too. Cracking five hundred eggs every day is entry-level work, and that number will double with a second cookie."

Icky pressed his lips together, revealing his reluctance.

"I'd like to pass that job off if I'm training a crew," Roy held firm.

"I'll look into it. But let me ask you this. You haven't supervised teams since you left Bolles," Icky noted. "Are you sure you're okay with handling that again?"

"What do you mean? I've been supervising *you* since Herta and I got back to Olean!" Roy grinned in jest.

Icky was going to disagree—until he caught the look on Roy's face.

He returned a half grin. He'd let the comment slide.

#

"Saturday morning: baking all by yourself again?" Millie slipped through her kitchen doorway to peek into the bakeshop. The sun was just breaking over the top ridge of the mountains, and the children were still asleep.

"I'm trying to solve a problem," Icky said quietly as he looked up from his reference books. A pitcher of eggs sat on the work table.

"What problem?" she asked.

"Roy said we should hire an apprentice because breaking eggs takes too much time."

"And you agree?"

"Well, he's right about the number of eggs. On our busiest days, he's cracking about five hundred—which of course we knew because we're paying for them, but . . . "

"Five hundred?"

"—which is well over two thousand a week," he emphasized, "And at six seconds an egg, that job equals a half a day's work."

"How do you know it's six seconds?" Millie asked.

"I timed it," he nodded at the pitcher.

"Did you allow time to remove broken bits of eggshell?"

"We don't break shells; we're professionals," he ignored her point. "Anyway, when we add our second cookie, somebody will spend a full day cracking eggs."

"No wonder he's asking for an apprentice," Millie wondered if that job could go to one of the new girls. After all, cracking eggs didn't require muscle.

"I can take that pitcher," she reached across the table. "I'll scramble the eggs to serve with beans for lunch."

"Okay with me," he returned to his reference books.

"And Roy is interviewing job candidates today," Millie reminded him. "We didn't advertise for an apprentice, but an entry-level candidate could come in. Maybe we could consider one of the girls to crack eggs."

"Better to hire a man," Icky said. "Then, when we need another guy to mix, we can move him up."

"But then you'd have to hire again," she countered.

"Yeah, no guy worth his salt will want to crack eggs for a career," Icky said. "But by starting at the bottom, he gets to see an entire operation. And we get to see if he has potential."

A part-time girl could move from cracking eggs to cutting dough full-time, Millie thought to herself. But as Icky was busy with his research, she'd argue her point later.

"Either way, I need to tackle this egg problem," he said.

"*Tackling* an egg could be messy," Millie lightened the conversation.

He grimaced. "I'll ignore that since I didn't have any coffee this morning."

"A pot is brewing. I'll get you some," she left for the hut's kitchen.

"Better make it a double," he called.

A few minutes later, she returned with two hot mugs. "Did you learn anything good—like which came first: the chicken or the egg?"

"Huh?" he said blankly as he sipped, adding, "Thanks for the coffee."

After a moment, he continued, "I did find some useful information."

"Like what?"

"Egg sizes," he tapped his reference book.

"Small, medium and large," she advised; after all, that's how they were sold.

"Right, but even within those categories, chickens don't have the decency to lay them all the same size," he said. "Large eggs can range anywhere from 1.75 to 2.25 ounces each."

"Is that such a big deal?"

"In large batches, it will be," he said. "Right now, each batch calls for fourteen eggs—which means an egg variance of as much as seven ounces."

"That's almost a cup," she recognized. "How are we fixing it?"

"It's been a judgment call," Icky said. "If the dough seems too sticky to roll, Roy usually just adds more flour. He also could adjust the bake time or temperature, but that would put us off schedule."

"So this is another example of thinking of temperature as an ingredient," she noted.

"Right! And sugar is affected, too. It acts like a liquid when it's heated."

"Is that why it's creamed into the lard or butter?" Millie asked.

"Sometimes," Icky said. "If we were baking cakes, though, we might want to mix the butter, sugar, flour, and baking soda at the same time. That's what Herta used to do in their bakeshop in Cuba.

"I didn't know she liked cake baking," Millie said with a note of surprise.

"It was her specialty," he said. "And lately, she's been borrowing cake baking books from the library."

"How do you know that?"

"She asked me *why* mixing all the ingredients into the bowl at one time makes a cake flat," he said.

"Does it?"

"Yeah," he said.

"And?"

"Creaming only the butter, sugar, and eggs adds air to the batter. But if dry ingredients are mixed in at the beginning, too, the batter can become tough—because the gluten is activated sooner."

"So?"

"So wheat flour that's overmixed is dense."

"Dense?"

"You can tell when you cut into it. It's flatter, too," he added.

"Well, a flat cake is probably easier to decorate," Millie allowed.

"When Roy and she ran their own shop, they mixed all the ingredients in one step because that was faster. They could bake more product in less time."

Millie wondered if Herta's questions were meant to hint that she was getting ready to start up her own cake baking business.

"What did you say about that?" she asked.

"Nothing to say," he answered.

"Baking gets complicated," Millie considered plans her sister-in-law might be making.

"It does—which is why I need to solve this egg problem," he returned to his work. "The mixer in the new bakery will handle fifteen times as much dough as this bench mixer, so the egg variance will be greater."

"How much greater?"

"By my calculations, fifteen times seven ounces means we could be off by as much as three quarts of eggs—and that's per batch."

"And then, if they're bigger eggs, the dough will be too moist," Millie followed.

"—which would mean our cookies could come out spongy," Icky said. "Or the rise could be off, since eggs can act as a leavening agent."

"All of this calculation is a different problem from the one Roy gave you," Millie noted.

"He said we need an apprentice. I'm checking whether or not we have other options," he pointed to a second reference book.

"Okay," she stood to leave. She knew he enjoyed research as much as his mother. "Have fun out here."

"Thanks," he returned to the index, and ran his finger down the alphabetized list, repeating, "eggs . . . eggs . . . eggs . . ."

"Ahh!" he flipped to a page:

> If Shelled Eggs are used, the following conversion basis will be adaptable where small amounts are called for: 1 lb. whole egg equals 9 to 11 shelled eggs; 1 lb. whites equals 17 to 20 whites; 1 lb. sugar yolk equals 19 to 22 yolks.

He leaned back and picked up his coffee mug.

"One pound equals nine to eleven cracked eggs. Nine to eleven," he drummed his fingertips on the counter, "means they're converting *numbers* to *amounts*! If I convert our recipes from *numbers* of large eggs to measurable *volumes* of liquid eggs: from how *many* to how *much*, then the issue with the world's inconsiderate chickens will be solved!"

Sort of, he paused. Shelled eggs are highly perishable, so we'd have to use all of that inventory immediately, even if it were refrigerated. . . . unless we could freeze eggs, and thaw them as we need them.

But would thawed eggs produce cookies with the same texture and taste? One way to find out!

"Millie!" he bellowed.

"I'm right here," she peeked into the bakeshop, calmly.

"Oh. Sorry," he acknowledged. "Freeze those eggs in the pitcher, okay?"

"Freeze?"

"Use your cupcake tin. Measure how much one of those little cups holds, then fill 'em to the brim, and freeze the pan."

"What are you going to do with frozen eggs?"

"I'm going to thaw 'em after dinner, and bake sugar cookies this evening," he said. "I want to see if Roy and Ma can tell the difference between fresh and frozen."

#

"So, what do you think?" Icky asked. "Do the cookies marked 'fresh eggs' taste as good as the ones marked 'frozen eggs'?"

"No difference," Roy said.

"You play a trick?" Ma asked.

"A test," Icky said.

"Same flavor, same texture, same cookie," Roy repeated.

"*Ja*, the same," Ma agreed. "Why freeze the eggs?"

"Roy says cracking eggs takes too much time, and he's right," Icky said. "So I want to find a vendor that sells shelled and frozen eggs."

"Because then we won't need an apprentice," Roy understood.

"We can't be the first bakery to need large quantities of cracked eggs," Icky moved on. He'd ask Jean to research vendors, beginning with Fleischmann's. "They sell a variety of products to commercial bakeries, and they deliver to Cold Storage downtown."

#

"Icky," Ma pulled her son aside as everyone left her kitchen, "You use my recipe for your sugar cookie, *ja*?"

"Of course. Why?"

"The recipe is German," she said. "The chickens are German."

"So?"

"The German chickens' eggs are bigger," she intimated. "The medium-sized egg in the Old Country is the large egg here, so you got to fix the recipe when you use eggs from the New York chickens."

"I did that when I started the bakery," he assured her.

"So, when you find the vendor for the frozen eggs, you will adjust the measure for the German chickens, *ja*?" Ma asked.

"I will," he confirmed.

"Good," Ma sighed gratefully. "I don't want people to say my recipe is dry."

"They won't," he promised. "If you want to be sure, you can inspect cookie quality when we move into the new building."

"No, the bakery work you do yourself," Ma refused, "but I thank you for the offer."

11

One for the Money

"Wow! They all booked meetings?" Icky thanked Jean for scheduling appointments with east coast distributors. "I bet the Pillsbury recommendation helped."

"Actually, the buyers just said to bring samples, so I didn't mention it," she clarified.

Icky rubbed his thumb across his chin as he recalled what Tom said about an increasing demand for bakery products. "We might be on to something bigger than I thought."

"Your hotel reservations and road maps are right there, under your itinerary," she added as she prepared to leave.

"Have a nice evening," he scanned phone messages, grateful that Jean knew how to plan a business trip.

"What's going on?" Millie came in from the bakeshop.

"Just reading messages," he held up three pink While You Were Out forms, "and thinking about all the meetings Jean set up. I'll be on sales calls next week."

"Again? You were out last week," she noted.

"That was local—to get orders for the new spice bites cookie," he answered.

"The package labels for that one arrived today," Millie noted.

"I saw them," he said. "Jean did a good job."

"When will that cookie be added to production?"

"Roy says the new crew is ready to roll it out, so it's on the schedule for Wednesday."

"Wednesday of this week?"

"Yeah."

"Did all the stores order it?"

"Yeah, just like Roy predicted, so sales doubled."

"Doubled?" she repeated. "We're doubling output, just like that?"

"With twice the payroll," he pointed out.

"But it's a *new* production crew!" she pressed.

"They've been testing this cookie all week," he said. "They're ready."

"But a new crew and a new cookie . . . "

" . . . go together if we're going to cover their pay," Icky interrupted. "Besides, the church staff chomped down platefuls of samples—without remorse, so we're ready to go. We got orders to fill."

"Then, how about this: If sales doubled, why are you meeting with customers again?"

"Future business. Hubbell recommended these accounts," he held up his itinerary.

"Distributors?" she asked.

"The ones on the east coast."

"That's an overnight trip!" she objected.

"Actually, I'll be gone three nights," he clarified, "and if Hubbell is right, our sales to individual stores will be small potatoes."

"I'm not sure we're ready for this east coast idea," Millie resisted.

"Why not?"

"Shipping out of our area seems like—oh, I don't know—like we're losing control," she cautioned, "like offering cookies to strangers."

"New England families like cookies just as much as Olean families," he insisted.

"Then tell me this: How can we claim to offer *fresh* cookies if they're trucked four hundred miles to some distributor, and then reshipped to stores?" she challenged.

"Bake 'em Monday, ship 'em Monday afternoon to arrive at the warehouse in the wee hours, re-box on Tuesday morning for delivery to store shelves by afternoon."

"Day old," she pressed.

"That's another benefit of using Numoline: invert sugar syrup improves shelf life," he pointed out.

Disbelief crossed her face.

"—by at least five days," he held his position. "I already tested it, and nobody at church could differentiate cookies baked Monday from the ones baked Friday."

"Well, I don't like the idea of you driving so far in that old Studebaker," she fortified her second objection. "If you have trouble on the road,..."

"I won't," he interrupted.

"Remember last week," she insisted.

He'd had to pump the accelerator and torture the starter to get the engine to turn over, which it did, but only after shuddering in defiance.

"That old rust bucket is dying," she maintained. And Millie could tell. Her father was a machinist and her brother, Gordon, was a mechanic; growing up with the two of them meant the sound of churning motors was the background music of her youth.

"I don't know what I can do about it," he said. "I want to meet these guys now, because once we move into the new bakery, I'll be too busy to make sales calls for a while."

"But...," she started to argue.

"Gordon can give the car a once-over," he conceded. "Okay?"

"It doesn't sound like I have a choice," she said, "so for now, that'll have to do."

"Good," Icky said, "because I gotta' go if we're gonna' grow."

#

As Millie finished the weekly laundry, she realized that Icky's one dress shirt wouldn't be enough for an extended business trip.

"You need two more," she told him, "so I'm headed to Carnahan's Men's Store tomorrow afternoon."

"Thanks," he said. "I didn't think of clothes."

"You're going to need a suitcase, too," she added.

He paused.

"Making sales calls is more complicated than I expected," he admitted. He'd never traveled overnight before, or stayed in a hotel.

Millie just nodded. If Icky thinks calling on customers is complicated, he ought to consider how tough it is to keep up with him when he's running in so many different directions at once.

12

Two for the Road

AFTER ICKY'S LAST APPOINTMENT, he stopped at a gas station to fill the Studebaker's tank and phone Millie. A pay phone was situated at the edge of the lot, so he dialed zero to reach an operator, gave her the number he wanted, dropped two quarters and a dime into the slots, and heard the call ring through. Millie answered. He imagined her standing next to the phone at Jean's desk.

"I'll get in late tonight," he said. "Yeah, the last buyer loved the cookies, too. I'll tell you more when I get home. I don't have enough coins to talk longer. . . . I love you, too."

Before he pulled out, he laid out his collection of maps on the passenger side of the car's bench seat and memorized the first part of his trip. Then, he prayed the car would start. The day before, the engine hadn't wanted to turn over, so he pumped the accelerator while holding in the clutch, and then revved the motor a couple of times. After a few dispirited coughs, the old clunker drew a bit of life into its pistons and finally settled into to a consistent vroom.

As he pulled out, he glanced at his wristwatch to begin the countdown to Olean: nine hours loomed ahead. He'd keep an eye out for a roadside diner to grab a quick cup of coffee and a slice of pie, probably late in the afternoon. He didn't want to eat more than that and risk feeling sleepy.

Spending days behind the wheel—which was essentially what he'd been doing since each of his meetings took only about an hour—taught him that making sales calls was solitary work. And two-minute long-distance calls home to let Millie know he checked into his hotel for the night wasn't enough time to catch up on family news or share details on his day. On the other hand, he found that being secluded afforded rare uninterrupted hours to reflect on how much he'd accomplished, and to consider what he still needed to do.

As afternoon waned, he crossed the state line into New York. His stomach was grumbling. He hadn't seen any open diners, but the car needed gas, so he stopped to fill up again, stretch his legs, and grab a candy bar. He tore off the label and read the ingredients as he took a bite. He'd begun differentiating various chocolate blends, and remembered how Hershey's competitor, M&M, developed a way to keep the candy coatings hard: "melts in your mouth, not in your hand," the ad boasted. He wondered about drizzling hard chocolate over the top of cookies, and jotted the idea in his notebook.

Five minutes later, he was back on the road, making a mental checklist of letters he ought to write and telephone calls he needed to make. He'd already penned a note to a distributor who signed a purchase order as soon as they sampled the cookies. Icky had to tell him to date it for spring when the new bakery would be operating—and the guy still wanted to sign a contract!

Not all of the meetings were so positive. A buyer for one of the big grocery chains said Icky would need a larger product line before they'd be interested. Variety and selection was the magic combination housewives look for.

"She wants to see that a brand offers three or more options before she forks over some of her weekly grocery budget. Then she isn't deciding whether or not to buy cookies. She's asking herself, '*Which* cookies shall I buy for my family this time?'" he explained. "And that increases sales at the cash register!"

Icky had already decided which two varieties to introduce next: peanut butter and hermits. He'd bake samples to take to Sunday dinner for evaluation. He'd talk with Roy about hiring and training a second shift, too, because if they ran two crews now in the make-do bakeshop, everyone could be offered the first shift when operations moved to the new building. That would mean they'd hit the ground running with a fully trained morning crew!

The sun retreated behind the mountains in the western sky, so he pulled out the headlight knob and adjusted the beam from low to high by depressing a floor-mounted dimmer switch with his left foot. The lights created a yellow tunnel penetrating branches arching over the road, and his thoughts shifted to home: one hour to go. As he drove through Hinsdale just north of Olean, he rolled each of his shoulders in circles, stretched his arms one at a time toward the dashboard, and then glanced at the mileage indicator to see how far he'd driven.

"Blast!" he said out loud. The temperature gauge had begun to climb.

Immediately, he assumed an alert posture as his eyes darted between the road and the gauge, back and forth, the gauge and the road. Was he seeing correctly?

He was. And the gauge was quivering nervously.

How long had it been climbing? He should have been paying closer attention.

Were all the fluid levels up? They were full before he left. And the engine didn't sound strange. No high-pitched whining or hissing. No shuddering. No coughing or chugging or hesitating. Maybe the problem was a faulty gauge.

His stomach muscles had begun tightening, so he forced himself to release a deep, jagged breath to calm down. He also loosened the death grip he'd imposed on the steering wheel. He'd pull over if he had to, but he'd like to make it all the way home if he could.

His eyes continued to dart between the road and the gauge. Only five more miles, he told the old car.

Then three miles. The gauge was definitely climbing, but slowly. He passed the Olean "welcome" sign; he could walk the rest of the way if he had to. He dropped his speed, guided the car down back streets, coasted into a parking place in front of the hut, and killed the engine. Immediately, he fell back into the driver's seat, relaxed his stiff jaw, and expelled a long, full breath. He was exhausted and keyed up at the same time.

Lights were on, so Millie was still awake. He grabbed his suitcase and briefcase, and slipped in through the bakeshop.

"We got a new account!" he announced.

"Shhh!" she stood quickly. "You'll wake the kids!"

"We got a distributor!" he repeated in a loud whisper.

Her forehead fell forward and her jaw dropped.

"Now?"

"As soon as we're in the new bakery," he said. "It's a small account, but it increases production by 15 percent!"

"But John can't deliver to the east coast!"

"No, definitely not," Icky said. "We'll ship these over the road."

"But we're going to need a larger crew!"

Then she stopped herself. She hadn't even greeted him yet.

"Wait a minute," she delivered a proper hello.

"It's good to be home," he answered with an extra hug. "I missed you."

"Did you stop for dinner? Are you hungry?"

"I had a Hershey bar," he ignored his stomach. "Anyway, about the production increase, I had time on the road to think through a start-up plan for the new bakery. If we hire an afternoon shift now, we can transfer everyone to the morning shift when we move. That way, we'll be able to handle this new order ahead of schedule."

Millie shook her head.

"I thought you were just going to meet people and learn what they're interested in. I didn't realize you'd come back with another account."

"To be honest, Millie, I didn't expect it either," he admitted, "but I probably should have known. Hubbell said they're hungry for baked goods. And they loved our cookies."

"When do they want deliveries?"

"I told them the new bakery is under construction, so we wrote in a spring start date," Icky said, "but we can update it if we're ready before then."

"Just so we don't have to increase production right away," Millie wanted to confirm.

"But the sooner the better," Icky insisted. "We'll see what Roy thinks."

"And you're adding a second shift?"

"Probably," Icky said.

"And doing it now—in this temporary bakeshop," she repeated flatly as she considered the impact of a crew operating on the other side of her kitchen door until eight o'clock in the evening.

"If Roy agrees," Icky pursued, "and a second crew will let us work two new cookies into the production lineup right away."

Millie sighed.

"Do you want a Manhattan?" she pulled down a bottle of Southern Comfort.

"Friday. End of the week. Yes," he allowed.

"I thought you'd be sapped, driving all those hours," she grabbed a jar of maraschino cherries from the refrigerator.

"My head is buzzing from being on the road." He decided not to mention the problem with the car. "I'll probably pass out as soon as I hit the pillow."

"At least you can sleep in," she set out a basket of crackers.

"Probably not," he disagreed. "Equipment maintenance is on tomorrow morning's list. When it's done, the afternoon will be free."

"Free for . . . ?" She'd like to have some "free" time.

"Formulating new cookie recipes. What else would I be doing?"

"Maybe we should hire someone to handle equipment maintenance," she suggested. "Then you'd have time to scale up a couple of the varieties that Mary Lou sold to the neighbors from her bike basket. Remember that peanut butter cookie?"

"Good point," he looked over the top of his drink glass. "And it's Mark's favorite."

"I only mean that you've got too much going on," she continued. "You're going to need a maintenance guy anyway, so why not find somebody now?"

"You're probably right," he leaned back, finally relaxing. He'd missed her end-of-the-day banter.

"Especially if you're adding a second shift," she reinforced her argument. "That'll mean the equipment will be doing double duty, so it's going to need more attention."

"You're probably right," he repeated, this time with a grin.

"All right, I'll stop," she allowed.

"No, don't," he said. "I like how you see the big picture."

"What do you think Roy is going to say about a second shift?"

"Don't know," he answered. "He trained larger crews at Bolles, so he'll probably be okay with it."

"But he can't supervise two crews."

"That's tomorrow's problem," he laced his fingers behind his neck and stretched his elbows over his head as he arched his back. "We'll hire a guy with supervisory skills. Or Roy will train someone."

"I just hope afternoon employees will stay with us," she noted. "Working next to that Blodgette isn't going to inspire loyalty."

"It'll be okay through the winter. Insulation in our make-do bakeshop is minimal, so the oven heat will be balanced by the cold winds outside." Changing the subject, he added, "I saw the brickwork on the new bakery when I got out of the car."

"Pa enjoys supervising construction," she said.

"Did you look at the architect's drawings for the house?"

"I gave them a once-over," she said. "Everything we asked for seems to be included."

"Good." To Icky's way of thinking, construction on the two buildings was one large job, especially since the bakery's business offices would be in the basement of the ranch.

Millie was quiet, but he saw a half-smile emerge on her face.

"What is it?" he asked.

"The bakery is growing so fast now, and we'd never dreamed it before you left Bolles."

"I didn't just leave," Icky admitted.

"I know." She'd never repeat that he'd been fired. She felt complicit since she encouraged him to develop cookie recipes, and they came from her kitchen. "I just keep waiting for our bubble to burst."

Icky reached over and patted her hand.

"Don't worry," he assured her. "I promised you that we'd be okay, and I meant it."

13

A Sweet Ride

Roy immediately agreed with Icky's plan to add a second shift, so Jean got to work on writing employment advertisements for *The Olean Times-Herald*.

"How does this sound: 'Wanted: Entry-level bakery positions. Must be able to lift one hundred pounds and work near hot ovens. M-F, noon to 8 p.m. Call 6849 to apply.'"

"Make it a hundred pounds for the men, forty pounds for the girls," Icky corrected. "The men need to haul bags of flour, and the girls need to slide heavy bowls of dough onto the rolling table."

"We'll need to buy two ads then," she said. "One under 'male employment' and one under 'female employment.'"

"They have two sections?" he asked.

"I thought you read the newspaper," she quizzed him.

"Not employment ads. And two sections seems like they get to charge twice as much."

"Employers probably just want to protect women from mistakenly applying for men's jobs," Jean suggested. Men were hired for their decision-making skills and ability to run major projects, while girls were expected to follow directions, escort customers to offices, answer telephone calls, type, make coffee, and take care of whatever else their bosses required. The separation of responsibilities was just common sense.

"If you say so," Icky said indifferently. "When will they run?"

"The Sunday edition has the largest employment sections," she answered.

"Roy wants you, Icky," Millie interrupted as she came in.

"Okay," he began to leave for the bakeshop.

"Wait, Icky! How many people do you want to interview?" Jean asked.

"Check with Roy on that one. He'll probably schedule Saturday interviews."

"What about an equipment maintenance guy?" Millie reminded him.

He looked at her wearily.

"Also," he said to Jean, "place an ad for a guy to do upkeep on the Blodgette and... other stuff. Maybe he can help Pa supervise construction."

"Part-time then?" Millie interjected.

"The position can go to full-time once we move," Icky clarified. He almost stepped into the bakeshop before he turned back again.

"And since you're writing ads, we're going to need one for a jam man."

"What's a jam man?" Jean asked.

"Guy who makes jams," he answered.

"So now you're going into the jam business?"

"No, I want to develop a fruit-filled cookie," he said over his shoulder. "And you can add taste testing to your job duties."

"I'll need a couple *dozen* samples!" she said loudly as he finally retreated. "Remember, I got kids!"

She had intended to help her husband by passing along his request that Icky help with usher duty on Sunday.

"Oh, well," she sighed. She'd just leave a note.

#

At the end of his shift, Icky called Gordon to schedule an appointment for the car.

"I know you just tuned it, but the gauge says the engine is heating up. Maybe the indicator is going bad—and no, I'm not an auto mechanic now," he anticipated his brother-in-law's retort. The two of them sparred like brothers, especially over cars.

Gordon's diagnosis didn't take long. "Your Stude-*baker* is Stude-*busted*," he reported. "It's okay for local travel, but I wouldn't take it too far without an engine overhaul."

Millie was within earshot, and added her own two cents. "Well, since you can't drive the delivery truck to make sales calls, it sounds like we need a new car."

"New *used* car," Icky insisted. "New to us, but used."

"As long as it's safe," she agreed.

"Which dealerships do you recommend?" he asked Gordon.

"Try a couple," he answered. "Next year's models are coming in, so everybody wants to get rid of this year's inventory. Maybe they'll negotiate."

#

O'Laughlin's Cadillac was on the route from Salamanca, so Icky stopped in on his way back from meeting with customers. He'd look around for a low-mileage used car: something economical and sturdy, with a large trunk to haul samples.

A salesman met him before he'd taken ten steps.

"How much driving do you do each month?" he asked once he'd said hello.

"About three thousand miles," Icky estimated, planning ahead.

"At that rate, you're traveling maybe forty thousand miles a year!" he calculated. "What, if I may ask, do you do for a living?"

"I . . . ," Icky was about to say that he was a baker. That wasn't quite right, though. He needed a car to meet with customers, and in that role he was a salesman.

That didn't sound right either. He should have asked Millie; she named everything.

What did it matter? He was only looking for a used car.

"I'm president of Haut's Cookie Shoppe," he tried to sound casual.

"Oh! My wife buys your cookies!" the salesman recognized.

"Thanks," Icky said.

"Well, then, back to business," the salesman continued. "At forty thousand miles, you're going to go through a car every other year or so."

"Guess so," Icky said. "Could make me a regular customer if you've got a good deal."

"Let me show you what's on the lot," the salesman offered.

"I was thinking of something used," Icky said.

"I can show you some options, but your mileage allows you consider something new, too—especially if you're meeting with customers. Then you might want to consider stepping it up, Sir."

Icky raised an eyebrow at the salesman's use of "Sir," but didn't reply. He had no intention of buying new, but maybe he'd look at a couple of models.

"Here's our Coupe de Ville," the salesman guided Icky. "This four-door sedan offers a V-8 engine and a four-speed automatic transmission. How does that sound?"

He waited for a response. His strategy was to get his customer to say "yes" as soon as possible, so he'd be in the habit of saying "yes" when the time came to close the sale.

"Looks expensive," Icky said.

"That depends on what you think expensive is," he answered. "Today's Cadillac is recognized as a symbol of success—designed for the man who has emerged above the crowd, so by that standard, it's an investment in your business."

He paused again, waiting for Icky's response.

There was none.

Should he say more? A luxury car indicates achievement, so when a man steps out of a Cadillac, he signals to the world that he's in an entirely different league: that's what his sales training taught him to say. But he couldn't tell how Icky would respond. He'd inch ahead slowly.

"Care to test drive it?" the salesman finally offered.

"Sure, why not?" Icky said.

Finally, a "yes"—of sorts. He'd work with it.

"Let me get the key, and we'll take it out for a spin," he said.

While the salesman stepped away, Icky circled the Coupe, wondering if arriving at a sales call in a Cadillac really would say something about the bakery's success. Would it prompt a distributor's confidence?

"Here you are," the salesman handed over the key. "You drive, I'll ride. That way I can tell you about the car's features while you're experiencing them."

They got in, and Icky adjusted the seat to give himself extra leg room. Immediately, he noticed the car's split bench, and realized Millie would be able to move her side up so her feet rested easily on the floor; she'd finally be comfortable, too.

"Now, you probably know all about high octane gasolines," the salesman suggested as they pulled onto the road.

"My brother-in-law is a mechanic," Icky revealed.

"Ah, well, you're in good hands then," he affirmed so as to build trust. "If he's keeping you up with automotive news, you know about GM's powerful high-compression ratio engines."

No response.

"Under this hood, you've got the equivalent of more than two hundred fifty horses," he continued. "All that power makes long-distance travel easier. And an easier ride means you arrive at your customer's office relaxed and ready to do business."

Icky had already noticed how much more comfortable the Coupe's ride was.

What would Millie say? Probably that they need a two-door car so that the kids wouldn't accidentally pull on or lean into the handle and fall out.

"Nice car," he finally admitted. "But I was thinking of something used. Something affordable."

"What if we can make you a good deal on this one?" the salesman asked. "Would you be interested in that?"

"It would have to be a really, really good deal," Icky said. "And it needs to be a two-door model."

"We've got a two-door on the floor. I'll work some numbers on it for you," the salesman pressed.

Icky would let the salesman do all the talking and put out his best offer. If it wasn't good enough, he'd go somewhere else. Like Gordon said, the Big Three were building cars every day. He'd find the right one soon enough.

Icky sat across the desk while a long column of numbers was scratched out, and noticed an interesting model across the showroom. His thoughts wandered to the first car he ever purchased: a Marquette. Millie was impressed by that one, he remembered, and imagined the look on her face if he drove a new car home. A moment later, he heard the salesman double-underline the bottom number.

"Here's what it comes out to," he turned the paper around so Icky could see it.

"Good start," Icky said, "depending on what you give me to trade in the Studebaker."

"Have you got a couple of minutes?" he asked. "I'll talk with the service manager."

Icky handed over the keys.

"While he's doing that, you can check out the two-door Coupe de Ville over there," the salesman nodded at the model Icky spotted a few seconds before.

#

"You did what?" Millie said when Icky got home.

"It's your favorite color, too," he smiled. "Want to go with me to pick it up?"

"When?"

"Tomorrow afternoon."

"Icky!" she crossed the room to hug him.

And I didn't even have to wait for a kiss, he grinned as he pulled her close.

14

Shifting Gears

"Need some help with that?" Icky lifted a couple of boxes onto the back of the panel truck. John had returned to the bakeshop halfway through his route to pick up more product before going out to Salamanca and Bradford.

"The truck was so full with Olean orders that I had to double back to load the second half of my deliveries," he reported.

"I saw you come in," Icky noted.

"Thanks for the help," John said. "Soon we're gonna' need a bigger truck!"

Icky had been thinking along the same lines, but he didn't know whether or not trading in the old truck for a larger one was the answer. Maybe the bakeshop should buy a second small truck, hire another driver, and split the route. In time, that would also allow him to enlarge each of their delivery territories.

Or maybe selling directly to grocery stores wasn't the best way to get products into the market anymore. Orders to east coast distributors would be shipped by an independent carrier—which on the downside was going to mean paying freight charges, but on the upside would mean no employee pay expense and no truck cost.

The question niggled him all afternoon. Millie saw he was distracted at supper, too. He hadn't even tasted the meatloaf on his plate.

"What's on your mind?" she asked.

"Huh?" he grunted.

"You're distracted," she persisted.

"Oh, John had to double back again today," he answered. "He thinks we might need a larger truck."

"He's had to split his route a few times," she said, "but probably not often enough to buy a new truck—especially since we just bought a car."

"And?"

"—and I'm glad we did!" she reinforced.

"But John got me thinking," Icky continued. "We won't deliver product to the east coast in our own trucks; we'll ship by overnight carrier. Why not do the same thing around here?"

"Because," she said slowly, "we already own a delivery truck. And John is a great employee."

"The truck is old, so regardless of whether or not it's large enough, we'll need to replace it next year. So there's one cost," Icky noted. "And adding a second truck would require hiring another employee, and double our maintenance expense and insurance, which means . . ."

"More cost," she said. "I get it. So, are you thinking about getting rid of the truck and hiring a local distributor?"

"We can't; we'd have to let John go," he admitted, "and we'd never do that."

"I agree," Millie said, relieved. "But why not ask him if he's ever considered becoming a baked goods distributor? Haut's Cookie Shoppe could be his first account."

Icky's brain had been grinding all day; he could almost hear the gears turning. Now, suddenly, his thoughts paused.

"That's it!" he exclaimed.

"Really?" Millie asked.

"Absolutely!"

"Well, ask John to come over Saturday morning to talk about it," she suggested. "See what he thinks."

Icky nodded, and finally took a bite of his dinner.

"And this time," she added, "tell Ma—so if John's mother says something after church, she won't be surprised."

"Good idea," he agreed. He sure didn't want to ruffle Ma's feathers again.

#

"How's it going, John?" Icky greeted him. "Thanks for stopping by."

"Glad to do it," John said. "I'm curious about the good idea you mentioned—because I don't remember suggesting anything."

"I was thinking about your comment that the truck isn't large enough to handle local deliveries," Icky answered.

"Oh! Right!" he agreed. "I had to double back twice last week again."

"And each time we add another product, your deliveries increase."

"Stores always order the new cookies," John noted. "I'm probably delivering four times as many boxes as when I started."

"And because you're already working a full shift, we're limited in expanding our market and adding new stores."

John nodded in agreement.

"And that got me thinking," Icky continued. "When we move into the new bakery, we'll use independent carriers to deliver product to our east coast distributors."

John stepped back and frowned; Icky quickly realized how his remark could be taken the wrong way.

"So, I've been wondering: Have you ever thought about becoming a baked goods distributor?"

John didn't say anything.

"Baked goods is the grocery trade's fastest growing market segment, according to our Pillsbury rep. And *my* guess is that if you get into the distributor side of the business soon, you'd have very little competition in western New York, and probably northwest Pennsylvania, too."

"I . . . I'm not sure what that would mean," John hesitated. He thought Icky was going to say he was losing his job. "What would I have to do?"

"You'd need to meet with all the area grocery store managers—which would be easy in Olean, Salamanca, and Bradford because they know you now."

"Then what?" he pressed. "I don't know what a distributor does."

"First, we'd stop selling to stores directly, and instead, divert our local and regional business to you," Icky explained. "You'd also become a primary source for a variety of other baked goods."

"I'm . . . I'm stunned," John planted his right fist under his chin, and supported his elbow with his left wrist. "How would I find other products? And wouldn't they compete with Haut's Cookie Shoppe?"

"Not at all. Stores always offer more than one brand—and of course, ours would be the only soft cookie you'd represent," he stipulated. "As for other pastries, you'd need to study the baked goods aisles in the grocery stores you want to serve, see what's popular, and figure out what they're missing."

"Don't they know that already?"

"Maybe—or maybe not," Icky answered. "Managers watch over an entire store. You'd focus on one department, and recommend a bakery combination that helps them control costs, increase sales, and become more profitable."

"I don't know anything about how to run a business," John admitted, but then added, "Don't get me wrong! It sounds interesting, but I'd have to think about it."

Icky nodded.

"That's what I'd do, too," he said. "And it's not a decision you need to make today."

"But if I don't want to do this, are you saying you're going to let me go?"

"No," Icky assured him. "I'm just saying that a couple of days ago you identified a potential problem before it got out of hand. Also, the first time we rode together, you suggested opening the Bradford market. You've got what it takes to run your own show."

In the back of his mind, Icky recalled how Roy said almost the same words to him years before, when he was only an apprentice baker.

"Okay," John sounded relieved. "Oh, man!"

"It's a lot to wrap your head around," Icky agreed.

"It sure is. A year ago I was in Korea, and socking away my pay to buy a car when I got out of the Army. But I sure don't have any big savings," he confided. "And I don't see how a bank will give me a business loan."

"That's the second hurdle," Icky said. "The first is whether or not this is something you really want to do, so give yourself some time to talk to your family and anyone else you trust. Maybe Frank Bauer can hear you out again. After that, if you decide to make the leap, come see me. We'll figure something out to get you started."

#

"Ah, accordion music," Pa announced as he tuned in the radio after Sunday dinner. "A good German instrument is this."

"I thought it was Italian," Mary Lou suggested.

"*Nein!*" Pa Haut held firm. "German!"

"Well, Mr. Carpoletti played accordion music at Bolles Bakery picnics," Mary Lou recalled. "And he's Italian."

"You remember those picnics?" Icky diverted a potential argument as he dropped onto the sofa.

"Of course! There were lots of kids and games, and you could go up to a big cooler for as many ice cream cones as you wanted!"

"And you never got a bellyache from repeat visits to that cooler," he joked.

"I asked for one . . . or maybe two," she said. She hadn't dared to ask for a third.

"Why don't we host an employee picnic?" Millie suggested. The bakery had grown to fourteen employees with the two shifts, so if everyone invited their families, they'd have a nice group.

"Great idea!" Icky said. "We could hold it at Allegheny State Park!"

"On the first weekend after the kids are out of school," she recommended. "That way, the weather will be good."

"I'll organize games," Mary Lou offered.

"And maybe the *German* accordion you would like to play?" her grandpa suggested.

"You have a few weeks to learn a tune or two," Icky concurred. "You could play while we eat!"

"And everyone will applaud!" Pa Haut added.

"No-o-o, thanks," she asserted. Some of her friends were taking piano lessons, and they complained about practicing scales every day. Strapping a heavy accordion over her shoulders would make playing an instrument even worse! "You can get Mr. Carpoletti for that."

#

"John didn't say anything after church about your conversation," Millie said as Icky and she settled down for the night.

"No, but I tell you, Millie, talking with him about it yesterday: that felt good," Icky said quietly.

"What do you mean?"

"I didn't know how to bring the distributor idea up, so I just told him what you said, and, well, it felt right, that's all."

"Hmm," Millie considered his response. "Maybe that's what Frank meant about vocation: a person is called when they have skills that someone else needs—and you believe John has those skills. And also, they enjoy the work they're asked to do."

"We'll see what he decides. He was smiling when he left."

"Maybe there's more to that smile than you and I know about," she suggested. "Jean said he's seeing someone."

"How does she know that?"

"Grapevine," Millie said. "John's sister, Dorothy, is the church secretary. She probably mentioned something."

"Well, that adds another ingredient."

"We'll see," she yawned. "Six hours 'til we're at it again. G'night."

"G'night," Icky said, pleased that John might say yes to becoming a distributor. A girl always has a settling effect on a man's life.

15

Divine Inspiration

John had two reasons to get to work early: first, Monday's deliveries had increased, so he'd be working a long day, and second, he hoped to grab a couple of minutes to tell Icky he'd like to try becoming a distributor.

"Great!" Icky encouraged him. "What made you decide?"

"A girl, actually," John answered. "When she and I talked it over, she said I should consider it seriously."

She actually said more than that, he reminded himself. She asked him what he liked about his job. The independence of it, he'd told her. He was on the road every day, doing the physical labor of delivering product and meeting great people. No one was telling him what to do; his boss just trusted him to get the job done.

He also liked being out in the countryside at the end of his route, noticing the change of seasons as he drove from town to town. It was relaxing, and helped him think about problems that needed to be solved.

And solving problems came natural to him. He even told her that his boss mentioned the way he showed initiative by handling a couple of issues for the bakery.

She asked whether or not being a distributor would be interesting enough that he'd want to make a career of it, and he thought it might be good, especially if he could grow it. But, he added, starting a company would feel like gambling. He wavered at the precipice of leaping into it—and at that, she dared to challenge him.

"Becoming a business owner isn't a gamble, John Heinz," she declared. And in that moment, he remembered the evening she addressed him by both his first and last names in front of the theater after he patted her on the head. She had corrected him for assuming she was still a schoolgirl.

"I'll have you know, John Heinz," she'd brought him to attention, and then, looking him squarely in the eyes, admonished his patronizing attitude. He was almost a foot taller, but she'd made him stand up straight and blink.

He saw her differently after that, and realized who she'd always been: full of poise and personality and pluck; someone not to toy with. No, she'd turned her back on his presumptions, and herded her younger sisters toward the bus stop.

And his eyes had followed her all the way down the block.

Now, she was confronting his hesitation over being self-employed, too.

"If you like this work, and you're good at it, then starting your own distributorship would just be taking a calculated risk," she reinterpreted the opportunity.

He argued that he had no experience other than the military. And when he said that fighting overseas wasn't the same as knowing how to run a company, she'd countered his reluctance with, "So what? How do you think people gain those skills?"

"But, . . ." he started to disagree.

She wouldn't let him diminish his experience, though.

"Serving in Korea was probably both bad and good," she allowed without asking him to dig into the losses he'd suffered. "It had to teach you to assess situations, decide who you could rely on, and figure out what you needed to do when the going got tough."

She was right. War had given him a view of heaven from a seat in hell.

And it gave him other skills that couldn't be taught in a classroom, such as sharp focus, informed caution, and dedication to a mission.

"Starting something new doesn't come with guarantees," she allowed. "But it seems to me that you know yourself well enough to estimate your own tolerance for uncertainty. And if your boss says you have a good head for business, why not use it?"

"It'll be a lot of work," he began.

"But if it's good work, isn't that okay?" she suggested. Then she reminded him that he had a strong family he could count on, and lifelong friends like her brother. All he needed was a deep breath of the Holy

Spirit. "Maybe it's time to inhale some courage, and trust a future that God might be putting in front of you."

Bertie wasn't afraid to speak her mind, that was for sure. And if he were to take on this opportunity, he'd need the sort of security that her sweet directness offered, for no matter what his decision was, she was on his side.

He also noticed that she didn't cross the line from telling him straight what he needed to hear to poking him to dredge up hard memories he didn't want to relive. No, she was kind. She'd be the right partner in his life, if she'd have him.

"Sounds like you two are serious," Icky noted.

"We're getting there," John said. "Once I work out how to get this business started, I'll ask her to marry me."

"That *is* serious!" Icky said.

"Talking all this out—well, it's been a crazy weekend," he admitted. "I didn't think I'd be able to propose for a long time. And becoming a distributor never occurred to me."

"Life is like that sometimes," Icky smiled. "Three years ago, Millie and I had no idea we'd be running a bakery."

"Well, if I can be half as successful as you are, I'll be doing good," John said. "First, I need to figure out how to get some money to buy a delivery truck, though."

"Well, maybe we could help. What if Haut's Cookie Shoppe provided a no-interest loan?" Icky offered. "You could pay it off as your accounts grow."

"You'd do that?" he asked.

"Like I said before, you'll be a great distributor," Icky assured him. Besides, hadn't the bakeshop been setting aside money to replace the old truck? Helping John move ahead was a sound business decision. "The sooner you get started, the better for both of us."

"I . . . I . . . Thanks!" John stuttered. "Wait 'til I tell Bertie!"

"Your girl?" Icky asked.

"Right," John said. "We've been seeing each other for a few months now—since I got home from the service. And if I'm lucky, soon she'll be more than a girlfriend."

"Let's finish loading this truck then," Icky suggested. "You'll want to get deliveries done early so you can ask her."

#

"What did he say?" Millie asked when the truck pulled out.

"He's going to give it a try," Icky said. "And we're going to give him a loan so he can buy a delivery truck."

"That sounds fair, especially since he's probably too young to have collateral."

"Yeah," Icky said. "Now that he's fired up to do this, I didn't want his enthusiasm to get knocked down by the banks. Also, he's solving a problem coming down the road toward us."

"When will all this happen?"

"We didn't set a date—speaking of which, John and a girl named Bertie may be setting a date of their own," Icky said. "He's going to propose, maybe this evening."

"Well, you're just full of good news!" Millie said.

"I thought I'd leave the best for last," he admitted. "Let's keep it to ourselves, though, until they announce it."

"You mean don't tell . . . anybody?" she asked, aware of how interconnected their personal and business lives had become. If she told Herta, she'd want to tell Ma, who always could be counted on to keep a secret, but in this instance would know before John's mother. John should have time to tell her before anyone outside their family knew so she could share the news with her friends.

And if she told Jean, the news would go back to Frank, and while he wouldn't say anything, he'd be waiting to hear which church John and Bertie would be married in. And since Bertie didn't grow up at Immanuel, the announcement also could mean one of them might leave their home congregation, with a potential conflict in the family of one of his congregants. And John's sister worked at Immanuel, too, so even more people could be buzzing around.

"Oh, I just hate it when I have to keep a secret!"

#

"You got to get the boy out in *die Natur!*" Pa Haut insisted. Ma and he would never interfere, but perhaps they could share a parent's concern. "You need to step away from the job, and give time to other things."

"But right now . . ." Icky defended.

"*Nein! 'Eile mit Weile!'*" Pa interrupted, adding a translation to another essential bit of German wisdom: "'You must make haste with leisure!' When Mary Lou was younger, you gave to her your attention. Now the boy is small. These years are gone once the children are grown."

"Starting up a business isn't easy, Pa," he justified. "I need to be working at it all the time."

"And the boy?" Pa leaned in.

Icky was silent.

"I thought we might rent a cottage at Cuba Lake next summer when the new house is under construction," Icky suggested.

"*Ja*, a good idea this is," Pa said.

"And a good way to keep Mark out of the way, so he doesn't get hurt," he continued.

"But also, a day or two you must take now," Pa insisted, "because before the house goes up, you move into the new bakery—and then you won't stop the work."

Icky pressed his lips together.

"Millie's dad invited us to go out on his new boat Saturday morning. I wasn't going to go, but . . ."

"Only fools rush around without noticing the most important thing," Pa insisted. "When the customers call, you change plans and go. And when the distributor calls, you change plans and go.

"This time, your father-in-law offers," Pa continued, "so stop rushing around only for the business. You go to the lake."

Icky sighed. "You're right," he acquiesced.

"*Ja!* I am!" Pa Haut said. "Doing things well doesn't mean doing them quick; it means choosing wisely the things that need your attention—and this time, it's the boy."

"I'll call Millie's dad," he promised.

#

The morning mist hovering over the lake gently parted as Gordon backed his truck down the ramp and eased his father's Peterborough 18 into the water. Pa Huff stepped easily from the pier into the boat, and stashed his rod and tackle box under the seat near the motor.

Icky parked his Coupe in the lot, and Mark exploded from the front seat. He was headed to the shore.

"What are we waiting for?" he demanded as he approached his grandpa's boat.

"Your Uncle Ed and your Uncle Richard," Pa Huff answered with morning gravel in his voice. "Hello to you, too."

"When will they get here?" Mark demanded again.

"Look behind you," he answered.

"Your grandson sounds like a chip off the old block," Icky laughed.

"Get yourself in here," he ignored the remark, and redirected his attention to Mark. "You take that seat up front, so you can see the fish."

Even more importantly, Pa Huff intended, we want to plant you where we all can keep eyes on you.

Mark's uncles climbed in right behind him, and Pa Huff pulled a rope to start the outboard engine—just enough to get its attention in the morning chill.

"Here we go," he announced. Gray fumes mixed with the vapor rising off the lake and then fell gently in obeisance behind them. After a short tour of fishing holes, Pa Huff slid into a quiet spot with tall grasses and rock outcroppings.

"Bass like it here," he said authoritatively, "so put lazy worms on your lines."

Pa Huff was the family fisherman: one with the water and sharing the same cycle of nature, so when he said it was time to fish, it was. Icky offered to help Mark, but the kid insisted he knew how to thread his bait "all by myself." A moment later, he snapped his little line, and cast out. Natural-born, his grandpa recognized.

The Peterborough floated toward the reeds in a stillness so quiet that the men could almost hear one another breathe.

"Where are they?" Mark asked.

No one answered.

"Grandpa, where's the Big Fish?" Mark's voice reverberated through the rising fog like an echo in a sanctuary.

"They're waiting for your worm to swim by," his grandpa answered quietly. "You keep talkin' loud like that, and you'll scare 'em away."

"I don't see anything," he complained as he leaned over the boat's edge.

"Shhh!" they all commanded.

It wasn't long, though, before the men started sharing local gossip in modulated tones. Among the four of them, they probably knew what everybody in Olean was up to. Eventually, Icky said something about funding a new truck, and making progress on the new bakery.

One of Mark's uncles admitted to not having the stomach to risk his family's welfare on a new venture. Icky didn't think of himself as daring. No, he insisted, the bakery was started so he could take care of his wife and children; he was being responsible.

Next, someone told a story about being *ir*responsible that made everyone chuckle.

"And we never touched Pa's hooch again!" Gordon added.

Pa Huff raised an eyebrow.

"What's a hooch?" Mark asked, picking up on a family tale.

They all clammed up, suddenly aware that they'd probably said too much in front of a kid who shared everything with everyone—even at church, and they didn't need the whole town to know that family secret.

A few minutes passed, and the men resumed grown-up talk: car buying and fixing; railroad stories, other serious stuff.

"Where are the fish?" Mark interrupted.

No one answered.

He knew he shouldn't fidget, but no fish were tickling his worm. No one was answering his questions either. Deciding he might have better luck casting out from another part of the boat, he ca-lomp, ca-lomp, ca-lomped his cowboy boots along the floorboards and headed back toward his grandpa.

But there was no room to sit at the rear of the boat. The fishing gear had been removed from under the seat, and spread out. The ice cooler was also using up space.

Hm. What to do.

He turned around, and decided that maybe the middle would be okay. One-by-one, he carefully ca-lomped back over the seats. His dad and his uncle were casting from opposite sides; he'd try to squeeze in between them. Once he sat down, though, he discovered that his arms weren't long enough to extend his short pole over the edge.

He stood, preparing to move again, and leaned forward to cross another seat.

Ca-lomp, ca-!

"Hey!" he protested as one of his uncles lifted him up. In a synchronous move, another one pulled off his cowboy boots and stowed them.

"Go up front and stay put!" his grandpa ordered from the rear.

"But there's no fish up there," Mark carped.

"Maybe there's no fish *anywhere* now," Grandpa Huff retorted. "You been clomping those boots on the bottom of my boat and scaring every fish off to the other end of this lake. Now sit down and be quiet! That's how we fish out here!"

Mark thought fishing rules were too much like being in church, but he did as he was told, and imagined himself being invisible like Johnny Ralph. A moment later, as he looked over the edge of the boat to see if he could make his reflection disappear, he spotted schools of small fish in the shallow water.

"Dad!" he whispered. "Baby fish! Right here!"

Icky nodded and smiled. "They're called 'small fries,'" he whispered in return, "and next year, they're gonna' be the Big Fish."

Mark's eyes widened, and he returned his gaze to the possibilities his future expeditions would bring.

"How was the Big Fishing Trip?" Millie asked when he dropped his pole outside the Quonset hut door at noon. "And where are your boots?"

"Cowboy boots aren't for going on the boat," Mark answered. "Fish don't like 'em."

"Then where are they?"

"Under a seat. But Mom, I found small fries that are going to be Big Fish next summer!"

"Wow! So you're going fishing again?"

"Yup," he assured her. "But next year I'll go by myself."

"Why? Didn't you have fun with Daddy and the rest of the guys?"

He paused.

"It was okay," he conceded. "They're just not very good at it."

16

Caring for the Flock

"Do I look like a sheep?" Bertie complained from the back seat of her parents' car. She'd been among the first to exit the church after worship. She'd even skirted around the clergy so she could wait outside until her family caught up.

Nobody responded to her question. They wouldn't dare.

"I cannot believe he shamed me in front of the entire congregation—and right after my engagement was announced!" she continued.

"It was . . . uncomfortable," her mother chose her words carefully.

"Uncomfortable? 'Uncomfortable' hardly describes the sin of wandering off and getting engaged to someone outside our flock," she continued to steam.

Mrs. Lucas knew her daughter was right. This particular man of the cloth was notoriously rigid, and unafraid to share his hardheaded opinions—even when he was wrong, as he certainly was this time. No reason existed in heaven or on earth for Bertie to decline a proposal of marriage from John Heinz, regardless of the fact that his family worshipped in a different church. She hoped Bertie wouldn't let the preacher's attitude tarnish her hopes for a beautiful wedding.

"We know you're not a lost sheep," her mother tried to smooth over the insensitive remark.

"Well, that's what he said," Bertie refused to accept his ridicule, "so I trust you won't be disappointed when I join John's church after we're married."

Her parents shared a knowing glance. They'd reared their children to not only be considerate, but also to demand the same respect for themselves. What did they expect?

Her mother sighed; it was her silent comment when she didn't want to argue.

A moment later, her father said, "When John asked for your hand in marriage, I imagined walking you down the aisle."

He didn't continue, but Bertie felt the tinge of sadness that accompanied his thought.

"Maybe we could still have the ceremony in our church," she allowed. Then, trying to lighten the mood, she added, "but I refuse to wear a wedding gown made of boiled wool!"

Her sisters smirked in sympathetic silence. Her brother, however, who was a lifelong friend of the groom-to-be, leaned into her ear and gently bleated, "baa-aa-ah."

Bertie elbowed him gently in his ribs.

"Good thing it's crowded back here, or she would have tried to butt me with her head," he taunted.

#

"What do I need to do to join Immanuel Lutheran Church?" Bertie asked Pastor Bauer a few days later when John and she met with him to discuss their marriage.

"Is that what the two of you have decided?" he asked.

"It's Bertie's decision," John answered honestly.

"I'd like the ceremony to be performed in my home church," she said, "but after that, my priority will be making sure that our children—when we have them—will know God's love. I think they will find it here."

"Well, I'm delighted to hear that you feel that way," Pastor Bauer said. "New member classes are held twice a year. And John can attend with you, if you like."

"I'll probably pay more attention than when I was twelve," John agreed.

Pastor Bauer nodded amiably. "For now, Bertie, how would you like to join our Sunday School teaching staff? We could use your help with the children's program."

"You want me to teach them now? Before I'm even a member?" she asked.

"Since you want your own children one day, I thought you might like spending time with some of ours," he answered.

"I'd love it!" she exclaimed. "And it'll make me feel so welcome."

"Good! That's what we want for our children," Pastor Bauer said. "I knew you were right for the job."

#

Millie arrived at Allegheny State Park with Mark and Mary Lou an hour before the start of the bakery's first employee picnic. She handed signs to her daughter and suggested that she pound them into the ground near the entrance, and add balloons.

"Then you can set up your games," she continued.

"All I have to do is line them up," Mary Lou announced. "I've got a pin the tail on the donkey game, an egg toss, and a bubble-gum blowing contest."

"I want some bubble gum!" Mark shouted.

"You can get in line when the time comes," Millie answered. "Right now I need your help with this," she handed him a small box of napkins. "Carry it to the picnic table over there."

"When can I go swimming?" he asked. "And where's my fishing pole?"

"We're not fishing today, but when the other children arrive, you can go into the water. Right now, we're cleaning tables and setting up."

"How come we have to clean tables and carry stuff?" he asked.

"Because we want everything to be nice," his mother continued to unpack.

"But how come we don't just do it later, when everybody gets here?" questions tumbled from his mouth.

"Because then I'll be busy helping Daddy grill the hot dogs."

"Oh." Mark understood the importance of hot dogs. "But how come they don't get hot dogs theirselves?"

"... hot dogs *themselves*," she corrected. "And they will. We're putting out the catsup and mustard and relish now, so they have it when they need it."

"I can do mine all by myself!" Mark said firmly. "How come . . ."

"How come you have so many questions? How come you talk so much?" she teased.

"I likes hot dogs, and I likes to talk, too," he answered, adding, "How come . . ."

"What?"

"I forgot," he said, distracted by the arrival of the bakeshop truck.

Icky, John and Bertie unloaded containers of food, including a large metal ice cooler filled with drumstick ice cream cones: the fancy ones coated in chocolate and peanuts, and individually wrapped in paper sleeves.

"This is my kind of picnic!" Mary Lou grabbed one end of the cooler to help carry it to the shaded spot she'd chosen. Her sign was already pounded into the ground: Free Ice Cream Cones! Limit = 0!"

"The limit is zero?" Icky asked. "You're not sharing?"

"No, there's *no* limit! So, 0."

She looked at her sign again.

"Maybe I'll change that," she agreed after a moment.

"The kids also get watermelon," Millie added.

"I don't know about Mark," Icky cautioned as he gave the kid a long look. "He might not be old enough."

"I am, too!"

"Watermelons have a lot of seeds," Icky cautioned.

"So?" Mark challenged what sounded like he was losing out of something good again.

"So if you swallow too many seeds, they'll grow inside your belly, and the leaves from the plant come out right here," he tugged the kid's earlobe seriously.

Mark watched his daddy walk off to get more boxes from the truck. He never saw leaves poking out of anybody's ears. The admonition was probably one of those pretend reasons that grown-ups give when they don't want somebody to do something. He'd ignore it.

Icky got the party started by cracking open a bottle of Iroquois beer, and handing it to John. Bertie preferred an ice cold bottle of pop.

"To your success," he toasted John's new venture as he lifted his bottle.

"Cheers!" they all clinked.

"John really appreciates your willingness to keep him on the payroll while he gets his distributor ducks in a row," Bertie said.

"I'm trying to line up other bakeries to represent," he added.

"Who have you identified so far?" Icky asked.

"Jonny Lang—you know: that distributor you introduced me to out in Cuba Lake?—he told me to look at Ann Dale baked goods in Fall River, Massachusetts; David's Cookies in Cedar Grove, New Jersey, and Farm Crest Bakeries in Columbus, Ohio," John said. "I contacted all three, and they're sending samples."

"That's a good plan," Icky agreed.

"If Olean stores like them, I'll offer the same lines in Salamanca and Bradford," he continued. "Their shelves could use some new product, too."

"You'll be up and running in no time!" Icky acknowledged.

"We'll see. Since you brought that up, how were you thinking I'd transition from employee to distributor?" Before Icky could respond, he added, "If possible, I'd like to wait 'til new truck models come out. To be honest, we've got this wedding to pay for right now."

"The bakery's delivery truck probably will last a few months," Icky answered easily. "It's an old beater, and not large enough to handle both our increasing orders plus your other products, so you're still going to have to double-back to deliver your entire route."

John hadn't expected to be allowed to deliver his other products from the bakeshop's truck. In fact, that wrinkle hadn't even occurred to him. He was grateful Icky offered before he needed to ask.

"I've already had to load up a couple of times," John said. "And in a way that's good, because it tells me what size truck I'm going to need."

"So, have you two set a date yet?" Millie changed the subject.

"We're still talking about it," Bertie answered, "but probably sometime in August."

"If you haven't asked anyone to bake the wedding cake, we could do that," Millie offered with a little smile toward Icky.

"Herta is an experienced cake decorator," he added. "Roy and she operated a storefront bakery before they moved back to Olean. I know she'd do a beautiful job for you."

"I'd love it!—or rather, we'd love it!" Bertie corrected herself. "Do you think she could make petit fours, too? I've always wanted those little cakes with tiny flowers on each one. Or is that too much to ask?"

"I think they'd be lovely," Millie said. "We'll check when Roy and she get here."

"While we're on the subject of the wedding, there's one more thing I'd like to ask," John turned to Icky. "Would you consider being my best man?"

"Me?" Icky said. "I've never been a best man! I'd be honored!"

"Thanks," John smiled back at him.

"And here comes the rest of the crowd!" Millie nodded as cars full of employees and their families pulled into the lot. "Time to get your games going, Mary Lou!"

"Let's get those dogs on the grill!" Icky directed.

#

"Where's Mark?" Millie asked as she packed up to go home. Icky had promised to keep an eye on him while she loaded the car with the leftover paper goods.

"I told him to stay put!" he defended, adding, "Mark! Where are you?"

"Right here!" the kid answered obediently from the ground on the other side of the picnic tables. He and one of the other boys were investigating a box of half-used condiments. The two experimenters had removed a couple of colorful bottles, and drippings of catsup and mustard were everywhere: on their hands, their faces, their clothes, their hair. Icky started toward them when Millie held up her palm to intervene.

"Nope, they got themselves into a mess; they can clean themselves up," she commanded. "Into the water! Both of you!"

She marched them to the lake and ordered them in, clothes and all.

"Dunk those heads, too!" she continued her tirade as she stepped in up to her knees.

A moment later, Icky heard splashing, followed by Millie yelling, "Don't you dare!"

He turned just in time to see his son doing what boys do best.

"Where's the camera?" Icky called to Mary Lou. "I want a photograph of this!"

"I'm going to kill that kid," Millie threatened under her breath as she herded the twin tyrants toward towels. She was soaked.

17

Smoking

As construction on the new bakery neared completion, Icky and Pa fell into the routine of inspecting progress each evening.

"Tomorrow they finish the painting," Pa reported. "And a good idea it was to make the walls white."

"Yeah, white really brightens the space," Icky agreed. He reached up to close four tilting windows that had been left open to air out the paint smell. "I like how this wall of glass lets in so much light, too."

"*Ja*, and the ventilation will be good in the summer," Pa agreed. With the authority of a man who worked most of his life as a fireman for Socony, he then challenged, "You sure the heaters should be installed in the ceiling? Heat rises."

"The ovens create enough warmth at floor level," Icky explained. "Ceiling heaters are just meant to maintain it in the winter, since that's the only time of year they'll be on."

"Okay," Pa nodded. "So long as you think it through."

They walked through production, and then entered the packaging and shipping department. Icky wanted to see that the new overhead door for the truck bay operated easily.

"Smooth as butter," he noticed how quietly it slid up and down.

"When do you install the new equipment?" Pa eyed crates near the back door.

"Electricians will be here Tuesday and Wednesday," Icky said as they went outdoors. He waved Roy over from the make-do lean-to bakeshop.

"The sooner, the better," Roy said, catching up. Second shift had just ended, and he'd worked a double to train the new supervisor. "We're running at full tilt."

"I hear you," Icky lit a cigarette. He worked first shift with Roy, and spent the afternoon hauling inventory in the trunk of his new Coupe. It was the only vehicle available at midday, so bringing in enough stock for two shifts required several trips.

"Leo Derby is doing okay then?" he asked.

"Yep, yep, yep," Roy pulled a Cuban cigar from his shirt pocket. "His experience from Swanson is making the transition easy. We worked the crew through four cookie varieties today without production delays."

"Good, because I have a pecan dandy ready to introduce, and after that, I'd like to try a fruit and nut cookie," Icky set priorities. "A shipment of raisins is due tomorrow."

"I'll get him started, though I don't know how we're going to fit both into the schedule," Roy cautioned.

"I only want to test them now, so we're ready to go when we move," Icky said.

"Are we still planning to do that next weekend?" Roy asked.

"Yeah, the movers will be here Friday after we close, and stay until the job is done," he confirmed. "If everything goes well, we'll test equipment Saturday morning."

"When will we be able to run through some product?"

"With any luck, Saturday afternoon," Icky said.

"Want me to ask if anybody wants to come in to help?" Roy asked.

"Do you think they would?"

"They're chomping at the bit to get over here and try out the new toys!"

"All right then!" Icky agreed. "Set it up!"

"Everyone is looking forward to working first shift together, too," Roy added.

"I bet," Icky said. "And two shifts in the temporary bakeshop equals one shift in the new bakery."

"And that means a whole new second shift will need to be hired and trained," Roy interjected, "because if you're right about those distributors, demand is going to jump."

"That's the plan," Icky said.

"I was afraid of that," Roy sent him a crooked smile.

#

"How goes the construction?" Millie asked when Icky came in.

"Good," Icky answered. "We're on schedule."

"What about John's distributorship?" she asked.

"Nothing will change for him," Icky said. "But once he's on his own, his income will depend on sales volume, so we need to be able to supply him with enough product."

"Maybe when he gets his new truck you can ride with him for a day, too. You could show him how to open a new territory," Millie suggested.

"What about you?" Icky shifted. "Are you excited about seeing your house go up?"

"I am, but today we all had eyes on Mark. Ma says that whenever he hears the builders working, he tries to slip outdoors."

"I bet she wishes he still fit in that harness," Icky said.

"She'd never use that," Millie disagreed.

"How about renting a cottage on Cuba Lake for the summer then?" Icky suggested. "You and the kids could spend a few weeks there, and Mark won't be in the way around here."

"But I'll be working first shift. And in the afternoon, I'll be busy with selecting carpet, paint colors, and appliances. Besides, . . . "

"We can hire somebody in packaging," Icky said. "We should have someone else who also knows how to do that job anyway. And you can drive back into town to pick out whatever the house needs."

She didn't respond.

"We don't need to decide tonight," he added. "But cottages rent fast once folks make plans for the summer season. We'll need to find one soon."

#

"Mom," Mary Lou crooked her index finger to bring Millie from the bakery into the house. When she returned from Marcus Park with the Bauer children, she heard Jean in the bathroom.

"I think she's sick to her stomach," Mary Lou said secretively.

"Oh!" Millie answered. She washed and dried her hands in the Quonset hut kitchen sink, and told Mary Lou to take the kids outside again. "You can play in the yard or go back to the park. Just give Mrs. Bauer some quiet time."

"Okay, but it happened once before," Mary Lou added. "She said the heat coming in from the bakeshop is making her woozy."

"I'll take care of it," Millie answered with confidence. She took an aluminum ice cube tray from the refrigerator and pulled back its handle to crack a few cubes. She also put a kettle on the stove to boil water for tea. She didn't know if Jean would prefer a cold drink or a hot one, so she'd prepare both. Heat from the bakeshop, my foot! she thought to herself.

"I guess you know," Jean said as she emerged from the bathroom.

"How far along are you," Millie asked.

"Ten weeks, I think," she answered. "I'll keep working long enough to get you into the new bakery."

"That's not important," Millie assured her. "This new baby is!"

"We always said we wanted three children," Jean shared.

"They come whenever God sends them," Millie answered knowingly, as Mark was ten years behind Mary Lou. "For now, just rest. Mary Lou took the kids outside, and she's the only one who knows you weren't feeling well."

"Thanks," Jean said. "And thanks for putting on the kettle. I'll take it from here."

#

"I thought about your idea of renting a cottage for next summer," Millie said after dinner, "and you're right. We should do it."

"What made you decide?"

"Kids grow up so fast, and we haven't been able to make memories with them since we started this bakeshop."

"Yeah, Mark arrived right before that," he noted.

"And there's a change coming in the staff," she added. "We're going to need to hire someone to handle office administration."

"Why?"

"Jean is expecting."

"Well, isn't that something!" he smiled. After a few moments, he added, "At least Ma won't be worried about us turning the pastor's wife into a *Rabenmutter*."

"A what?"

"Literally, mother raven," he translated. "Ravens are notorious for neglecting their young, so in Germany they say a working mother is a *Rabenmutter*."

"She doesn't neglect her kids!" Millie insisted, hoping that Ma didn't have that opinion of Jean or her. "They're right here—with Mary Lou to take them to the park for fun!"

"Jean isn't going to be easy to replace."

"No, she's not," Millie agreed.

"But when you retire, you two moms can spend time together."

"Retire?" Millie repeated.

"From working in the bakery," he clarified. "It'll be standing on its own once we move, so you can get back to being a full-time mother. That is what you want, right?"

"I thought you'd always need me to help—the way Herta works with Roy."

"They ran just a two-person storefront bakery," Icky differentiated. "Ours is commercial, so we're going to be bigger—and that means we'll soon have greater staffing flexibility."

"Bigger, hm?" she questioned. "I think our ideas on growing this bakery have become vastly different."

He inhaled a shallow breath through his nose, and bit his lips.

"Don't get me wrong; I know you can grow it, but 'it' keeps changing," she waved toward the new building. "How far do you want to go with it?"

"To the moon!" Icky said automatically. How could she not know that? She worked alongside him every day. True, expanding the business had been an evolving mishmash of possibility. And sure, it was born on some combination of necessity and hope. But he'd fed it on the dream that if he worked hard enough, maybe, just maybe, he could make it into ... something.

"I think we ought to grow it as much as we can, while we can," he finally admitted.

"Then why do you want me to quit?"

"I don't want you to 'quit,'" he disagreed. "I just want you to be free to get back to caring for our kids. Like before." Suddenly, it dawned on him that he'd never asked. His sister enjoyed baking. What if Millie wanted to work outside the home, too. "Or did you want to work in the bakery?"

"No," she confessed easily. "Being a wife and mother is all I ever wanted."

"All?" he challenged gently.

"Yes," she answered easily. "All—and everything."

18

Getting Out of a Jam Jam

"This guy's got great credentials," Icky said with enthusiasm. "And when he gets here, we'll finally be able to add a fig jam cookie to our product line!"

"Where is this jam man from?" Millie asked. Icky had expected applicants from New York's nearby Finger Lakes region or the Lake Erie grape belt.

"Small town near Pittsburgh," Icky answered.

"It seems strange that he's willing to shut down his own business to join a start-up." It was the same concern she posed about Roy and Herta: Why work for Haut's Cookie Shoppe when they could open their own bakery again?

"We're not a start-up anymore," Icky defended, "and our new vat room has everything that a guy who specializes in jams could ever want. Like Pa says, we've got a real *Mittlestand!*"

"But why would someone with experience want to work for us? I mean, we're definitely a small- to medium-sized business now. But this guy had his own small bakery."

"He says he doesn't like catering parties or waiting around the store until people come in to buy a few pastries. It's tough to cover costs that way. I wouldn't have liked it either."

"But you wanted a *jam* man," Millie contested.

"And he's good at that," Icky insisted.

"Did he bring samples?"

"Of course," he said. "Roy said he knows what he's doing, and gave him a tour of the vat room."

She should have known that Roy was already involved.

"What's his name again?"

"Frank Neiler," Icky answered.

"And when does he start?"

"In four weeks," Icky said. "A shipment of figs is coming in next month from the Middle East."

"I've never seen a fresh fig," Millie said.

"The agent said they'll be fully ripe when they arrive, which means 'good enough to eat'," Icky repeated. "That's also when they're ready for jam."

"I think I'll remove a few from the crate for the kids to try," Millie said. "Mary Lou will like sharing something unusual with her friends."

"Take as many as you like," Icky agreed.

"Hiring this jam man is the first time you're bringing in a guy who knows more than you do," Millie noted.

"Roy knows more, too."

"That's different. He's family and you apprenticed under him," she insisted. "But for crew, you usually hire inexperienced people you like to hang around with and then train them."

"Yeah, well, Roy does all the training," Icky corrected. His brother-in-law was patient with new hires. Icky, by contrast, told new guys to pay attention while he delivered a gung ho demonstration. No questions allowed.

"And more than skills, we want guys who can't see themselves doing anything other than baking."

"Like when you were first promoted from your apprenticeship," Millie recalled.

"Just like that," he confirmed. "I want the sort who'll be happy here."

Millie nodded. "Well, if they're also good at their jobs and you need them, then that's their calling."

"—which is why Neiler is going to fit in."

"If you say so," she said.

"He also likes to bowl, and says he can bring in an occasional 300 game."

"He bowls," she failed to see merit in that credential.

"Jonny Lang wants to put together a team for next fall's league," Icky explained, "and we're going to sponsor it. Maybe Neiler will want to join up."

"Wait. What does 'sponsor it' mean?" she asked.

"We're paying for the team's bowling shirts with our name across the back. It'll be good advertising."

"'Icky's Cookies' printed on *bowlers*' shirts is good advertising?" she said dubiously.

"Bowlers eat cookies," he insisted.

"Not with beer!" Millie challenged. "If we're going to sponsor teams, we ought to support kids' sports."

He paused to consider her suggestion. "Until then, we're sponsoring bowling. Lang is a good distributor, and he's helping John Heinz get started."

Millie didn't respond.

"He also likes our cookies," he added.

"And as you always say, if you're not right about something, you're never completely wrong either," she noted.

#

"What happened?" Icky frowned as he inspected a large bowl of fig jam with fuzzy gray mold across the top. "This is one of the problems I had when I tried to make jams myself!"

"That's why I called you in," Neiler said, honestly. "And I'm working on it."

"Working on it how?"

"Well, I'm considering options."

"Such as?"

"First of all, I could have just added benzoate of soda," he said.

"What does that do?"

"It's a preservative," Neiler said. "Commonly used, too—except in fruits that contain citric acid; then it can become benzene, which can be a problem."

"What sort of problem?"

"I tested it once in a key lime pie filling; it tasted like gasoline," he admitted.

Icky grimaced. "Figs aren't citrus, so . . ."

"Right, it would be okay in figs, but I'd still like to avoid it if I can."

"So what are you doing?" he pressed Neiler. It seemed that the guy had the same wandering way of answering questions as Pa: doling out alternatives that would *not* work before finally—finally!—giving the one that would. Ma did it, too, so maybe it was a German trait. Regardless, it tested his patience.

"I'm working on it," Neiler continued dribbling out his analysis in small portions. "Figs contain a lot of water; that's one thing to consider. Also, the corn syrup might be feeding the mold."

"So?" Icky urged.

"Well, like I said, reducing the amount of corn syrup is my first thought. After that, we might need a higher proportion of pectin—and if that's the case, the next question is how much," he offered another nibble.

"Pectin is a sugar polymer," Icky tried to encourage details.

"Sugar can be a thickener, too," Neiler continued thinking out loud since Icky seemed to understand what he was talking about, "like when it's boiled in water to make syrup."

"Invert syrup," Icky confirmed. "Numoline."

"Right, like that," Neiler agreed. "We wouldn't want to use that to set fig jam, though. It'd come out cloyingly sweet!"

Icky remembered adjusting Numoline in his sugar cookies for the same reason.

"So, we'd still be using pectin," Neiler concluded, "again, without that benzoate of soda."

"Why am I here, then?" Icky asked.

"I just wanted you to know that something went wrong."

"And the problem could be the corn syrup?"

"Like I said, I don't know yet," Neiler conceded. "And replacing corn syrup with cane sugar probably isn't the answer."

"What about other thickeners?" Icky pressed, offering alternatives that might be stocked in the bakery's inventory. "We got plenty of flour; cornstarch, too."

"We could try 'em," Neiler considered. "Figs aren't too acidic, so one of them might work."

"Well, you're the expert," he dropped the whole problem back into Neiler's lap. "Let me know at the end of the day how it's going."

At the end of Neiler's shift, Icky circled back to the vat room to check on his progress.

"Won't know 'til Monday," he said, "but so far, the jam is setting up."

Icky took a small paper cup and dipped it into the bowl.

"The flavor is fruity. A honey quality, too, but not overly sweet," he approved. "How'd you do it?"

"What you said about cornstarch pointed me in the right direction," Neiler said. "I hadn't considered it before because I usually make jams from strawberries and raspberries, and they can be acidic; cornstarch loses its thickening property with acidic fruits."

"So you're using cornstarch?" Icky asked. Neiler was trickling out his negatives again.

"Well, I could have given it a try, if I'd had more time," he defended. "But you know how cornstarch is; it needs to cook out."

"And this has no starchy taste," Icky held up the paper cup.

"And you wanted an answer by the end of my shift, so with that time crunch I had to come up with something else," Neiler wanted to emphasize the deadline pressure he felt he'd been working under.

"So?" Icky crossed his arms, hoping Neiler would get to the point. "What is it?"

"Okay. Well, first, I added 25 percent more pectin," he said without taking offense. "And then—and here's the surprise: I cut the amount of corn *syrup* because I think that was feeding the mold—and then I added corn *flakes* as a thickener."

"Corn flakes!" Icky said with surprise. "Cereal?"

"Not sugar-frosted; just plain corn flakes. Here," he handed over a breakfast cereal box. "I got a few of these at Richardson's on my lunch break."

"Breakfast cereal," Icky confirmed.

"I got a rolling pin from production, and crushed the flakes to powder," Neiler revealed. "The result is less boiling, and more figgy flavor."

"Corn flakes," Icky repeated.

"If it works," Neiler cautioned. He didn't like over-selling a formula until he was sure about it. And this one wasn't done yet. "It's got the flavor, but remember: we won't know for sure 'til it's completely set up. We don't want mold again."

But Icky was already thinking about how to source a large volume of corn flakes. The bakery couldn't buy its inventory from a local grocery store.

"We also need to know that this jam won't burn once it's baked in the cookie," Neiler cautioned.

"These flakes are from Kellogg's," Icky tapped the rooster logo in the top corner of the box. "General Mills probably makes corn flakes, too."

"Corn flakes also are sold as 'toasties'," Neiler added. "Post makes 'em."

"We'll have to see which cereal maker has the best price," Icky decided as he walked toward the door.

"Wait! If you're going to start looking for a source, you want to ask for *confectioner's* corn flakes," Neiler specified in a loud voice. "They're finely ground, and that'll save us the trouble of crushing them ourselves."

"Good point," Icky stepped away again.

"Or ask for fine bran," Neiler called out louder.

Icky stopped in his paces and turned.

"Bran? You said corn."

"Bran is technically the husk of the seed, so you can ask about corn bran. It's just got to be finely ground," Neiler repeated. "But don't go making any large purchases until we know this works—and that won't be until Monday."

"Monday, okay," Icky said over his shoulder.

"We also gotta' test the jam in the dough," Neiler insisted loudly enough to be heard over the mixers in the next room. "We gotta' be sure this formula doesn't boil out in the oven. We gotta' give it time."

"I hear you," Icky yelled back. Hiring Neiler was a good decision, he told himself. Even if the guy didn't like the pressures that come with the business side of running a bakery, he sure is accustomed to thinking through production challenges.

When he got to his office, Icky thumbed through his notebook of fruit-filled cookie recipes to find the one he'd been working on. As he handed it over to Derby, he said, "We got a vat full of jam that should be ready next week. Frank Neiler—you know, the new jam man—"

"Right," Derby said. "Met him already."

"He's got this jam problem solved—or probably solved," Icky said. "He'll know for sure on Monday. So, next week we need to test it in the dough."

"That store-bought jam we tried a few weeks ago had too much sugar," Derby recalled; he wouldn't mention how Icky's attempt at making jam resulted in mold. "By the time the dough baked, the fruit burned."

"He's aware of that," Icky said, "so you two need to team up."

"I'll get working on it," Derby confirmed.

On Monday, Derby and Neiler perfected the boil out on the jam so that it was thin enough to layer on dough, but still had enough moisture to withstand the heat of the ovens.

"When are you moving this cookie into production?" Jean asked, "because we need to give it a name and order labels for the packages."

"We'll do a limited run," Icky said. "Heinz can offer it locally as a specialty product."

"Are we just testing the cookie then?" she asked.

"No, we wouldn't sell a test cookie. This has to be customer ready before it goes out."

"Then, why . . . "

"We can't get enough figs this late in the season to offer it to east coast distributors this year," he interrupted. "And I'll ask Millie for a name; she's still in charge of that."

He found her in the bakery, packing cookies.

"Simple is best," she said, "so maybe 'fig' should be in the name. Like those Fig Newtons: everyone knows what's in them."

"Ah, but do people know they were named for the town of Newton, Massachusetts?" Icky pointed out, adding, "It's just a bit of cookie trivia. One of our distributors told me."

"Really!" she said. "I thought 'newton' was the shape."

"Nope. The bakery that developed that cookie names each of its products after some town in Massachusetts. There's also a chocolate Beacon Hill, and a fruit-filled Shrewsbury cookie."

"Are we going to get into a jam by baking the same cookie under a different name?"

"Are you trying to be funny?"

"Huh?"

"Get into a '*jam*'?" he repeated.

"Oh," she then realized. "Okay. Then, more to the point, are we going to 'get into a *jam* jam'?"

He shook his head at her attempt at humor.

"First, our cookie isn't exactly the same as Fig Newtons. And second, it needs its own name," he finally answered.

"Then, how about 'fig filled cookies' for this one? We can add 'strawberry filled cookies', or 'raspberry filled cookies' when those fruits come into season. Then, housewives won't have to guess."

"Okay by me," Icky said.

"Me, too," Mark grabbed a cookie.

"Hey! What are you doing in here? And save a couple of these for Jean and Marion!"

The kid just smiled and took a large bite.

"How is Marion doing?" Millie asked about the new office administrator.

"Jean says she'll be ready to take over at the end of the week," Icky answered. "She types, organizes the production schedule well, and solves office problems without asking a lot of questions."

"Jean also tastes cookies when new recipes are developed," Millie directed her comment to Mark.

"I can taste cookies," he insisted.

"And you like these?" Icky asked.

"Yup," Mark said through bites.

"Don't talk with your mouth full," Millie cautioned. "And why aren't you next door with Grandma?"

The kid slipped out, a second cookie stolen for Buko.

19

Digging In

"Climb on up here so you can get a better look," George reached down from his big red International Harvester Farmall tractor and hauled Mark up next to him. An excavator was being unloaded from a flatbed trailer, and he wanted to restrain the boy with a front-row seat to the action.

George Burlingame was a plumber by trade, but he also knew a whole lot about building anything and taking care of everything. That's why Icky hired him to handle maintenance—for starters. The job expanded quickly to include all sorts of projects, including construction oversight on the house, with special attention to the basement where the bakery's business offices would be located. Today, it seemed he was volunteering to manage a curious kid, too.

George had a narrow face, full of edges and hollows. He shifted Mark from one knee to the other, and the boy turned to look up at him.

"You got a neck like my Grandpa Huff," he announced.

"How's that?" George asked.

Mark pointed at his taut neck muscles and said, "Right here. And here, too," he touched George's leathery tanned face. It was rough with silvery stubble.

"Look over there," George redirected the boy as an excavator crawled stealthily across the curb and situated its bucket over the spot where the basement was going to be dug out. Sharp teeth were ready to chew into the earth. Next, a dump truck rumbled into position and stood at attention, waiting for orders. Its driver climbed down from his cab to inspect the lot, and sidestepped a large mud puddle remaining from a deluge that pelted the neighborhood the night before. This lot must be full of clay, he thought to himself. We're gonna' have one tough dig.

He waved to George on the sidelines. Mark thought the gesture was sent in his direction, though, and saluted.

The driver returned the boy's salute, and within seconds, swung the excavator into action.

RR-rr-rr-rr-rr. . . Crash! Chomp. Chomp. Chomp.

RR-rr-rr-rr-rr. . . Crash! Chomp. Chomp. Chomp.

RR-rr-rr-rr-rr. . . Crash! Chomp. Chomp. Chomp.

The brutal pounding called out to all the other boys in Olean's west end, and lured them away from their cereal bowls. Patrols formed quickly and moved up sidewalks *en masse*, intent on forming an army. Each intersection added more troops The mission: Identify the source of the noise, reconnoiter, and protect the neighborhood.

Crashes continued to reverberate against the crisp morning air, each collision verifying that they were headed in the right direction: Marcus Park. But when they arrived, nothing was there.

Boys turned in every direction, and finally split their platoon into squads to patrol nearby properties. Were the trucks at Topper's beverage distribution center up to something?

No. Nothing there.

What about the railroad tracks? Had a train dumped its load?

Nope. Nothing.

What about . . . but the pounding had stopped.

Up and down the block, boys looked over their shoulders, waiting for the metallic monster to reveal its hiding place. A couple of quitters were ready to break out of formation when . . .

RR-rr-rr-rr-rr. . . Crash! Chomp. Chomp. Chomp.

Behind them!

"Bakery!" one of them yelled, his fist pounding the air over his head as he led the way toward N. Fourteenth Street. In unison, the entire regiment turned, crouched, and charged down the block. They all knew the location. Haut's Cookie Shoppe gave out samples anytime a kid asked. They would protect it!

The platoon stopped at the edge of the park across the street from the excavator trailer just as the huge yellow monster dropped its head violently into a hole: Crash! Jagged metal teeth tore into the earth, brutally seizing a mouthful of dirt. Then the head yanked out of the hole and turned in their direction. It seemed to gaze at them, one by one.

Satisfied that the boy army wasn't going to launch an attack, the monster's bucket head spun around, paused momentarily, advanced slowly, and positioned itself midair over a dump truck. Then, without warning, it thrust convulsively forward, and disgorged itself of the earth.

Again and again, the monster tore and chewed and spit and puked, charming every boy hovering across the street. Young recruits assigned to reporting to higher-ups at headquarters could only speculate about what was going on. Maybe, if they got just a little closer, they could figure it out, so they inched in, step-by-step . . . until one of the men on the job site held out both of his palms to keep them back.

Danger lurked inside that hole. They knew it.

At noon, each member of the boy company returned to his duty station for mess—which could be sloppy joes or fish sticks or canned spaghetti—and reported the monster's violent action in lurid detail to his commanding officer. Mothers up and down the block expected frontline intelligence: grist for afternoon telephone mills. Lines would be buzzing about what the Hauts were building now. A new bakery just opened. What could be next?

Maybe that old Quonset hut was being torn down! Wasn't it an eyesore? . . . How could Henry and Emma stomach seeing that old metal barracks outside their window? . . . For years! No one else would tolerate a view like that. . . . Well, you know that their son and daughter-in-law live in it with their two children. Yes, even in the winter! . . . Didn't the girl sell cookies door-to-door from her bike basket one summer a couple of years or so ago? . . . Test market? No-o-o. Well, maybe. But someone said the family was having trouble making ends meet. . . . They should have had the sense to haul that Quonset hut off as soon as that red brick bakery went up. . . . No, it was still there. . . . Yes, they supposed they did need to sleep somewhere, but how long could they all live in an old World War II Army barracks! . . .

While the Command was busy on the telephone, each boy soldier got afternoon leave (and dimes) to see a gruesome old movie at the Haven Theatre, and caught up with one another to march uptown.

Afterward, they marched past the damage wrought on the lot at N. Fourteenth and Sullivan Streets. The alien perpetrator was gone, but tracks left in the earth bore grisly evidence of its power: proof that a monster tried to destroy the neighborhood that day.

They told their mothers that the kid who lived in the Quonset hut watched from a seat on some guy's tractor. Mark also got a good look at the boys who were surveying the action from Marcus Park. He could hardly wait to follow them.

But instead, George escorted him back to his grandmother, and picked up a $165 check that Icky left for the foreman in payment for digging out the basement.

"Tomorrow they're going to start laying block," he reported to Ma Haut. "Then they'll coat it with tar."

She remembered when Mark once leaned over the edge of a kitchen stool to dip his toe into his dad's molasses bucket. Then he fell in. She couldn't risk the boy trying that with tar!

"The smell will stink up the whole neighborhood for a while," George continued, "and that's just the sort of thing a boy wants to look into. I can take him over to check it out, and talk to him about it. Maybe then he'll leave it alone."

Mark listened quietly as a hint of the next day's adventure was being discussed.

"I think they leave for the cottage tomorrow morning," Ma Haut said. "This vacation cannot come too soon!"

#

"Thanks for making calls with me," John said as Icky and he pulled onto Route 17 and headed north. "I'd really like to open up the Williamsport territory, and with you along, I'll have a good chance of bringing on enough stores to cover delivery costs."

"I'm happy to spend the day in this new baby," Icky patted the dashboard on John's new 1951 GMC 100 half-ton panel truck. "This sure is better than the bakery's old wreck."

"I got a good price, too," John added.

"Like I said when you started looking: They're building 'em every day. All you got to do is wait for their best offer, because they need buyers more than you need any of the vehicles on their lot. And in the end, standing your ground gets you a better deal."

"It sure did," he agreed. "And look, Icky, I don't know how to say this, but thanks for the loan. I never expected the bakery to bankroll my business like you did, but . . . thanks."

"Your success is our success," Icky said. Returning the conversation to the truck, he added, "And this is one smooth ride!"

"I thought so, too," John agreed. "Bertie said that since I'm spending most of the day behind the wheel, I ought to pay attention to the way the truck feels on the road."

"How are the wedding plans going?" Icky asked.

"She's got it under control," John said. "I just need to show up."

"That's how it usually goes," Icky admitted.

As they continued toward their first stop, Icky's mind wandered, first, over the way that western New York's mountains rose sharply and then sloped slowly downward into a long valley, and then, over John's courage in taking on a new business. After a couple of minutes, he said, "Look, I know you thanked me for the loan, and I appreciate that. But I want you to know this: Helping you get started is a two-way deal."

"What do you mean?" John asked. Had he missed part of their agreement?

"You're getting to be a really solid distributor, and that's going to grow our local and regional sales," Icky hoped to build his confidence. "What I'm saying is that we're helping each other, because long-term, our bakery wouldn't grow without you either."

"Well, I sure hope we add a couple more accounts today," John said. "Store managers will like meeting the top guy of one of the bakeries I'm representing."

"Then, let's go get 'em," Icky said.

20

Work Hard, Play Hard

Telephone service at the cottage was connected soon after Millie and the kids moved in so Icky could handle bakery calls on the weekends.

"I'm not sure I'll like talking about business on a party line," he said.

"You can hear a little click if somebody picks up the receiver. Tell them that the line is in use and that you'll be off in a few minutes," Millie asserted. "They'll hang up."

"Not me. I'd listen anyway," Mary Lou exaggerated. "Then I could get in on all the good gossip!"

"Don't teenagers have enough to do without listening in on other peoples' conversations?" Millie challenged.

"I was only kidding," Mary Lou rolled her eyes in exasperation. After all, I'm not Mark—and on imagining the possibility that her mother might ever, ever! confuse her kid brother's behavior with hers, she began to raise her adolescent defenses.

"Maybe you'll want to invite one of your friends to come out to the lake," Millie tried to diffuse Mary Lou's pout before it sprouted into teenage angst. Besides, two girls would be too busy talking to one another to pry into who-knows-what-rumors might be spread around on the telephone. Modern communications were a breeding ground for insensitivity, speculation, and conjecture, that was for sure.

"Cool!" Mary Lou agreed, and invited her friend, Sylvia, to spend the following week.

#

"You girls can take your things upstairs," Millie directed as they hauled Sylvia's bag through the door. "Then, when you're settled in, follow Mark down to the lake and keep an eye on him. He wants to dangle a worm off his rod."

"He won't catch anything," Mary Lou said.

"But it'll keep him occupied," her mother contended.

The girls shrugged in unison. They could work on their tans.

Mary Lou kicked off her canvas sneakers and slid her feet into the water, while Sylvia sat cross-legged on the dock. Mark found a good fishing spot, threaded a worm onto a hook, drew his boy-sized yellow rod over his head, and snapped his line. The worm flew out, out, out about ten feet, and dropped into the lake.

Good, really good, he decided. It was the first time he fished without his Grandpa Huff's supervision, so he prepared to wait just like he'd been taught—but it wasn't long before his fishing line gave a little tug. Something was going on with his bait!

He sat up straight and stared into the water, recalling how Grandpa Huff told him about fish behavior. "At first, your fish is only bumping into that worm, maybe giving it a sniff or two, maybe taking a little taste. You just give it time to grab on."

The line tugged again, gently.

And again. The third snap was full on.

"I got one!" Mark announced gleefully as he jumped to his feet and started reeling in his fish. Round and round his mighty hand rotated the spool.

The girls looked over their shoulders to see what was going on.

"Oh, my gosh!" Mary Lou stood up. She didn't expect him to actually catch something.

"Get the net!" the kid shouted eagerly. "Get the net!"

Grandpa Huff would have been right there with a net; Mark expected no less of his sister.

"What net?" Mary Lou shouted as Mark pulled a little sunfish out of the lake. A small spray of water followed as his prize whipped back and forth.

"Augh!" both girls shrieked, backing up so they wouldn't get spattered.

"Get him!" Mark demanded.

He circled the rod over the dock, and his fish flopped around on the boards.

The girls didn't want to touch it. And Mary Lou didn't see a net anywhere.

"Here!" she finally stepped on the line. She thought she might be able to extract the hook. She'd seen it done before.

"Augh!" she repeated as she tried to grab the fish with only the tips of her fingers. "I can't get it! It keeps moving!"

Sylvia stepped in and unexpectedly planted her sneaker squarely on the fish's tail in the same moment that Mary Lou exerted some control and yanked on the hook.

"Eeew," Sylvia shrieked loudly, pulling her foot back. But she wasn't quick enough to avert tragedy.

"You tore off my fish's head!" Mark accused the two of them, his jaw jutted out and his eyebrows crossed at the girls' clumsiness. How could they take over like that!

"That's my fish!" he asserted.

Both girls were shrieking then.

"*My* fish," he complained. "*I'm* the one who gets to gut it."

He gathered up his catch and stomped toward the cottage. Mary Lou had expected him to be upset at seeing the fish's demise. But no, the boy's vast fund of knowledge, accumulated at Grandpa Huff's hip, prepared him for his first solo catch—except that his incredibly inexperienced sister was too inept to bring a net.

"I got a fish!" he announced to his mother as he dropped it onto the kitchen counter. "And we're having it for supper!"

Wasn't that what his grandparents always did? Sometimes the feast included a few more fish, but that didn't matter. Mark's prize was always centered on the platter, the star of the meal. He expected no less honor to be awarded to this hard won sunfish. And somehow, with everything else she was doing, Millie made sure that it was.

21

The Icing on the Cake

LUCUS-HEINZ WEDDING IS CELEBRATED

On Sunday, August 18, Kathryn Roberta (Bertie) Lucas was given in marriage by her father to area businessman John Heinz during a celebration of their nuptials among family and friends.

The happy bride wore an elegant full-skirted gown covered in silk tulle with a sweetheart neckline and short puffed sleeves. A matching fingertip-length veil, lace gloves, and an orchid bouquet with satin streamers completed the ensemble. The groom was handsome in dark trousers and a white double-breasted jacket with a white satin shawl collar over a starched white shirt and white bowtie.

The wedding party included the bride's sister, Shirley De Groff, as matron of honor, with bridesmaids Laura Heinz and Dorothy Heinz; and Edward (Icky) Haut, as best man, with groomsmen Al Palmer and Preston Leroy Lucas. Denise Ruane was the flower girl, and Robert Mooney was the ring bearer.

A reception was held at the Weston Firehouse where guests enjoyed a wedding cake and dainty petit fours from Herta Fischer, who is employed by Haut's Bakehouse.

The groom is owner of John Heinz Distributing, a baked goods supplier serving grocery stores in southwest New York and northwest Pennsylvania.

The couple will reside on Green Street following their return from a honeymoon to Lake George in the Adirondack Mountains, where they hope for good fishing.

#

"Icky! Appearing in the newspaper are your name and the bakery name!" Ma exclaimed with happy excitement. "The story says that to John Heinz marries Kathryn Lucas. And Herta's cakes also were enjoyed!"

Icky stepped away from the hot oven and wiped his forehead with a small towel he kept in the back pocket of his baker's whites. Ma held out the newspaper for him to read.

"Look! At! That!" he punctuated his response. "The paper also mentions the name of John's new business! He's going to like that!"

"I'll leave the paper in the hut for Millie. She comes in from the cottage today, *ja*?"

"She just arrived. She's talking with painters about room colors," he said. "Then she'll go over to the parsonage to visit Jean and the new baby."

"The Reverend and Mrs. Bauer have a daughter," Ma acknowledged. "Is this not their third child, after John and Mary?"

"She is," Icky said. "They named her Anne."

Ma nodded, approvingly. Then, returning to the topic of the new house, she inquired, "If Millie picks colors, construction must be almost done, *ja*?"

"We got a bill for the appliances, and they'll be delivered soon."

"New refrigerator and stove together: these are expensive, but not so much as the bakery," Ma said. She wouldn't pry into how much everything cost, but she would like to know, if Icky cared to share.

"The refrigerator was three hundred dollars," he said; he knew his mother always liked to keep track of prices. "The oven and countertop burners were just over two hundred dollars, and the fan over the burners was about fifty-five dollars.

"Then, we blew our wad on a KitchenAid dishwasher," he admitted proudly, "—over three hundred sixty bucks."

"A washer for the dishes!" Ma exclaimed. "This you need?"

"Yes," Icky said decisively. "Millie was willing to live in an old Army barracks while we got this bakery running. Putting a dishwasher in her new kitchen is the least I can do."

Ma nodded, happy enough just to have a toaster in her own kitchen. Its twin wire cages lowered and raised warm bread the way Pa liked it, and that was good enough for her.

"Excited she must be to finally see her house," she said. "You still move this fall?"

"October or November, I think," he said. "I gotta' get back to work, Ma."

She waved him away. They'd never say it, but Pa and she also were looking forward to moving day. Soon thereafter, that old Quonset hut would be removed, and the view from their kitchen window would be restored.

#

"I thought you were on your way back to the cottage," Icky said when Millie appeared in the new bakery's doorway a few minutes later.

"I wanted to show you the bedspread I found for Mary Lou's bedroom," she lifted a corner out of the shopping bag. "It's expensive—$12, but it will look really nice on her new poster bed, especially with the paint color I just chose. I want to hide it at Pa and Ma's house so she doesn't see it until it's on her bed when we move in."

"Ma left a newspaper article on John and Bertie's wedding. It's on the desk in the hut."

"I'll look for it. And I have some news, too," she said. She'd been saving this surprise for last. "Frank and Jean asked if we'll sponsor their baby's baptism in a few weeks."

She paused to see his reaction.

"What did you say?" the words stuttered from his mouth.

"Yes!" Millie answered with delight. "I said 'yes!'"

"Wow! That's a big responsibility," he exclaimed, "but it feels more like a privilege."

"I thought so, too," Millie said. Jean was, after all, her closest confidant.

"And of course, we'll never have to worry about this baby's upbringing in the church—not with those two as parents," Icky continued.

"I know," Millie said, "but it's awfully nice to be connected to them in this way."

"We have to tell Ma," Icky said.

"I'll leave that to you," Millie acknowledged.

"Why me? This is good news—great news!"

"You get stuck with telling them unpleasant stuff, so this time you can share something good. And while you're over there, can you drop off the bedspread?"

"I can," he agreed. "Enjoy the last couple of weeks at the lake!"

"We will," she kissed him good-bye. "And we'll see you on the weekend."

#

"How is Derby working out as afternoon supervisor?" Icky asked.

"He's doing great," Roy said. "And a couple of the girls from the morning operation say they want to move to second shift, too, so that gets him started with an experienced crew."

"Why would girls want to change to second shift?" Icky asked.

"Their husbands work days," he explained. "Their kids are in school, so they can do their housework in the morning, prepare dinner fixings for their husbands to reheat in the oven, get in to work at noon, and still be home in time to tuck in the little ones. It's a good schedule for them."

"Sounds easy enough," Icky said. "And good for us, too, as long as they can handle the afternoon heat."

"Your sister never had a problem with it—and that was in Cuba," Roy pointed out. "The islands are a whole lot warmer, even with the trade winds."

"Maybe we should try to find another two girls who want the same schedule," Icky suggested.

"Do you expect enough orders to support additional staff?"

"Won't be long," he answered. "Distributors are asking what our next new cookie will be."

"What are you telling them?" Roy asked.

"A fruit cookie," Icky answered. "Neiler and Derby should have samples by week's end."

"No chocolate? The girls are asking for that," Roy noted.

"We could mix chocolate chips into our pecan dandies dough."

"That would be easy to add to the production schedule, too," Roy said.

"Good!" Icky agreed. "Tell Ma we'll have two new test cookies on Sunday."

22

Too Much Salt

The best place to purchase pork for Ma's Sunday dinners was Ray Wittenberg's butcher shop, just three blocks down the street, so Icky took Mark for a short walk to pick up the order. While they waited in line, they stared through the showcase at their family's favorite meats.

"Don't breathe on the glass," Icky instructed.

"I need to see!" Mark defended as he moved back a bit and wiped off the condensation. His fingerprints left a kid-level smudge, just like Buko's nose bumps on Grandma's windows.

"Grandpa likes pork," Icky pointed at the selections, "and he likes to eat it every day."

"I likes hotdogs!" Mark said, enthusiastically. Both of them decided that sausages were really good, too. A moment later, they paid for their order, and exited onto the sidewalk. Icky bent down to pick up Mark.

"You hold on to this package," he said, sliding the pork roast between them as he stood up, "and I'll hold on to you."

Suddenly, two blasts penetrated the air close by, and Icky jerked around just as someone fell to the sidewalk across the street.

"What the—!" he said, and in the same moment, turned his back to the attack to protect Mark, and bolted toward home at a full run.

A third discharge went off.

Mark tucked his head into Icky's shoulder and tightly gripped the package to his belly. It felt cold.

When they got home, Icky finally took a full breath, grateful that Mark wasn't sobbing. But as soon as the boy's toes reached the ground, he pushed through the back door, and like soda pop effervescing out of its bottle, loudly yelled, "Mommy! Mommy! Two guys got shot!"

"What?" she exclaimed.

"I didn't think he saw it," Icky followed him in.

"What?" Millie repeated with alarm as she checked Mark for wounds. "Are you okay?"

"Yup," he answered. "They got shot! It was loud!"

"Where?" she demanded, wide-eyed.

"Across the street from Wittenberg's," Icky reported. "It looked like one of them put some daylight into the other."

"What is this red on your shirt!" Millie shrieked.

Icky and she immediately lifted it up, scrunching the garment into Mark's chin as they searched his belly for a wound. Seeing that he was okay, they searched the meat package he'd been holding and figured out that the kid had clutched it so tightly that a small amount of liquid leaked out.

Mark defiantly pulled down his shirt. He didn't want to be inspected. He wanted to talk.

"I don't know what the red is," he said indignantly. "I didn't do it!"

"Okay," Millie said. Distraction was needed, so she led him down the hall to his bedroom. "Let's get your shirt changed. Then we can make you a peanut butter sandwich for lunch."

But Mark wouldn't be put off.

"I saw it, Mommy!" he insisted.

She shuddered at how close they had come to bullets.

#

Ma led Sunday's dinner table conversation with comments on the Bauer baby's baptism.

"Wonderful it was that the Reverend and Mrs. Bauer invited you to be Anne's sponsors," she said.

"An unexpected honor," Icky acknowledged.

"When we met with Pastor Bauer and Jean yesterday, he also asked Icky if he'd become the new Sunday School superintendent," Millie added.

"*Ja?*" Ma said. "This job you can do?"

"Yeah," Icky agreed. "I just need to attend meetings and review financial statements."

"But two hundred children! A lot of responsibility this is!" Ma insisted.

"Pastor Bauer also said we can be proud of the two kids we're rearing," Icky said.

Grandma smiled broadly at them, and agreed that they were well behaved. But as too much doting could spoil a child, she shifted the conversation to the morning newspaper.

"On the front page is a story about a shooting yesterday morning," she said. "Just down the street it was."

"We were there!" Icky exclaimed.

"Me, too!" Mark interrupted.

"What is this?" Ma asked.

"Mark and I were coming out of Wittenberg's when it happened."

"Then what?" Pa asked.

"We got out of there, that's what!" Icky said. "What does the story say?"

"That a triangle led to two shootings on State Street." Ma wouldn't call the dead man a lover, not in front of the children. "And then the shooter takes his own life."

"That sounds right," Icky said. "Two shots. Then another."

"And Mark saw it, witness to a murder before he's out of kindergarten," Millie said.

Suddenly aware that the attention was focused on him, Mark decided to showcase new linguistic skills he'd picked up when he went to the park after the shooting. He wanted to brag about the crime he witnessed to a few of the boys who were older and wiser. They must have been impressed, because in response, they told him a couple of things, too.

Looking his grandma straight in the eyes and enunciating with great pride over his expanding vocabulary, he said, "Pass the salt, ya' sons-a-"

"Mark!" his mother cut him off.

The kid blinked.

Grandma sat up as straight and stiff as her wooden chair, and gasped with such strenuous civility that her breath sizzled through her teeth with a loud "s" sound.

Stunned silence sucked the rest of the air from the room.

Sparks flew from his mother's eyes.

His father's ears turned crimson. Mark couldn't be sure, but he thought he saw smoke coming from them.

Mary Lou muttered something about getting an Ivory soap mouthwash.

Finally, Millie ventured into the vacuum, and asked, "Where did you hear that?" She'd grown up with three older brothers, so there was little her son could say that would shock her.

"I don't know," Mark shrugged. He began to sense that something was wrong. Images of a cartoon flickered in his thoughts: rabbit and coyote unexpectedly faced one another, wide-eyed, with the toe-curling realization that they were caught behind some fence, together. Everyone at the table had eyes like those two characters, but the funny "*Bo*-ing!" was missing.

"I think you do know," Millie forced him back to reality.

"I don't remember," he pouted, the lie floating in front of his innocent lips. Grownups were breathing down on the top of his head, their laser beam eyes aimed in his direction. He scrunched his shoulders toward his earlobes, and shut his eyes in a desperate attempt to become invisible.

After the hollow void of a moment's silence, he peeked open one eye to see if everyone was still staring. They were, so in one last ditch effort to save himself, he finally blurted, "It's not my fault that stuff just comes out."

Slowly, Icky allowed, "That's true." But then, with calm precision he added, "but I want to know this: How. Did. It. Get. In. There. In the first place?"

Mark glanced at Mary Lou for a clue on what might happen next. The look on her face was grave.

Only one way out seemed open. He'd have to tell the awful truth, even if it meant he'd be banned from talking to the older boys ever again for the rest of his whole entire life. With great regret, he accepted his fate and answered in the smallest possible voice, "Ronny said it, and everybody laughed."

His parents lifted their heads and nodded at one another while his grandparents dropped back into their chairs. Knowing looks revealed that they all were familiar with the Wilson family. It was sad, really, that Mark's comment revealed the sort of language those boys were accustomed to hearing.

Intent on showing that he wasn't the only one at the table who said the wrong thing, Mark argued his defense. "You're supposed to laugh, too, and then pass the salt."

Millie could only hope her son would forget not one, but two, unfortunate experiences that weekend: first, the shooting across the street from Wittenberg's butcher shop, and secondly, the rough language he learned at the park. She passed the salt to lift the weight of consternation from the kid's shoulders.

"Wasn't that a beautiful baptism?" she redirected the conversation. She expected Icky to respond, but his thoughts were elsewhere; perhaps their pastor's comment about rearing model children was offered too soon.

Finally, Pa passed the coleslaw across the table. He could see when a guy needed a way out of a hole he dug himself into, and this time, both his son and his grandson needed help.

"Only a couple bites are left here. Anybody want it?" he prodded. "Better it is to be sick from overeating than to be wasteful!"

#

"Where are those samples of Icky's new fruit and nut cookies?" Pa asked. He'd like to nibble on one while he watched the television before nodding off to sleep. "That one I'd like more of!"

"Only one remains, and hidden it is for your lunch box tomorrow," Ma said. "Over to the bakery you can go if you want another."

"Maybe that I will do," he lifted his chin in defiance. "More than a ton of those raisins he bought, so a few cookies he can spare for his father."

"A ton of raisins *and* a half ton of nuts: that's what he said," she nodded. "And he always shares."

"What think you about the dinner talk today?" Pa asked.

"Two sons we reared," Ma responded quietly, "but never were the words on their tongues so foul that they curdled the milk."

"The boy doesn't know what he said," Pa defended their youngest grandchild. "Besides, our sons had three sisters to keep them in line. Mark has only Mary Lou."

"Then, for her also we will pray," Ma suggested as she picked up her darning. "A blessing the girl probably needs."

23

The Devil in the Details

"Okay, here's what we're going to do," Icky directed. "The two ladders are spaced out at the exact width of the sign, so we'll each grab an end and walk it up. You hold your side next to the building while I put in the first screws over here at this end. Then I'll climb down and bring the drill over to you."

"Aren't you gonna' mark the building with chalk to be sure we get it straight?" Roy disagreed.

"Extra work. Just line your end along the same row of bricks as mine," Icky insisted, noting how Roy told new crew to measure ingredients twice and pour once, too. "Let's go."

"Okay. It's your sign."

One step at a time, the men lifted the sign to their shoulders and climbed up the ladder until they both were on the third rungs from the top. Nodding to one another, they lined the bottom of the frame along a row of bricks. Icky drilled in the first masonry screws, quickly descended the ladder, and walked the drill and orange extension cord to his brother-in-law.

"I'll hold your end," he handed over the tool and reached up for the bottom of the sign. The third corner was anchored into place just as the city building inspector pulled up in his old Ford pickup.

"Hey!" the guy yelled from the truck window as he leaned halfway out. He looked like a tortoise emerging from its shell, open-mouthed, with eyes squinting into the bright morning sun. "What are you doing there?"

"What does it look like? I'm putting up a sign!" Icky held back irritation from being interrupted in the middle of a job. The guy tightened his mouth as if he'd swallowed a bug, and cocked his head to one side. Icky realized who he was then. They served on the church council together.

"You know," he said with authority backed up by city government, "you need a permit to do that. Got to comply with the law if you're going to put up a commercial building—not to mention hanging a sign on it."

He had to admit it looked good and solid, though.

"Seems like you know all about this compliance thing," Icky answered with his own voice of authority. "I'm busy here, so if you want a permit, you go get one and I'll sign it when I'm done."

The inspector slowly shook his head in disbelief. But since he knew how hard Icky had worked to start his bakery, all the while also devoting time to church projects, he said, "I'd say 'no' if anybody else told me to do that. But seeing how you've been handing out those cookies we've been tasting at church, I'll just drop off the forms. Fill 'em out, and get 'em back to my office."

"Okay, see ya' later," Icky ended the conversation and pressed the drill into the last screw.

"You put this building up without a permit?" Roy probed as he climbed down.

"I thought the one for the house covered both buildings," Icky defended. "And besides, you know how busy we've been working. We got orders to fill!"

"I hear you. But that argument won't hold water if you get fined," Roy pointed out. "I'm surprised he didn't stop by sooner."

"I guess the building looks like a big garage, situated next to the house. Maybe he didn't realize 'til now that this is the bakery. He sure knew we were putting one up."

"Well, your sign definitely identifies it," Roy pointed out, "so you want to turn in those forms right away, before somebody else downtown decides to reverse his decision."

"It'll be done Monday," he agreed. "Thanks for the help with the sign."

#

Millie finished preparing snacks to go with drinks just as Jim and Helen Freitas arrived to celebrate the new bakery.

"A toast: A guy's baking bread career goes up in flames and returns as a pastry expert!" Jim pronounced dramatically as he raised his glass toward the new sign: "To Icky's Cookies... The House that Quality Built."

"To Icky's Cookies!" Helen and Millie repeated.

"Thanks," Icky said, swallowing hard.

"This building is huge compared to the bakeshop you attached to the back of that hut," Jim said.

"Almost eight times larger," Icky acknowledged. "The lean-to was eight by thirty feet, and the new bakery is thirty-six by sixty feet."

"Four years is a long time to live and work in an old barracks," Jim said. "You two worked hard to get here."

"The commute is still short," Icky added. "Building the bakery next to the house is sort of like a church and its parsonage."

"Come on in and see the ranch!" Millie invited Helen and Jim up three steps into the kitchen.

"Nice!" Helen admired the birch cabinetry.

"Try some of these," Millie handed Jim a generous plate of deviled eggs and bite-sized ham balls in a brown sugar glaze.

"Why do they call these eggs 'deviled'?" Jim asked. He expected Icky to know everything there was to know about food. But this time, Millie answered.

"The paprika sprinkled on top looks like embers burning on the floor of hell," she said. "The name comes from Spain."

"This morning, I thought it was the building inspector who had the devil in him!" Icky said. "He stopped by as Roy and I were drilling in the new sign, and said we didn't have a permit to build the new bakery."

"I didn't know about this!" Millie exclaimed.

"No big deal," Icky continued. "I thought the one for the house also covered the bakery."

"So now what?" Millie pressed.

"He dropped off the forms after lunch. We'll fill 'em out, and turn 'em in. That's all."

Or he'll get Marion to do it, Millie thought to herself. Icky hated paperwork.

"Wait a minute. The inspector delivered the forms to you—personally?" Jim repeated with surprise in his voice. "That's a switch. Usually they threaten to tear down your building and make you start over."

"We attend the same church," Icky said nonchalantly. "I guess that helped."

Millie nodded then. She knew who the inspector was. And they were lucky—this time.

"Follow me," she led Helen from the kitchen through the living room, and then down a hallway. "And here are the bedrooms. Each of the kids has their own space now."

"I like how you furnished everything," Helen said. "It could have come out of *Ladies Home Journal*!"

"I went to Bender and Riggs Furniture," Millie said. "The sales lady was really helpful."

Jim finished his third deviled egg as the girls returned to the kitchen. He was about to turn the conversation back to the bakery when Helen handed him a paper napkin and pointed to the corner of her own mouth. He dabbed yellow yolk from his lip.

"So after the building permit, what other paperwork needs attention?" he turned to Icky. "I know you're working with Pete Sheeser to file your business taxes."

"Yeah, thanks for that referral," Icky said. While Jim could have handled the bakery's records, they agreed not to mix business into their friendship.

"How about your new product name: *Icky's Cookies*? Did you get it trademarked?"

"I think I'm covered," Icky dismissed the question. "I'm the only 'Icky' around here. Besides, how many cookie bakers do you know?"

"None," Jim agreed. "But the way your business is growing, some other bakery that wants to offer pastries could steal the name from you."

Icky eyed Jim skeptically.

"Why bother with a situation that's not likely to ever occur?" he challenged, even though he knew that Jim was probably right, legally. "I got enough to do with . . . "

"Like not getting a permit to build the bakery?" Jim interrupted as only a good friend could.

"We're small," Icky avoided concern. "Seems to me that registering a trademark is ahead of the game."

"No, your name is your reputation," Jim continued to press, "and that's your income and your future. You've got to protect it."

"Nobody's going to steal the name 'Icky's Cookies.'"

"It probably wouldn't be a first choice, if that's how you want to look at it," Jim allowed.

"Which is my point, precisely," Icky felt he'd won. "And what's wrong with 'Icky's Cookies'?"

"I'd call it 'Jim's Cookies,'" he smiled self-indulgently. "But this isn't about whether or not somebody likes the name; it's whether or not they can use it to make money. And if your product is selling well, then the name has value. A trademark protects that value."

"Okay," Icky finally conceded. He moved the deviled eggs and ham balls to the kitchen table, and grabbed a chair. "I'll talk to Sheeser."

"Not Sheeser," Jim said, taking the opposite chair. "You need an attorney—somebody like Sid Shane."

"Shane," Icky pondered. "Why does that name sound familiar?"

"He chairs the Cattaraugus County Democratic Party, so his name is in *The Olean Times-Herald* all the time," Jim answered.

Icky grimaced.

"Don't go holding politics against him," Jim cautioned. He knew Icky voted Republican. "He's a ripe old businessman with a lot of experience, and his son Mike is starting law school at Georgetown. Shane will take good care of you."

Icky didn't say anything.

"He's also represented the Seneca nation on cases against state government," Jim continued, "so he's got a good head on his shoulders. He's the right guy for this stuff."

"If you say so," Icky allowed. In the back of his mind, though, all the nonsense of filing a trademark was just one more impediment to getting back to work. Building a new bakery and being on the road had taken him away from operations long enough.

#

"Nice space!" Tom Hubbell said on the first sales call he made to the bakery's new business offices.

"It's working out for us," Icky said. "Have a seat."

Tom settled into a comfortable chair opposite Icky's desk, and admired the pine-paneled walls. "When you said you were running the business from the basement in your new house, I didn't know what to expect," he said. "This is great—and convenient!"

"And only thirty seconds from the bakery," he agreed.

"But I bet it's difficult to leave work at the end of the day," Tom noted.

"Sometimes we head across the street to Marcus Park," Icky picked up a baseball shirt from the credenza behind his desk. "The bakery is backing a men's team in the town's Amateur Baseball League this summer."

"So, Icky's Cookies is a corporate sponsor!" Tom smiled.

"I never thought of it that way," he grinned broadly, "but we are incorporated, so yeah, I guess we are! But it's just a team of neighborhood guys."

"Neighborhood?"

"Right across the street. Teams play every night. If it's not fast pitch, it's slow pitch. And there's leagues: industrial, tavern and church—we've got 'em all," Icky listed.

"Do you play?"

"No, I get enough exercise hauling hundred-pound bags of Pillsbury flour!"

"You're still working production?" Tom asked.

"Often enough," Icky said. "When Roy is short a guy, I'm it."

"So, Roy is supervising operations?" Tom asked. He remembered how he was Icky's supervisor at Bolles's bakery.

"Yeah, and we added a second shift," Icky said.

"You guys are busy!" Tom noted.

"I'm not complaining, that's for sure," Icky said. Moving the conversation to the reason for Tom's visit, he asked, "So, what do we need to talk about?"

Tom pulled paperwork out of his briefcase, and asked, "Do you remember a meeting a few years back when we discussed fortified flour for the first time?" At the onset of World War II, Pillsbury and other millers had agreed to fight malnutrition by adopting National Research Council recommendations on the addition of essential vitamins and minerals to bread flour—which Mace Bolles had balked. Cost was one reason for his resistance, but at a quarter a sack it was only two-tenths of a penny per loaf, so he couldn't launch a good argument.

"We're using fortified flour, too," Icky confirmed.

"Well, now we're getting another mandate," Tom said. "This one comes from the Food and Nutrition Board and the American Medical Association. They're jointly supporting 'revised minimum daily food requirements.'"

"So what does this bunch of regulations mean?" Icky asked.

"Most of the change is on our end," Tom said. "The flours we mill have to be enriched with folic acid at a level of 0.43 to 1.4 milligrams."

"What about cost? Is this a big deal?"

"Less than a nickel per hundred-pound sack," he answered.

"We can handle that," Icky said, though he'd run quick tests on his recipes. Even if an added ingredient didn't alter taste, it might have an impact on texture or bake time.

"Also, your labels will need to be updated to show that your cookies contain folic acid," Tom added. "Making sure you do that is the other reason for my call."

"I hear you," Icky made a note to tell Marion to update the packaging. "Just so I know, what does folic acid do?"

"It's a B vitamin that helps the body make red blood cells," Tom said. "Adding it has something to do with preventing anemia."

"The flour milling business is always in the middle of something new," Icky said.

"Soon you'll need your own proprietary cookie flour blend, too," Tom suggested. He'd been expecting Icky to develop it for quite a while—just as he did when he worked at Bolles.

"I'll get to it. For now," Icky ended business, "how about a drink? You've been on the road all day, and you got to eat somewhere. It might as well be with us. The food's pretty good."

"I'd like that," Tom agreed.

"And afterward, we can walk across the street to Marcus Park to watch a couple of innings of baseball," Icky continued. "My team is playing tonight."

"Are they any good?" Tom asked.

"They're up-and-comers," he led the way to Millie's kitchen. She'd already set an extra place at the table so Tom would know he was expected. Icky reached into the cupboard and took down a bottle of liquor and glasses.

"The first one I pour for you," he said. "The next one you make yourself. Mixers are in the refrigerator if you want them."

"To your continuing success," Tom toasted the new bakery.

"With Pillsbury," Icky added.

"Thanks," Tom said. "We're glad to grow with you. And speaking of growth, where are your kids?"

"They should be home soon," Millie said.

"Both of them?"

"Both," Millie said. "Mark is in the first grade, thank goodness. Mary Lou is a sophomore."

"They sure grow up fast," he said.

"They do," she answered. "At the beginning the term, we asked Mark if he made any new friends..."

"And he answered, 'Yup, and some of the normal ones are in my class, too,'" Icky finished.

"Normal, huh?" Tom laughed.

"We're working on his vocabulary," Millie added.

"What news is coming from the grocery trades?" Icky pulled out chairs at the table. Tom could always be counted on for industry trends.

"Sales of prepared foods are curving upward," he answered, "especially products like canned spaghetti and luncheon meats."

"I can believe that," Icky said.

"And specialty frozen foods are topped with processed 'American cheese food,'" he added. "We're seeing it on everything, especially vegetables."

"Some kids don't like vegetables," Millie acknowledged. "I can see how a product line that coats green foods with cheese would be popular."

"But why use fancy wording?" Icky asked. "Couldn't they just call it 'cheddar', or whatever cheese it is?"

"Not really," Tom said. "'American cheese food' is less than 51 percent real cheese curds, so technically, it can't be called 'cheese', according to the FDA."

"So calling it 'cheese food' is how they get around that?" Icky sought clarification.

"Yes, because it's food that happens to contain cheese," Tom said.

"What else *happens* to be in it?" Millie asked, critically.

"I think they add whey..."

"Which is milk," Icky inserted.

"Right," Tom agreed, "and maybe vegetable oil. Then they emulsify it to get a smooth texture that coats the tongue."

"So, picky eaters won't turn up their noses at broccoli coated in 'cheese food,'" Millie surmised.

"Isn't calling it 'cheese food' stepping across the line with regard to truth in labeling?" Icky asked.

"I don't know," Tom answered. "They're doing it, and nobody's telling them not to."

"Well, I think it's deceptive!" Millie pronounced. "If I buy a new product, I'm trusting it's good for the children!"

"I'm not saying 'cheese food' isn't safe—or good," Tom corrected. "It's just not plain cheese anymore. It's cheese that's been . . . "

"Don't say 'improved,'" Millie interrupted. She didn't like sneaky labeling.

"How about 'altered,'" Tom suggested, "or 'transformed'. That's probably closer to what they'd say: that they've taken the work out of converting a hard block of cheese into a sauce by 'transforming' it."

Millie decided that children just need to be introduced to fresh vegetables when they're little. Then they learn that they're supposed to like them.

"And they'd probably add that they're doing all the work for you," he added.

"Uh-huh," she said, flatly. She'd be reading labels more carefully.

"What else is trending?" Icky moved the conversation along.

"Like I said, foods that take work out of the kitchen for busy mothers are hitting the shelves," Tom said. "Soon you'll see frozen pre-made meals called TV dinners."

"TV dinner?" Icky repeated.

"They're kid-sized portions of factory-cut white turkey slices wrapped around stuffing, plus a small portion of peas, and a scoop of apple crisp for dessert. It all comes in individual aluminum foil containers. Moms just heat them in the oven for a half hour, and deliver them to tray tables for kids to eat while they're watching their favorite television shows."

He had a disgusted look on his face.

"You don't like that idea," Icky observed.

"Distracting kids with television screens is a crude imitation of family dinner together," Tom said. He was on the road enough to appreciate good home-cooking. "But we'll see if the idea improves over time."

Icky nodded.

Millie didn't think that the TV dinners idea sounded so bad. Icky was on the road a lot, too, and she wouldn't mind packaged meals she could feed the kids at a moment's notice—once in a while. She'd look for that product.

"Even with all this innovation, grocery stores still eat up high quality home-baked cookies like yours," Tom concluded with a smile as he lifted his glass. "And that's what we want to be part of, too."

Icky picked up his glass and tipped it in Tom's direction. "Here's to that!"

24

Just Making Conversation

"Jim was right," Shane said when Icky asked about trademarks. "Registering your brand gives you exclusive use of it."

"For how long?" Icky wondered. Would he need to renew it every year?

"It's yours for as long as you want it," he said. "Trademarks are like naming your children; their names are registered on their birth certificates. You started this bakery, so essentially, you gave birth to it. Once you register its name, no other bakery can use your brand to sell their product."

"Some other kid might be named . . . 'John Smith,'" Icky contended.

"Okay, you got me there," Shane said, "but what I'm saying is that no one else can try to make a profit off stealing your business name—or your product name—so both Haut's Cookie Shoppe and Icky's Cookies need to be registered.

"But I thought that naming the business was covered when we incorporated."

"No, incorporation is entirely different, but I'm glad you did that," Shane said.

"Our accountant got it done," Icky revealed.

"That's Pete Sheeser, right?"

"Right," Icky answered. "He said we had to do it to file taxes as a corporation."

"And to protect your personal assets," Shane said. "Incorporation gives the bakery its own status, separate from you as an individual. If anything were ever to happen—say, your bakery's delivery truck driver were in an accident, and somebody decided to sue the business—an injured party wouldn't be able to automatically attach their claims to your personal property, such as that new house you built.

"Or I should say, they wouldn't be able to attach liability to your personal property without proving you were personally negligent," he added.

Icky nodded, recalling how one of Mace Bolles's drivers got into an accident with a company truck a few years back. It led to a nasty lawsuit, but it was against his bakery, not his home.

"I guess we better get this trademark thing done then," he finally agreed.

"I'll draw up the documents," Shane shook Icky's hand and walked him to the door. "Checking records to be sure no one else already owns these names takes time, but I think you can relax, and get back to baking."

#

"How was the meeting with the attorney?" Millie asked Icky over dinner.

"Shane is doing the paperwork. He says we also need an advertising agency. This brand thing is bigger than naming cookies and listing ingredients on labels."

"What else?"

"The artwork has to be consistent, too."

"Artwork?" she repeated.

"Packaging, labels, anything that identifies the bakery and its products, including our baseball team's shirts," he sliced into his pork chop. "Trademark is a whole big deal."

"How much is this going to cost?" she asked.

"We'll get quotes," he ended the rehash of the attorney meeting. "It was good to invite Jim and Helen here to toast the new sign. I bet you missed having friends over while we lived in the hut."

"I did," Millie admitted, "but we couldn't entertain in that tiny space."

"It was the only home Mark knew," he nodded at their son.

"I know Grandma's house, too," he lifted his chin with authority.

"And you like to eat," Millie redirected him, "so you do that while Daddy and I talk."

"How do you like your new kitchen, now that you've worked in it?"

"It's heaven," she smiled.

Mark wondered when he'd be allowed to talk. Mentioning heaven could mean that he had to sit quietly, like in church.

"You worked hard to get it," Icky said.

"We did," she insisted.

"I helped, too," Mary Lou reminded her parents. She was more adept than her brother at navigating the moment when they could be included in a dinner conversation. Besides, she felt she could claim some involvement in the family business, for hadn't she sold cookies door-to-door from her bike basket when the bakery first started testing favorite varieties?

"You sure did," Icky commended her. "We would have starved to death if you hadn't brought in all that extra income."

She knew what he meant. He'd never let her forget how she negotiated a 20 percent commission, and then boldly deducted it before turning over all the pennies she collected.

"Well, I haven't asked for money since then," she defended. Like her father, she didn't like to be financially indebted to anyone. Besides, she had a lot of expenses: roller skating and movie admissions, sodas with girlfriends, jukebox selections, records, magazines—all sorts of collateral supporting a teenage lifestyle.

"Yes," Icky allowed. "You're quite independent now. Maybe it's time to start charging you rent."

"For what?" she said, aghast.

"Your new room," he suggested in jest. "From the time I was thirteen, I was expected to give most of my pay to your grandpa and grandma every week. And since you're older than that, you also probably owe a couple of years' worth of expenses."

"We just moved here!"

"So?"

"I had to share a room with Mark when we lived in the hut!"

"Okay, we'll charge less for that one," Icky allowed.

Mary Lou frowned, and wished she hadn't brought up the whole conversation.

#

As soon as research on the bakery's trademark application was approved, Shane called Icky to pick up the papers.

"How's the business going?" he asked.

"Growing as fast as the kids who eat our product," Icky said, adding, "including the ones who knock on the bakery's back door to ask if we're giving away broken cookies."

"They do that?"

"Every so often," Icky said. "And we can always find an extra cookie."

"Then, let's hammer out these details so you can get back to business," Shane slid paperwork across his desk. "This document assures that you'll never have a hassle on ownership of your bakery's name. Just get your labels right."

"I handled labeling at a bread bakery a few years ago."

"I bet Mace Bolles wishes you'd stayed on and started a cookie line for him," Shane speculated. Clearly, the attorney didn't know about how badly they'd parted.

"Let's just say it's not a problem," Icky allowed. Reconciling that relationship had taken a couple of years, but once Haut's Cookie Shoppe was running two shifts and Icky felt less vulnerable, he was ready to talk with his old boss. In fact, he made a point to seek him out, and put their argument behind them.

"Good," Shane pressed ahead to review the rest of the work he'd prepared. When the signatures were dry, he sent his secretary off to assemble copies. She also brought cups of coffee to the two men so they could chat for a few minutes while she finished.

Shane leaned back in his leather chair. It squeaked comfortably.

"Olean is becoming quite the food center," he suggested. "*The Olean Times-Herald* says Butch Butchello is gearing up to sell his spaghetti with meatballs dish in grocery stores' frozen foods aisles."

"Yeah, our Pillsbury salesman says frozen meals are a growing trend," Icky said. "Personally, I'd rather make a reservation at Butchello's Castle restaurant."

"Me, too," Shane laced his fingers together across his stomach. "But twelve hundred dinners a day is a lot of pasta. And most of his employees are girls."

"We hire a lot of girls, too," Icky said.

"Kitchen jobs," Shane agreed knowingly. "They're probably good at that sort of thing."

"The story said Butchello also will sell his restaurant's salad dressings. They're under the Loretto Foods label," Icky added.

"The commercial food industry is big business," Shane curved the conversation back around. "Swanson, Birdseye, Morton—the list goes on and on."

"Pillsbury, General Mills, and Kellogg, not to mention Entenmann's and Archway cookie brands," Icky added millers and bakers. "They've been around for decades."

"Lots of opportunity," Shane urged.

"I like to think so," he said. "And baked goods is reportedly the fastest growing sector."

Shane nodded. "When I take on a new client, I like to dig into the sort of business they're in."

"Ours is limited to baking cookies," Icky nodded in return.

"Bake: that's the operative word," he pointed the tip of his index finger into his thick walnut and black leather desk pad. "You know, since you've spent your entire career as a baker, that your employees will eventually be approached by the Bakery and Confectionery Union."

"Maybe. But Haut's Cookie Shoppe is a family-owned business. Millie and I own it, and my sister and brother-in-law help run it," Icky shrugged.

"And a few employees," Shane pointed toward the ceiling to make a point.

"We've hired a dozen or so more people, and we'll add a few more to our second shift. But even then, we're small."

"I see that Icky's Cookies is big enough to sponsor a men's baseball team," Shane contended.

"And soon we'll be sponsoring a boy's midget football team," Icky added.

"Community involvement gets noticed," Shane noted, "especially if you continue to grow."

"So?"

"I just want you to be prepared," Shane gestured broadly. "This bakery union has been around a long time—since 1886. They've got more than three hundred locals, and nearly a hundred fifty thousand members. It's not huge, but it's nothing to sneeze at either."

"Look, we probably will grow some, but even when that happens . . . ," Icky waved his hand, dismissing any idea that his bakery would be infiltrated by a union. Didn't Mace Bolles always say he'd close down before he let outsiders tell him how to run his business? He ran a much larger operation, and it had never been targeted.

"Our new building is about the size of two garages, end-to-end, and it sits next to the house," Icky countered. "If a union wants to fill its coffers, it'll go after somebody bigger than us."

Shane's secretary returned with the documents.

"Just making conversation," he allowed. "Here's your set of the trademark papers. We'll file the originals with the government, and keep copies here, just in case you ever need them."

"Thanks," Icky said. "I appreciate your willingness to look into the legalities of the food business, too."

"I always like to keep up with things," Shane said.

25

Can't Read Your Mind

"What's that?" John Heinz looked over Icky's shoulder to see what Millie was holding up.

"Shirts!" she said. "Our advertising agency had them made."

"We're sponsoring a boy's midget football team," Icky continued, "so each kid who signs up for the Icky's Cookies team will get one."

"You wouldn't have any extras, would you? Bertie and I might be interested."

Icky and Millie glanced at one another, trying to make sense of John's request.

"In case it's a boy," he continued.

"When?" Millie demanded a confirmation.

"When what?" Icky asked.

"The due date is in about six months," John hinted.

Icky finally caught on. "Wow! And yeah, if it's a boy, let's sign him up!"

#

"Another new cookie you add?" Ma asked as Icky brought a plate to the table after Sunday dinner.

"This one is almost the same recipe as the spice bites cookie," Icky explained.

"*Ja?*" Ma said with a small smile. "How many varieties do you bake now?"

"Sugar cookies, spice bites, peanut butter, hermits, fruit and nut bites, pecan dandies, molasses—that's seven."

"And we added chocolate chips to the pecan dandies recipe, so that's eight," Roy said.

"First shift is hustling," Herta brought coffee to the table, "especially since the two experienced girls moved to second shift. Now I'm training two new girls, and they're not keeping up yet." She felt she was carrying the bakery's largest burden. She also thought it would serve her brother well to hear how hard he was pushing the crew. He wasn't always around, after all. No, the way she saw it, he took little breaks by traveling to the east coast, staying in hotels, and eating in restaurants.

"Even when the new cutters can keep up with Herta, which will be in only a couple of weeks, I see a problem coming," Roy shifted the conversation. He wasn't ignoring his wife's feelings; he just didn't want to reinforce her antagonism—most of which he believed came not from the bakery, but rather, from not knowing where their own lives were headed. The nature of their living situation—staying with her parents to save money so they could start over and decide where to settle—had been heavy on her heart.

"These two shifts are nearing capacity, so if existing accounts increase orders, which they always do," he emphasized, "we'll struggle to handle it."

"You can't add a third shift?" Pa asked. He'd worked the night shift when he was first hired on at Socony-Vacuum Oil Company. Lots of employers operated around the clock.

"We still need to shut down for equipment maintenance," Roy answered.

"That's what weekends are for," Pa suggested.

"And you don't want a third shift working through the night right next door, do you?" Roy doubted.

"The bakery is quiet, so why not?" Pa believed pragmatism outweighed preference.

Ma frowned, however. While many employees lived close enough to walk to work, an increasing number drove over and parked along Sullivan Street. She already was concerned that their neighbors might complain about the steady lineup of cars all day. If bakery employees crowded the street all night, too, what would people say?

"But a third shift won't really solve the long-term problem," Icky said. "We're outgrowing our space."

"So you're going to grow larger than a *Mittlestand*?" Roy asked. Herta and he would have built a small storefront bakery; that's what they operated in Cuba.

"When we started, I hoped we'd one day grow as large as we are now," Icky admitted. "But that was before I knew what was possible. I'd never turn down more business, not when all we need to do is expand."

"You're thinking of adding on to our bakery?" Millie asked.

"Maybe. Eventually," Icky said. "Right now I'm still developing new product. And I need to meet with our accounts on a regular basis.

"And," he added a third demand on his time, even if his sister didn't see it, "I still work operations. I don't know where I'd get enough hours to oversee construction again."

Millie and he didn't usually enter into discussions about the business side of the bakery in front of family, but the topic was already on the table, so she decided to continue it. Besides, Herta's comments about being overburdened were irksome.

"Should we hire a salesman so you're not on the road so much?" Millie suggested.

"Maybe. Again, eventually. For now, since orders keep increasing we might buy an existing operation. I just heard that Tasty Bakery might be up for sale."

Herta looked to Roy. Did he know about this? She couldn't tell.

"Where did you hear that?" Roy asked.

"Shane," Icky said. "He pays attention to that sort of thing."

"Doesn't Tasty bake bread?" Millie asked. "And aren't they over in Salamanca?"

"They do—and they are," Icky said. "We'd have to convert the production floor, and train their people."

"Have you been inside to see the equipment?" Roy asked.

"Not yet," Icky admitted. "But it's got to be like Bolles Bakery."

"How would you find out?" Roy asked.

"I'll just call the owner," Icky said. He'd met Sam Fenice through business connections; the guy seemed approachable. "If he does want to sell, maybe we can work out a deal."

"So you've already decided to do it," Roy surmised, raising ire in Herta's eyes.

"It could get us through this crunch," Icky returned to his original point.

Millie thought Herta seemed irritated. And Ma's lips were pursed. Maybe she'd been wrong to discuss business at the dinner table.

#

"Mark! Cut it out!"

"I'm not doing anything!" he answered loudly. The kid was embedded in a world of high intrigue and drama, played out by three-inch-tall green plastic Army men, each of them posed in a different battle position. He'd perfected his "eh-eh-eh-eh" machine gun sound, and was just about to send one of the figures flying across the carpet into an imaginary fox hole under the sofa. He wondered how his mom always read his thoughts, and decided that she must have a pair of those x-ray glasses, the kind featured in the back pages of comic books. The ad said they let you look through walls or around corners.

This was dangerous. He had to get outside the range of their power. Marcus Park would be far enough. He abandoned the carpet battleground and took to the field across the street.

"Does your mom read your thoughts?" he asked the guys when they took a break from circling the baseball diamond on their bikes.

"Sometimes," one of them said.

"Why?" asked another.

"Mine yells at me when she's not even in the same room—like she's got x-ray vision," Mark said. "Or she knows what I'm thinking."

"Cover your head with aluminum foil," the first kid said. "That's how comic book heroes protect themselves from aliens."

Mark didn't think his mom would give him a piece of foil, not without asking what it was for, and he sure couldn't tell her.

But wait, he realized; she'd already know . . . because she'd be reading my thoughts.

"Jimmy—you know, over on Thirteenth Street—he covered his head with foil and it worked for him," the kid insisted.

Mark had seen Jimmy in a Davy Crockett coonskin hat, not running around with aluminum foil on his head.

"You're full of boloney," he disagreed.

"No, I swear," the kid held firm. No one bought his story, though, so he dropped it.

The guys went back to racing bikes around the baseball diamond. As they approached the bases, they slammed on their brakes to practice skidding sideways to a stop.

"Just like race cars," one said.

"You gotta' dig in harder," Mark advised. He'd practiced skidding in the loose dirt often enough to be a neighborhood pro. "Lean sideways as you come in, and shove your weight into it."

They practiced every angle, envisioning how they'd one day be commanding wheels on big engines, fighting their ways around the track at the Cuba Lake Racetrack.

"Let's go to Bill's," one of guys finally suggested. They headed out, packages of dots, sweet juice in two-inch wax bottles, and wax mustaches flashing in their imaginations. Mark thought he'd choose a wax mustache this time.

Or maybe a grape soda pop. Or Tru Ade orange—that's the best! But grape was good, too. The choices were huge, and he had to get it right, because once the cash register went ka-*ching*, his choices were over. No kid ever got more than a nickel a week, which was the same as never.

"Wait!" Mark said. "I need money."

He yanked open the back door and yelled, "Mom!"

"What?" she answered abruptly. "You don't have to scream."

"I need a nickel!" he begged. "The guys are going to Bill's."

His reference to "the guys" said it all.

"A nickel, huh?" she reached for her purse. "Five cents. Let me see if we even have a nickel."

"We do," he jiggled his knee impatiently. "Hurry! They're waiting."

"Hur-r-r-ry?" she dragged out the word as she sorted past Chicklets and Beechies peppermint gum to find her wallet.

"Hurry, please," he repeated politely. "They'll leave without me."

She handed over the precious coin.

"Thanks!" he yelled over his shoulder.

That kid has a septic tank for a stomach, she said in his wake.

26

Out of Nowhere

"Tasty has a good operation," Icky told Millie when he returned home from inspecting the bakery.

"You got a good look at it?" she asked. He hadn't been gone long.

"I saw enough." He'd toured the floor set up, eye-balled the ovens and refrigeration capacity, opened the fuse box, and decided to buy the place.

"Are we going to talk about this?" she asked.

"What do you mean?"

"Are you and I going to discuss whether or not we should do this?" she asked again.

"I didn't think we needed to go over it again," Icky said, a bit taken back.

"We didn't really talk through it in the first place," Millie insisted. "At Sunday dinner, you said you heard about it, and you wanted to pursue it—which you just did. But that doesn't mean you and I have talked about whether or not we ought to go ahead."

"Okay. What's your problem with it?"

"Going in debt again: that's my problem," she revealed. "The bakery is doing fine as is. We don't need to increase sales. We don't need to expand."

"We do if we want to keep our market share," Icky insisted. "We're not the only bakery our accounts can buy from. If someone else gets in there with a better deal: with more varieties or greater volumes or lower prices, we could be shut out. I don't want that risk."

She didn't say anything.

"Okay?" he asked.

"It seems like buying Tasty increases our risk," she said. "Debt is risk."

"Debt isn't the only kind of risk," Icky said. "Losing accounts because we can't meet increasing needs is also a risk."

"You're determined to buy Tasty then?"

"I think it's in our best interest—for now," he said. "It doesn't solve our long-term needs, but it helps keep us going until—well, until I figure out the next step."

Millie heaved in a deep breath. "What about staffing? You can't run a bakery without crew."

"They've got a couple dozen employees and a weekly payroll around thirteen hundred dollars."

"How does that compare with ours?"

"The payroll per person is in line. Our cutters earn more by exceeding quotas, though; that's not an option in a bread bakery."

"Merit pay ought to suggest how good new ownership will be," she noted.

"Yeah, the girls do seem to like it," he agreed.

"But Tasty has more people," she noted.

"More than twice as many—which will allow us to offer more cookie varieties."

"How many more?"

"Twice as many, probably."

"Probably," she repeated. She recognized that answer: the beginning of one of his new plans, yet unformed. "We'd keep the entire Salamanca staff then?"

"An experienced crew is easier to train than new hires," he confirmed. "And Sam says he'll stay on for a while, so I'll ask Shane to draw up the purchase agreement that way."

"What's the next step then?"

"We'll finalize an agreement, and file tax paperwork with City Hall," he said. "Then, since we're doubling our payroll overnight, we'll move full steam ahead with training."

"What's Roy going to say?" Millie asked.

"He'll probably be okay with it," Icky assumed. "And I bet he'll like having an experienced guy like Sam to rely on, too."

"A transfer in ownership can be disconcerting," Millie noted. "You'll have to figure out how to tell everyone."

But before Sam and Icky had a chance to tell employees about the change in ownership, City Hall disclosed the deal to the mayor. Seeing an opportunity to boost his administration, he told the *Republican Press* that Icky's Cookies was leaving Olean and moving to Salamanca—which wasn't true, of course, but served his purposes well enough.

"It's just a bunch of shade and shine," Sam reported when he called Icky about the article. "This mayor likes to take credit wherever he thinks he can."

"I hate politics," Icky grumbled.

#

"Got a minute?" Roy poked his head through the doorway of Icky's office.

"Hey, Roy! Are you ready to train a few more guys?" Icky asked immediately. "You've baked both bread and cookies, so I'm hoping you can lead Sam through the Tasty conversion."

"How long?"

"Probably a month or so. You decide," Icky answered.

"I don't know," Roy hesitated. Ever since Icky started talking about operating in two locations, Roy wanted to tell him about plans Herta and he were making. She wanted to keep them a secret until the details were worked out, but he'd finally convinced her that sooner was better than later.

"I thought you'd like managing a new operation," Icky assumed.

"You'll do fine running that bakery without me," Roy edged toward his reason for stopping into the office.

Icky looked him straight in the eyes. "What's the problem?"

"Time," Roy hesitated, "and temperature."

"Time and temperature?" Those were baking terms.

"Time: before the snow hits; and temperature: warm and sunny. Herta and I are moving south."

"How far south?" Icky asked, stunned.

"Florida."

"Florida! You're sure about this?" Icky blinked.

"Being back up north made us sure. We're done with blizzards and icy roads, Ick."

"But Florida is so far away."

"With warm days and cool nights breezing off the ocean," Roy contended.

"What about Ma?" Icky asked immediately. "Does she know?"

"I think she suspects something," Roy scrunched his shoulder. They'd tell her once they hammered out their moving date. If Ma suspected anything before then, she wouldn't ask because that would suggest she'd been listening in—which she wouldn't do intentionally, of course, but a person couldn't help but hear a few things when they all lived under the same roof.

"At least she won't worry that we'll be out of the U.S. this time," Roy added. "And they speak English in Florida"—which was a challenge when they moved to Cuba. Neither Herta nor he spoke Spanish when they arrived, so they struggled to communicate with their customers and neighbors. Learning the language was worth the effort, though. They loved the island: the way the locals leaned out of their windows and lounged on balconies and called out to one another. And Havana literally vibrated with energy. It was intoxicating.

At the same time, while everyone was friendly, Herta and Roy learned that even their friends considered them mere transplants: interesting to have around, but not essential to the community. "You think like outsiders," one explained as political tensions began to rise. "Sure, the U.S. preaches liberty and democracy, but the neighbor to the north practices tyranny on those outside its borders. It's in the American blood."

About that time, Ma's letters said newspapers were reporting trouble on the island. Roy and Herta decided that they needed to leave.

"What are you going to do for work? Open a bakery again?" Icky asked.

"Yep, yep, yep. We want a small shop we can handle ourselves," Roy said. The way he saw it, managing crews meant solving problems that drank down his energy. He'd do it for Icky, but he didn't want a large operation on his own shoulders—especially one as large as the one they'd be taking on in Salamanca. "And Herta likes creativity more than production goals," he continued. "She wants to take up cake decorating again."

"Well, this is a surprise," Icky said. He wouldn't call it good news; good news would be Roy and Herta finally settling down in Olean.

"Yep, I know," Roy admitted, "and don't get me wrong; it's been great working with you. But Herta and I need to get our own business going again."

Icky nodded.

"I'll talk to Herta about sticking around 'til Salamanca is set up," Roy offered. "I'm guessing she'll be okay with that, because family is family: that's what she always says. Besides, the realtor down in Ocala is moving slow."

"That's where you're going?"

"Middle of the state," Roy clarified. "Everybody's on island time down there, or maybe it's called peninsula time. Or tourist time, or orange time. Whatever they call it, it's a whole lot slower."

"Slow is not how we've been running," Icky acknowledged.

"Which is another reason. We like an easier routine—not that I'm complaining!"

"Didn't take it that way. And I'm grateful you're willing to stay long enough to help us transition," Icky assured him.

"Just 'til the crew is assigned to their new positions," Roy reinforced. Then, with a crooked smile, he added, "Besides, you really don't need me anymore."

"I wouldn't say that," Icky insisted.

"Let's just get this Salamanca thing done as quick as we can."

#

Icky sequestered himself in his basement office all afternoon, hoping to work off the sting of Roy's news. Herta and Roy were gone for nearly a decade the last time they moved south. This time, their decision to leave Olean probably would be permanent. And Roy was right; this would be especially hard on Ma.

The bakery would struggle without them, too. Roy was the only man with as many years of baking experience as Icky.

After an hour or so, he realized that none of the work on his desk was getting done.

"I'm gone for the day," he passed Marion's desk on his way upstairs.

She raised the palm of her left hand to stop him from interrupting as she said, "I'm counting."

He paused.

"Okay. Now, what did you want?" she looked up.

"What are today's totals?" he asked.

"First shift baked 6 percent more than scheduled, and second shift was short," she reported. "It evened out."

"Thanks," he said. "I'm leaving. Have a nice evening."

She rolled a sheet of paper into her typewriter.

"I'm almost out of here, too," she said as she heard Icky's feet retreat into the kitchen upstairs, "as soon as I finish typing tomorrow's production schedules."

Millie looked up as Icky came up the last two steps.

"You quit early," she noticed.

"I need a Manhattan," he took down the bottle of Southern Comfort.

"Mid-week?" she quizzed.

"A strong one," he continued as he justified silently, this is the only "comfort" I'm going to get out of anything "southern" this evening.

"Dinner is at six o'clock, unless you have a meeting," she said.

"Staying home," he answered.

Sentence fragments, she noticed.

He watched her cut potatoes. He was proud that he'd kept his promise to build a house for her. And he could understand why his sister wanted to get settled into her own home, too.

He took a sip, sagged into a kitchen chair, and sighed.

"Spill it," she insisted. She was done waiting.

"Roy and Herta," he set his glass on a coaster. Sentence fragment again.

She put down her knife.

"What about Roy and Herta?" she repeated.

"It's not public," he recalled Salamanca's mayor stealing the thunder on the Tasty purchase before it could be announced to employees, "so if I tell you, you can't say anything, especially not to Ma. This news is theirs to share when they think the time is right."

"So?" she persisted.

"They're moving to Florida."

Her jaw dropped. Hobbling along without Roy and Herta was precisely the threat she'd always feared, although the business probably had grown large enough to survive now.

"Why now?"

"Weather," Icky said. "Roy said they're done with snow."

"So, what does that mean for the bakery?" she asked.

"He said they'll stick around long enough to convert the new operation from bread to cookies. Then we're on our own," he answered. "That's all I know."

"Are they upset?" she asked.

"No, they just want to start their own shop again. We'll have to hire somebody to take over operations here. Until then, I'll work production in Olean for a while."

"You can't do everything yourself," Millie warned.

"And I'll need to get ahead of sales before they leave."

"You're going out on the road again?"

"I don't see any way around it," he answered. "While Roy helps Sam with the transition, I'll meet with our accounts to see if I can increase orders to cover the new payroll."

"I hope so, because we paid cash for Tasty, and our bank reserves are nearly depleted," she reminded him—and then wished she hadn't, for in that moment she realized the precariousness of their situation. Roy always kept operations running smoothly, so Icky could balance new product development against increasing sales.

But with Roy gone, he wouldn't have the freedom to develop new accounts or formulate new recipes. That was how the bakery always strengthened its bottom line.

Millie guessed Icky might be worried that they were in over their heads.

"At least you have time to work it out," she suggested.

"Not much," he answered grimly as he downed the last of his drink.

"But our accounts always increase their orders," she pointed out. "Right?"

"They always have in the past, Millie, but part of that is because we keep up with what housewives want to buy. We're always offering something new," he said. "If we can't do that, we could be headed for trouble."

#

While Roy helped Sam convert the Salamanca operation, Icky hit the road to meet with distributors—and the headquarters of a store he'd been serving only locally: A&P. Icky thought his bakery was finally large enough to handle a larger bite of their business, and the buyer sounded open to considering another supplier when he called for an appointment. He packed samples of each variety of cookie in the trunk and prayed they'd sign a purchase order.

A few miles down the road, he let his mind wander to the problems he left on his desk. A while back, he told Hubbell he'd develop a proprietary flour blend, for both improved production control and cost management. He'd been putting off that chore, as revising every recipe according to new bakers percents was going to take a considerable amount of focused time. Of course, once Roy was gone, he'd have less of that. He chided himself for not getting it done.

He also hadn't added a seasonal cookie to the line yet. That also would strengthen the bottom line. If production were limited to Olean, they might be able to push it through this year. A macaroon might be a good addition. Coconut was expensive, but if housewives were willing to pay a little more for something special—available only in December—we could run it in a smaller market, like Heinz Distributing. That would be good for John, and save me time from calling all of our other accounts.

Wouldn't it be great if the macaroon was so popular that families counted on it as an annual treat? He felt his spirit lift. What kind of coconut? Shredded? Or flaked? Maybe desiccated coconut; that's what Hostess snowball cupcakes are coated in. He remembered that they came out in 1947, the year Mark was born—and they were popular! He'd write a note to run a trial over the weekend: one more thing to do when he got home.

27

Expert Opinions

"The report says that the average American family now consists of a father working outside the home, his wife, and their two children—so, a family of only four," Jean shared the latest news from the church mothers' meeting.

"You have three kids," Millie held the telephone receiver between her ear and her shoulder while she finished breaking lettuce into a bowl, "so I guess you're above average."

"We missed you today," Jean diverted. "And it sounds like you're in the middle of something."

"Salad," Millie answered. "Ma's garden is growing an abundance of tomatoes and cucumbers, and Icky is on his way home from a business trip, so we'll all have dinner together."

"Frank's hours have been crazy, too."

"They're handling the problems of the world; we're handling meals and kids."

"Sounds about right," Jean concurred.

"And you know what they say: being a mother isn't a rose garden."

"Well, my parenting skills were tested after the meeting," Jean admitted.

"What happened?"

"You know how Mary always wants to be Mommy's helper?"

"Ye-es," Millie waited.

"I let her push the stroller down the block from the church to the parsonage. We were halfway home when the thing just folded up—with Anne inside."

"Oh, no!" Millie said.

"Then, Mary started screaming about breaking the baby."

"What did you do?"

"We pried open the contraption, and Mary saw that Anne was okay. She calmed right down," Jean said.

Mark slammed the back door and pounded up the steps into Millie's kitchen. Ignoring the fact that she was talking on the phone, he demanded, "What's for dinner?"

"Daddy will be home in a half hour," she whispered over the top of the handset, "and I'm on the phone."

"I'll let you go," Jean allowed. "My brood will expect dinner soon, too."

#

Child-rearing experts would say that a boy who challenges the family dinner menu isn't a picky eater; he's developing a discerning palate. Millie would say that since she served the same basic menu each week, Mark ought to be able to guess what was going to magically appear: chicken on Monday; meatloaf or spaghetti with meatballs on Tuesday, and pork chops on Friday. On Saturday, the kids might get fish sticks or pancakes if the grownups decided to go out. And of course, Sunday was dinner at Ma and Pa Haut's house.

That left Wednesday and Thursday open—which could be good or bad. Hamburgers or hotdogs or macaroni and cheese were really good options. But if liver was on sale, Mark would tell his mother he wanted to croak.

"Not again!" the seven-year-old put his hands around his throat, and made a gagging sound.

She ignored him.

Clearly, more drama was required, so he dropped to the floor, and pretended to be choking.

"And canned spinach," she added.

"Can't I have something else?" he begged. He considered folding his hands in front of his face. He saw cartoon characters do that, and this situation seemed to warrant begging.

"Liver is good for you," Millie answered.

"It's not!" he argued. "I hate it!" He made his gagging sound again, low in his throat: "Acckkk-kk-kk. . .."

"Stop that!" she reprimanded. "You'll ruin your vocal chords."

"I won't need them. I'll be dead from the liver."

Millie sighed. She could see he was cranked up.

"All right, we have leftover ground beef," she gave in. "You can have a burger."

Mary Lou came in the back door, and Millie turned her around to get some flour from the bakery just across the driveway. "Enough to coat the liver," she handed her a small cup, "and don't dillydally," not that Mary Lou ever would.

Millie looked at the clock, poured canned spinach into a saucepan, and turned the burner on low. Then she fried bacon and drained it, leaving grease in the frying pan to flavor a couple of sliced onions. They glistened in the fat, caramelized and sweet. She dredged the liver, and dropped the limp raw organs into the bacon grease. Icky liked his liver firm and well done, so everyone had it that way. Dinner was ready just as he came in the door.

"Smells great!" he said gladly.

"Something special," Millie said, "just for you!"

"I'll be right there!" he called out as he tossed his tie onto the bed and washed his hands. He'd been looking forward to a home-cooked meal all day.

"How come Mark gets a burger again?" Mary Lou challenged as she set the table. She didn't remember ever dictating what was on her plate. And if Grandma Haut knew the stunt the little ingrate was pulling, she'd have something to say about his pester power, too!

"Never mind," Millie said. "He doesn't get any of what we're having." She decided not to defend herself against another kid's complaints.

"That really looks good!" Icky sat down. "And I'm famished! I was rushing to get home so I didn't even stop for lunch." Millie glanced around the table to be sure nothing had been forgotten. Mary Lou had done a nice job: *Vollkornbrot* was piled into a bread basket and ready for sopping up all the salty bacon sauce. A serving fork was on the platter, and Icky had a tall *Pils Flasche* in front of his plate. She noticed him smiling as he cut into his meat. At least one person will appreciate the meal.

Or not.

"What the . . . !" he spat the beginning of a curse—and stopped himself, realizing that they'd just said grace and asked the Lord to bless the meal. The tip of his tongue poked out in front of his teeth.

"What?" Millie looked up, surprised at his reaction. When he didn't immediately reply, she looked at the morsel suspended on the fork in front of her mouth, and decided she was obligated to taste the liver herself. A dainty corner ought to be enough.

"Oh, dear!" she restrained the urge to spit it out.

Mary Lou looked at the liver on her plate. She didn't need to try it. She took her parents' reactions as permission not to sample.

Millie swallowed her bite, and looked at Mary Lou. "From which bin did you get the flour?" she asked.

Suddenly, the girl froze in her chair, eyes rounded wide, forehead wrinkled, and face slackened into an unexpected frown.

"Uh, I think it was . . . I don't remember," Mary Lou answered, shocked that she could have been the culprit.

"That's it then," Millie said. "I think the liver is coated with baking soda."

Icky dropped his fork onto his dinner place with a clink, and evaluated the platter as if he might find a few good morsels nestled beneath the onions. He'd been looking forward to the liver, especially once he smelled the bacon and onions. Now, everyone looked to him to pass judgment. Inhaling slowly and deeply, he finally allowed, "I can see that you two are feeling bad because you wanted to put a nice dinner on the table."

Millie and Mary Lou nodded.

"I assume you had no part in preparing the meal," he turned toward Mark, as the kid was usually the one responsible for raising Cain. This time, though, while the liver drama played out, he'd been chomping down his hamburger, seemingly delighted by all of the confusion. It was like live television at the dinner table.

"But somehow," Icky admitted as he continued to stare at his son, "I want to blame you for this. I just can't figure out how."

Mark smiled widely. The tension at the table was broken. And for once, he could revel in the glory of getting away with . . . nothing.

"Let's go out to dinner," Icky shoved his chair back from the table. He'd have preferred a meal at home, but what he was most hungry for was time with his family.

"What about Mark?" Mary Lou asked. "He already had his meal."

"Just a hamburger," Millie said. "He could eat more."

"We still have canned spinach," Mary Lou suggested, happy to have the attention shifted to someone else.

"No!" Mark protested. The situation seemed to be turned into a game of Gotcha, and he was going to be the loser. Again!

"So, you'll be okay eating whatever vegetable the restaurant is serving tonight?" Millie closed an argument before it could begin.

"Okay," Mark said. But while anything would be better than canned spinach, he felt that something had gone terribly wrong. Hadn't he been enjoying the perfect hamburger his mother prepared just for him, little prince that he was, while Mary Lou was almost getting yelled at? Then, suddenly, he had to eat some mystery vegetable he just knew he wasn't going to like.

Why does this always happen to me?

28

On the Floor and Out the Door

"Here's how Sam and I see it," Roy reported on the transition. "With the experienced people you got in Salamanca, you ought to put Bill on mixing dough. He's been hauling hundred-pound sacks of flour for bread production, so he's strong."

"Promote him now?" Icky asked.

"Yep, yep, yep," Roy said. "He's got some learning to do, but give him a couple of weeks. He'll step up."

"What learning?" Icky wanted to know now, before announcing a promotion.

"He's used to yeast," Roy explained, "and needs experience with baking powder and baking soda."

A proprietary flour blend would have gone a long way to solving that problem, Icky regretted not getting it done.

"Also, Sam says that seeing one of their own guys get promoted tells your crew that you're interested in doing good by them," Roy added.

"Good point," Icky said, "but we've got to move into full production quick. Bill's got to be ready for that."

"He will be," Roy moved on. Holding out the Personnel Assignments list he prepared, he added, "So here's the rest of your lineup. In your top positions, Florence and Madge will lead the cutters. They're fast enough to start, and can train the rest of the crew."

"How many cutters?"

"Eight," Roy said. "And that's just one shift."

Icky computed output in his head. At eight hundred cookies per person each hour, cutters put out sixty-four hundred cookies per shift.

And with eight cutters, that's over a half million cookies—or over forty thousand packages. If he had time, he'd be able to add more varieties.

"Then, Frances and Rose are supervising the ovens, and each said she can move to second shift if you grow."

Icky nodded.

"For wrappers, you got Gladys, Jette and Joyce—all three experienced with cellophane envelopes. They're quick at stacking and packing without breakage."

"How's that new machine working?" Icky asked. The wrapping equipment had been expensive.

"Works great," Roy answered. "Next, you're gonna' need a floor coordinator, and with all these gals, the best person is Leanne. She's a good organizer, and everyone likes her.

"Then," Roy stepped back because he knew Icky probably wouldn't like his last recommendation, "you oughta' move Harry Truman over from Olean as your general manager. You need eyes over here to see that this operation runs your way."

Roy was right. Icky hated to lose Harry in Olean, but the move would place an experienced operations guy in Salamanca where he was needed most.

"What about the rest?" Icky asked about the back end of the business.

"They can stay in their same jobs in inventory and the loading dock," Roy said with finality.

"Anything else?" Icky scanned the list.

"The snow's comin'," Roy changed the subject.

"We saw a few flakes yesterday," Icky acknowledged without picking up Roy's point.

"Yep, yep, yep. On its way. Herta donated our winter clothes, and we're ready to hit the road."

"Oh!" Icky finally caught on.

"We got one more Sunday dinner together," Roy said. "Monday morning we're heading south."

"Now? Before Thanksgiving?" He thought they'd be around at least long enough to celebrate the holiday season.

"We want to be on the road before the snow sticks," Roy corrected.

"Well," Icky took a moment to gather his thoughts, "then I—I don't know how we would have built this bakery without you, Roy."

"You already had it going in the right direction when we got here," he said.

"And thanks for staying around to help with this transition," Icky added.

"Glad to do it," he said. "Herta, too."

"I'll catch up with her. And when you're ready to pack up, we'll help you load your car," Icky promised.

"No need," Roy said. "We got just two suitcases of clothes that we can still wear in the Sunshine State."

Icky blinked in surprise. He'd been so busy with customers that he hadn't noticed the urgency with which his sister and brother-in-law were preparing to leave. The reality of their departure felt like he'd slammed into a wall.

The two men looked at one another long and hard.

"We know you'll continue to make a go of this," Roy assured Icky. He wouldn't say goodbye.

"You will, too," Icky blessed Roy and Herta's new adventure. "Write and tell us all about it."

#

The mountains to the east of town were silhouetted against a crimson sunrise as streaks of morning light pierced through gray-purple clouds. The Olean crew heard Roy and Herta's car trunk being slammed shut, and interrupted their production schedule to pour out onto N. Fourteenth Street to bid them farewell. Those two had trained everyone in that bakery, and no one was going to let them just slip away unnoticed.

Pa had already gone off to work, just like always, leaving before dawn. The sky is black as dirt—just like my heart, he thought to himself. He'd been steeling himself for the loss of their presence. Herta was the first-born, the one who changed Ma and him from a married couple to a family—and the first close-by blood relative since they were young. With that baby, Ma vowed to provide the care and comfort she hadn't known herself, and made the same promise four more times, as the rest of their children came into the world. Pa did, too, but he'd been especially protective of that first one: the one who gave him the title, "Pa." He'd never forget. He'd said his formal goodbyes the night before, leaving only a brisk farewell for the morning as he released them, silently gripping Roy's hand, and blessing his daughter with a kiss on her forehead. Ma watched him from her kitchen window as he rode his bike down the street. Roy and Herta may have thought that their leaving Olean didn't faze him. But she knew her man was grateful that pre-dawn's shadows would protect his heart from revealing itself.

Ma stood on the porch, watching everyone's goodbyes. Icky and Millie walked across the lawn and stood next to her.

"Missed they will be," she said as she wrapped her arms in her shawl against the morning cold. "But forget us for long? That they will not be able to do."

"How is that?" Icky asked.

"Cookies are packed into their suitcases," she revealed, guiltily.

"You did that?" he asked.

She nodded gently, exposing how she had invaded Roy and Herta's privacy by sneaking something into their belongings while they bade Pa goodbye.

"That was nice of you," he said.

"They will find them when they stop for their rest," she tried to rustle some contrition from her heart. But genuine remorse could not be summoned. "They will think of us, as we also miss them."

Icky watched her back up toward the door, and realized that only Pa and she would sit at their kitchen table from now on. Maybe that was why she always held herself at a safe distance when people said their goodbyes. This time, though, her loss was more obvious, given away in one little birdlike wave, barely a flutter, as she turned and went in.

"We should make plans right away for spending Thanksgiving with Ma and Pa," Millie suggested quietly as Roy and Herta's car disappeared down the street.

"That would be good," Icky agreed. "Maybe we can host the meal. That way, Ma won't notice so much who's missing this year."

"I'll find out if she'd like that," Millie agreed.

"Okay, I'm headed out to Salamanca," Icky advised.

"Oh? I thought you'd step into Roy's shoes here in Olean."

"Derby is working double shifts here for a week or so until we get someone trained to take over Truman's job. He's moving over to run Salamanca," Icky answered, "and I need to see for myself what's going on over there."

"What about Sam?"

"Sam knows the people, so he'll provide oversight and help Harry get the crew moving."

"You're expecting problems?"

"Not exactly," Icky said, recalling Roy's feedback. "Switching from bread to cookies is just more challenging than we expected."

He kissed her goodbye, and slid into his car. He had half an hour to think about how to explain leavenings to Bill, because if Roy was right and the guy had worked only with yeast—which was entirely possible since most bakers learned their trades on the job—then he couldn't be expected to know how to use them to control the production schedule.

And that, Icky told himself, would be a problem. Still, it was one he could solve.

29

Chemical Reactions

"We've been watching for you," Sam welcomed Icky.

"How's the morning crew doing?" he asked.

"Slow start, but not bad for a Monday," Sam allowed.

Eight o'clock is halfway through the first shift, Icky thought to himself. They ought to be warmed up by now.

"G'morning, Icky!" Harry said enthusiastically as he came around the corner. "How was the drive? Did Roy and Herta get on the road okay?"

"They did," he answered. "What's the news?"

Harry knew exactly what Icky was asking for: numbers. "We're backed up about 30 percent. I think you'll spot the problem as we make rounds."

"I'll do a walk-through myself first," Icky said. After all, he hadn't met with employees since Roy laid out the new assignments. He'd check in with everybody and follow the dough all the way through production—starting with Bill.

"Roy says you've had your hands in the baking trade for years," he greeted the new head baker.

"Almost ten," Bill said. "But only on bread. I don't think I've got cookie production down yet."

"What do you mean?" Icky asked.

"With bread, I control production by timing the yeast," Bill began. "But all I know about chemical leavenings is when to pour 'em in. I don't really understand how they work."

"Okay, let's start at the beginning," Icky offered. "Our two leavenings are baking soda and baking powder," he tapped the recipe card posted alongside the mixer. "Baking *soda* is activated by acids like lemon. Baking *powder* works in heat."

"But how do I control the rise with them?" Bill asked.

"I know it's been a while, but remember high school science experiments when we mixed baking soda with vinegar, and it bubbled up out of the top of our beakers?" Icky asked.

"Carbonation," Bill recalled.

"Right—and baking soda creates that carbonation with any acid," Icky said. "Buttermilk, fruit juice, molasses, brown sugar—even unsweetened chocolate. And our sugar cookie recipe calls for buttermilk."

"Okay," Bill paused.

"Next, the recipe also calls for baking *powder*, right?" Icky tapped the card.

"Right," Bill said.

"Baking *powder* is a blend," Icky paced his explanation. "First, it contains some of that baking soda."

Bill nodded.

"Plus, it has a starch, and monocalcium phosphate, or MCP. We use a brand that also has sodium acid pyrophosphate, or SAPP, in it, too."

Bill inhaled a deep breath as he memorized soda, starch, MCP, SAPP. This is getting complicated, he thought.

"MCP is a *fast-acting* acid salt," Icky said. "It gives the dough a quick boost in the bowl."

"And the SAPP?" Bill moved right along.

"SAPP," Icky repeated the initials, "is a *slow-acting* acid salt. It keeps the rise going in the oven."

Bill nodded. "What about the starch?"

"Don't worry about the starch; it's just a filler," Icky brushed if off. "Okay, now like I said, the SAPP's reaction is slower and it works when it's *heated*."

"Is that why the label on our baking powder says it's 'double-acting'?"

"Right," Icky confirmed.

"But how do I use leavenings to control production?"

"Control the temperature: SAPP reacts with heat," Icky said.

"This is probably where I'm messing up," Bill interrupted.

"See those refrigerators?" Icky pointed. "They're located near the mixers so *you* can use 'em. If the girls aren't keeping up, roll those thirty-inch bowls of dough into the cold to halt the rise."

"Because in the cold, the SAPP isn't activated?" Bill put the pieces together.

"Right," Icky repeated. "You got about 30 percent of your rise still coming with heat, and you want to save that for the oven, not the bakery's ambient temperature."

"Got it," Bill confirmed. "Baking powder gives two rises: on the bench, and again in the oven."

"And since our recipe calls for both baking soda and baking powder, you can guess that's because the first rise on the bench needs a boost," Icky clarified.

"Okay, I think I'm getting it," Bill said.

"Who's your floor person?" Icky moved the conversation ahead to solve Bill's concern about timing.

"Leanne."

"Okay, Leanne ought to be watching production. When the cutters are ready for more dough, she'll take a bowl out of the refrigerator and roll it over."

"Okay," Bill confirmed.

"And if they're working ahead of your mixing . . ."

"That hasn't happened," Bill interrupted. "I'm mixing faster than they're cutting."

And that's the real production problem, Icky realized. Just like Harry said: the cutters aren't keeping up.

"You'll get the hang of it," Icky walked off toward the cutting station.

#

"The challenge they're facing is precision," Sam observed. Even at a distance, he could see that the dough wasn't being rolled to one-eighth inch thickness.

"That's causing problems with package weights, too," Harry pointed out.

"I think they're just not accustomed to working with five-pound steel rolling pins," Sam defended.

"They're going to need to get this right, and work faster, too, because we need to start filling orders by the end of the week," Icky joined the conversation. "The girls over in Olean can't be expected to carry Salamanca's slack."

Especially with Herta gone, he justified, his concern building. Without her, the Olean crew would be struggling to meet its own production numbers.

"Also, those inspectors can show up anytime," Harry returned to his original point.

"Truth in labeling has always been high on the inspectors' checklists, so everyone understands how important product weight is," Sam defended his people.

"Then we shouldn't be having a problem," Icky restrained his irritation.

"Let's give it a closer look," Harry suggested as he moved in.

"How's production going?" Sam joined the cutters.

"We're trying to catch up," Florence admitted.

"This schedule says we each need to cut eight hundred cookies an hour," Madge reported, "but we're not there yet."

"Who says we've got to cut a certain number of cookies every hour?" one of the girls immediately challenged. Her back was turned, so she didn't realize the Boss had come in.

"It's the same pace the crew in Olean keeps," Harry answered.

"And I saw them do it," Madge agreed. "When we were over there, the Boss showed us how they timed production."

"And the same standard is required at both locations," Icky repeated Harry's answer.

Hearing his voice, the girls immediately straightened up, looked over their shoulders, and nodded.

"The Olean crew is more experienced than we are," Florence tempered the mandate.

"What she's saying is that everyone knows we're learning, but the Boss still wants us to try to reach our goals—if we can," Madge softened.

Icky grimaced.

"Well, what if we can't do it?" another one of the girls countered.

"You got half of that rack filled already," Sam tried to move past complaints and focus on production. "Eighteen cookie sheets done; eighteen to go."

As soon as two racks were filled, Frances and Rose took turns wheeling them to the ovens and sliding them in. After seven minutes, the timer rang, and Frances pulled out the two racks of freshly baked cookies and wheeled them to the cooling and packaging area, while Rose was supposed to wheel in the next two racks of raw dough.

"I'm seeing a quality problem," Icky stepped back to speak with Harry. "They're not cutting fast enough, so the dough on first of those two racks sits there, deflating and flattening."

"That's why Harry thinks his timing is off in mixing," Harry noted another inefficiency. "With a seven-minute turnaround, Frances and Rose ought to be constantly moving those racks, in and out, without all this delay."

"They could roll the first rack into the oven as soon as it's ready," Sam joined them.

"No, the oven can handle two racks at a time; rolling in just one rack slows the schedule and doubles oven energy cost," Icky disagreed. "It also sets a false expectation."

Sam called Madge and Florence aside.

"Look," he began, "the girls need to pick up the pace. You two are meeting production standards, so how about getting the rest of them to step it up."

"We can do that," Florence agreed.

"We can try," Madge hesitated. But as they returned to the cutting crew, she leaned in to Florence and whispered, "Even if you and I are doing it, I still say that eight hundred cookies an hour is awful fast for some of these girls."

Florence shook her head in disagreement. The night before, she'd computed production standards by the hour, minute and second.

"It's just twenty cookies per minute," she corrected. "Twenty per minute is three seconds per cookie. Just think of it like an old-fashioned folk waltz: cut, two, three; cut, two, three; cut, two, three."

"You sure?" Madge challenged.

"Positive," Florence assured her. "You and I have been working at that rate all morning."

"If you say so," Madge doubted. "Maybe we should all count out loud."

By the end of the shift, the crew was exhausted from focusing on the nonstop cadence of their work, but they also felt like they were finally getting into the groove.

"How many did they average?" Icky asked.

"With the delay at the start, they probably averaged six hundred an hour," Harry reported.

"They need to improve that tomorrow," Icky said.

"And if they don't, Bill needs to tell Leanne to push Florence and Madge," Harry added. "I'll work with him on that."

"By the end of the week, they should be up to speed," Sam hoped.

"They don't really have a choice," Icky said. "We got orders to fill."

#

On Friday, Millie gave Mary Lou two dollars, and told her to take Mark to Gomez's Drive-In for dinner. "Daddy and I are going out to the Castle Restaurant tonight."

She'd decided Icky could use a quiet diversion, and the Castle was his favorite. An hour before guests arrived, servers readied the tables and themselves for the night's service. Napkin tents were positioned at each guest's place, and flatware and glasses were polished. Leather-bound menus stood at attention like soldiers next to the reservation book. At five minutes before opening, the necktie that had been dangling around the barkeeper's neck was snapped into place, and waitresses' freshly starched aprons were tied. Butch Butchello stepped forward and unlocked the door.

"We've been missing you around here!" he greeted Icky and Millie.

"It's been too long," Icky agreed, shaking off the cold wind.

"Then let me get you seated," Butchello handed over a coat check and passed their wraps to the closet attendant. On the way toward the Haut's favorite table, he leaned into the bar and ordered their usual drinks.

"You've been busy with that Salamanca expansion, eh?" he said to Icky as he pulled out Millie's chair and waved his arm with a flourish to invite her to be seated.

"We're growing," Icky answered. "How are sales on your new product lines?"

"The grocery stores love those spaghetti dinners," he said, delighted to talk shop, "but my packaged meals don't come with dessert, so housewives still buy your cookies. Am I right?"

"That's a good plan," Icky nodded.

"Your drinks are on the way," Butchello smiled and nodded snappily as he retreated. "We hope you enjoy your evening with us."

After a moment, Icky leaned in and said to Millie, "Thanks for making the reservation."

"Is Salamanca still having problems?" she asked.

"When I got there Monday, the girls complained that we're imposing Olean's production standards on them."

"Eight hundred cookies an hour seems high when you're not used to it," Millie defended. "I mean, no housewife cuts cookies as fast as we do."

"But it wasn't just the number of cookies. The girls wrapping product reported weight discrepancies because the dough wasn't being rolled thin enough."

"Did inspectors show up?"

"No, but they could have. They like to catch a new bakery getting something wrong," Icky frowned. "And we couldn't ship the ones that were off-weight."

"So?"

"We gave 'em away, like always," he said. "Today's sugar cookie production was on target, though, so they're finally ready for a second recipe."

"The spice bites cookie?" Millie guessed as their drinks arrived. She'd been watching their waitress weave her way around tables in a practiced choreography.

"I think so," he answered, adding, "Thank you," as their drinks were set in place.

"Are you ready to order?" she interrupted. "Or are you having today's special?"

Icky looked at Millie.

"The special-of-the-day is good for me," Millie decided.

"Make it two," Icky confirmed. "Prime rib is my favorite."

After the waitress left, he wrinkled his brow and admitted, "I'm sorry, I lost my thought."

"You're just tired," she allowed. "You were saying that you're moving spice bites into production. I bet the smell of Saigon cinnamon will perk up their spirits."

"Let's hope so," he sat back with his drink.

"Marion told me that your floor supervisor wants to put up balloons to celebrate the official start-up next week."

"Seems silly to me, but she says it will mark their first official production day, and get everybody moving in the right direction."

"A festive tone can do that."

"If you say so."

"I do," Millie encouraged, adding, "I guess we've been doing things one way so long that our way is the only way."

"Well, our way is the right way," he defended. "We've got enough experience now to know what works best. We need to stick to that."

"Which is why you're the boss," she assured him.

"That's another thing: they call me 'Boss' over in Salamanca," Icky said. "Like, 'Hey, Boss!' Or, 'The Boss says do it this way.'"

"Where did they get that?" Millie asked innocently. She knew Icky wasn't aware of how authoritative he sounded: shouting orders like a drill sergeant, even though he was just trying to be heard over the mixers. He also moved with the bearing of a man who was accustomed to having his orders carried out. And it wasn't just his broad, muscular shoulders; he also stomped when he walked. Of course, most of the employees were aware that the softest cookie in the bakery was its founder; the Olean crew figured it out soon enough. But she bet Salamanca hadn't caught on. Not yet.

"Are you doing something different out there?" she continued.

"I don't know. Maybe one of them started it, and the rest picked it up," he supposed without much consideration. "But calling me 'Boss'—it just doesn't feel the same as working with people who know they're part of a family operation."

"Well, maybe that's because you work shoulder-to-shoulder in production with the people in Olean, but Salamanca reports to Harry and Sam." After a moment, she expanded her thought. "Also, you've been wearing your suit all week."

He didn't say anything. He hadn't realized that employees might be seeing him as a businessman first, and a baker second. Nothing could be further from the truth! He'd make a point to show up in his baker's whites and work the line with Bill for a couple of days!

"You also can tell them to call you by your name if you prefer it," she suggested.

"Right now, I just want everybody to meet standards and put out good quality product."

Their meals arrived, and they placed napkins onto their laps.

"Enough talk about business," Icky decided. "How are the kids?"

"They're good," Millie answered, adding, "I told Mark to use his manners when Mary Lou took him to Gomez's this evening."

"Uh-huh," Icky smirked, adding, "Um, pass the sodium chloride please."

"The what?" she blinked.

"The sodium chloride," he nodded toward the salt shaker, "since I'm asking more politely than Mark did at Sunday dinner."

"Good thing Ma didn't hear that." Millie passed it to him. "Our salty kid got permission to order root beer with his hamburger tonight. He's happy."

30

First Fruits

"Look! Our pictures are in the newspaper!" Florence held up a copy of the *Salamanca Republican Press*.

Everyone immediately gathered around the break room table.

"It's a story about those Maple Street third-graders: the ones who toured the bakery last week," she continued. "Remember when that reporter and photographer were here?"

"Remember trying to keep up with those blasted production numbers while thirty-two children pranced through!" another one grumbled.

"Oh, those kids were well behaved," someone insisted. "They just hoped they'd get a cookie."

"And that photographer was everywhere," Florence added.

"Oh! Here's Bill!" somebody pointed to another photo. "It says, 'Foreman William Johnson mixes dough for a 540-dozen batch'!"

"And here we are together: 'Mrs. Florence Shinners and Miss Magda Rieter roll and cut dough.'"

"There's Frances and Rose!" Magna announced.

"Where?" Frances pushed in.

"Right here," Florence tapped the page.

"'Miss Frances Emborsky and Mrs. Rose Miskowic transfer dough into an oven that bakes seventy-two dozen cookies in seven minutes,'" Frances read aloud. "We're famous!"

"Here's a photo of our packaging area," Florence tapped the page again.

"Let me in there," Jette insisted. "'Mrs. Jette Lee Cole and Miss Gladys Bowley operate the wrapping machine.' They even spelled my name right! I gotta' get some extra copies of this newspaper. This is going in my scrapbook!"

#

"How's production this morning?" Icky asked when he called Salamanca for the daily report.

"Good," Sam said. "The girls are smiling ear-to-ear over seeing their photographs in this morning's paper."

"What photos?" Icky asked. The *Salamanca Republican Press* didn't deliver in Olean.

"Some local school kids toured our operations last week, and a newspaper photographer came along," he answered. "It's a big spread. All the girls got their pictures in it."

"Save me a copy," Icky said. "I know this is a short work week with Thanksgiving on Thursday, but do you think the crew will show up Friday?"

"They always did when we baked bread. Besides, numbers are up at over forty-two thousand cookies on each shift, so they're earning merit pay," he reported.

"That is good news!"

"We'll all have something to celebrate," Sam ended the call.

#

"Grace, mercy and peace be to you from God our Father and from Jesus Christ our Lord and Savior," the Reverend Bauer welcomed the congregation on the Sunday following the Thanksgiving holiday.

"Today, most of us are probably still recuperating from the bounty we enjoyed on Thursday, and working off calories from extra helpings of the dressing we piled onto our plates," he began. "I know I am."

He saw nods throughout the congregation. A couple of the men patted their bellies.

"Thanksgiving is often thought of as a particularly American holiday. But today's Old Testament text reminds us that communities coming together to give thanks goes back further than the birth of this nation. The Book of Proverbs was written at least seven hundred years before Christ. And chapter 3, verse 9 tells us that during the harvest season, farmers delivered to the temple the best of their crop and the healthiest of their flock: the first fruits of their labor.

"Let me remind you of verse 9 again: "Honor the Lord with your substance and with the first fruits of your produce.'

"Giving to the Lord these *first* fruits means two things. First, the way that we celebrate God's many blessings is by sharing!

"And secondly, what do we share? *The best* of our abundance! The Book of Proverbs isn't limiting first fruits to apples or grapes here. Neither does the text suggest we offer up the crumbs remaining in the bread basket after we've enjoyed our fill, or the dregs remaining in the wine bottle after we've filled our own cups.

"No, if we're celebrating what's already been done by the Lord, we take up our first portion—that is, our best portion—and offer it to others. For it is in this way that we reflect God's glory.

"Sharing our best, whether it's what our gardens produce or what our labors provide is what God hopes for from us." He paused to allow the congregation to consider the possibility that a loving God could experience hope.

"As I look out at this congregation, I can see that we've been richly blessed, each of us in different ways. And in response—in gratitude—we share the best of our gifts. You see, in the harvest, God invites us to be the Lord's people: people through whom God's purposes are accomplished.

"And in so doing, again we say: we reflect God's love, for love reveals God's care for the creation.

"There's no denying that Thanksgiving is an American holiday. For us, however, this holiday originates with our faith. So, as we continue to enjoy this celebration of God's gifts, I offer you this short message: Give the first fruits to the glory of the Lord!

"Let it be so. Amen."

#

"I've been thinking, Icky," Millie gathered her thoughts on the drive home from church, "that maybe we could make some special contribution to the church—you know, to commemorate the expansion in Salamanca."

"Oh?" he glanced at her. "What do you have in mind?"

"Well, you're the Sunday School superintendent, so I was thinking of some sort of fund to help people who want to become teachers in Lutheran schools—or maybe even for people who want to become pastors."

"That's probably a good cause," Icky agreed.

"Do you think it's the right one?" Millie sought his support.

"It fits Frank's sermon."

"Maybe you can talk with him about it after the church council meeting on Wednesday."

"Wednesday—this week?" he asked. "Again?"

"Once a quarter," she confirmed.

He rubbed the creases in his forehead, and said, "Yeah, I can talk with him," though he could do without a midweek evening meeting.

#

"Icky!" Ma stomped snow off her boots before coming through the back door and up the steps into Millie's kitchen.

"He's in Salamanca, Ma," she answered. "What do you need?"

"This!" Ma thrust a chilled newspaper into her hands. "You know about this?"

"Oh, my goodness," Millie glanced at the page. "I knew Frank—or Pastor Bauer—invited Icky to join him for lunch with someone from the synod office yesterday. This photograph must have been taken then."

"They say Icky gives to the church two thousand dollars!" Ma rustled the page with her fingertip. "See? The bakery awards scholarships to pastors, parochial school teachers, and deaconesses!"

"Icky didn't waste any time in getting this done," Millie scanned the article.

"You know about this?" Ma asked in surprise.

"Uh, we talked about it," Millie said. She wouldn't reveal it was her idea. "It says the money will go to people who have financial need, good character, and high academic standing."

"Also, Icky will add another thousand dollars every year! And," Ma tapped the cutline under the photograph, "this man, the Reverend William A. Drews, says the gift 'will pay dividends for eternity'!"

"I see," Millie nodded.

"For *eternity*!" Ma repeated with quiet emphasis.

"Shall I tell Icky to stop by when he gets home?" Millie suggested. It would be good for him to experience Ma's surprise when she read about her son in the newspaper. After all, he had to realize they'd print something when they took his photo!

"*Ja!*" Ma said. "Tell him to bring back this newspaper. Pa hasn't seen it yet!"

"You can keep your newspaper," Millie said. "Jon always delivers our copy to the bakery, so I'll grab it."

"*Ja*, the paperboy likes to be tipped with a warm cookie," Ma noticed.

"It's only fair, since he's always on time," Millie agreed. "I'll tell Icky to see you as soon as he gets in."

31

Raucous and Rowdy

Canadian winds rolled southeast across Lake Erie, churning up moisture and dumping lake-effect snow on Cattaraugus County. First shift bakery employees prepared to head home at noon, digging out their cars in the parking lot, while second shift employees inched in, hoping to safely slide into a cleared space. No one was in a good mood.

"Sorry I'm late," one of the new afternoon girls finally joined her production team. "Getting in was treacherous."

"Is that white stuff still coming down?" someone asked.

"Sure is," she answered. "And piling up. When we leave, we're going to have to dig out, too."

"Ugh. It's so dark at eight o'clock now," another member of the crew noted.

"I'm just praying my old heap starts. The temperatures are expected to drop into the teens."

"At least you got a car!" someone else complained in a loud voice. "My husband works six miles out of town, so he gets the car while I walk eight blocks to work. I was froze to the bone when I finally got here!"

"Hustling to meet production numbers: that's the best way to warm up," one of the girls at the next cutting station suggested. "And meeting standards puts more merit pay in Friday's check."

"I don't know if this job is worth it to me," the complainer disagreed in an even louder voice.

"Think of your kids," another one encouraged. "You'll give them a nice Christmas this year."

"Oh, yeah?" the grump refused to give in. "Who's giving me a nice holiday?"

#

Icky fell into a chair at the kitchen table as Millie set a reheated dinner in front of him.

"You worked both shifts again," she said. It was almost eight-thirty.

"Had to do it," he said flatly. "We haven't replaced Roy."

"He's not replaceable," she noted. "And you're the boss; or, that's what they say."

"So?"

"So, you're the only one working double shifts—almost every day."

"Bad weather: one of the guys didn't show up again," he nodded. "I can't just sit in the office when we got to fill orders."

"At least the staff shortage was in Olean this time," she nodded toward the bakery across the driveway.

"Yeah, but the Salamanca crew had trouble getting in to work on time," he said.

"I bet!" She wouldn't have liked driving in this weather either.

"Marion called over for the numbers, and she said the whole schedule was off. Bill held dough in the refrigerators, but the cutters never caught up."

"So?"

"So it'll be there tomorrow morning, waiting for the first shift."

Millie nodded.

"Anyway, we pushed Olean to make up for some of the loss."

"That's really why you worked both shifts then," Millie noted.

"I'm sorry not to finish this, Millie," Icky put down his fork and pushed back the plate. "It's good, but I won't be able to sleep with food in my stomach."

"Maybe we can do something to cheer up the crew and give everybody some energy," Millie suggested as she removed his dish.

"Like what?"

"Like an employee Christmas party. We could include their spouses, and make it a dinner with dancing afterward."

"Okay. Do it," he answered automatically.

"Me?"

"Right, you're in charge."

"But I've never planned a large party!"

"It's your idea," he repeated. "Besides, all of us are busy with extra orders this season."

"I thought sales would drop off during the holidays."

"Why?" Icky asked.

"Most housewives bake holiday cookies, so I thought they'd buy fewer of ours."

"Well, sales are up," Icky stretched his arms over his head. "Maybe they don't have time to bake."

Millie disagreed. She knew that every family had its own special recipes, passed down through the generations. Even working wives and mothers would be expected to keep up traditions and bake those treats.

"But back to your idea," he interrupted, "a party would be a great time to announce a bonus plan I worked out last weekend."

"Bonuses?"

"Actually, I've been thinking about it for a while," he revealed. "Lots of companies hand out end-of-year bonuses to their top executives. I thought we could, too. But instead of limiting the recipients to the top brass, we'd recognize everyone's contributions."

"But Salamanca is still a new operation—and just breaking even."

"And because they're new, now's the time to do it," he insisted. "I know we've got a few slackers, but most of the crew is stepping up. We need to recognize folks who are contributing the most!"

Millie nodded. She also noticed that Marion was busier in the office, too, now that she had to keep up with two bakery schedules. The keys on her typewriter tapped faster than Gene Kelly and Vera Ellen moving across a dance floor. Clearly, no one had considered how a second operation would add to her workload.

"When do I get a bonus?" Millie asked since she was in charge of the party.

"You?" Icky said with surprise in his voice. "You are my bonus."

"Nice try," she pressed.

#

The next morning, Millie called a number of halls, and finally booked St. Stephen's Club on N. Union Street for the employee party.

"They have space for up to two hundred people—all twenty-seven of our Olean crew, plus the fifty-four we added in Salamanca. Plus their spouses, and a few official guests," she told Icky. "And there's a kitchen that can be used for a catered meal."

"St. Stephen's would have been my first choice," he said.

"Did you decide to give Friday off to everyone?" she asked.

"Yeah. They got Thursday off for Thanksgiving, and increased production the other days to make up for most of it," he said. "They could do it again."

"Setting expectations leads to results," she agreed.

"What's this?" he glanced at Millie's checklist. "You invited the mayor. That's Davis in Olean, right?"

"Of course! The party is here, so I asked Marion to call his office, and his secretary said she'd check his schedule. Police Chief George Finger will be there, too, and he'll make some remarks. And further down on the list you'll see the Bauers's names," she added. "Frank agreed to offer a prayer before dinner."

"It looks like your wing-ding is coming together," Icky said.

"Dinner will be at six-thirty," she began.

"What are we serving?"

"The caterer is working up options. After the meal, you'll hand out your bonuses. Then, we'll dance until one in the morning—assuming I find a band," she finished. "And I'm going shopping for a new dress."

"New dress?" he questioned with exaggerated intentionality. "You're too busy with this party to shop. Besides, don't you have something in the closet that would do?"

She narrowed her eyes.

He smiled. "You win," he said. "New dress it is."

#

Recuperating in a stupor from the bakery's Christmas party, Millie and Icky dragged themselves to the children's Christmas pageant at church Sunday afternoon, and crammed themselves into pews with all of the adults at Immanuel Lutheran Church. Mary Lou crowded in next to her grandparents.

"I remember when you used to be part of this program," Grandma Haut whispered to her.

Mary Lou nodded, relieved to be too old to participate, as she never enjoyed delivering presentations.

"Now it's Mark's turn," she pushed attention to her brother. The kid probably had the heebie-jeebies, but better him than me, she thought to herself.

Mark's second-grade class was expected to read from the Gospel of Matthew. Just before marching them into the sanctuary, his teacher lined up everyone and gave each child a small slip of paper containing a verse. Mark glanced at his, grateful it was just two sentences: "When they heard the king, the wise men departed. And behold, the star which they had seen in the East went before them, till it came and stood over where the young Child was."

For nearly an hour, parents and grandparents smiled indulgently as each group of children paraded in. The youngest, dressed in halos and angel wings, stumbled over one another to make their ways up the two steps before the altar, and then struggled through an animated version of "Away in a Manger." Next, sweet-faced cherubs dressed in wide white collars over short capes were led in to sing "O Little Town of Bethlehem."

Finally, Mark's class marched in and lined up in two rows: seven girls on the lower step, four boys behind them. Donnie Swartz, Jerry Colf, and Bradly Ford processed in ahead of Mark; he'd be the last one to speak, and for good reason. He was best reader, and the teacher wanted a strong closing to the pageant.

But as soon as the children faced the congregation, their eyes glazed over. Two hundred pairs of eyes stared at them, waiting for something to go wrong. One of the boys intentionally elbowed the kid next to him. Retaliation ensued, followed by whispers of "cut it out." Goofing off progressed down the line until Bradly nudged Mark. With no one to pass his revenge to, he elbowed Bradly again, and in the process, dropped his wrinkled Bible verse. He watched helplessly as it floated to the front step and vanished among the girls' shoes.

Horror of horrors! All three boys saw Mark's eyes widen. Then, his forehead crinkled like corrugated cardboard, and his lips sucked in. Immediately, they covered their mouths to keep from laughing, and clenched their own verses—because if they didn't, Mark might exact reprisal and grab one.

The girls ignored the rustling irritation coming from the boys behind them as they lifted their petite little chins, and politely read their verses. Mark felt their word-by-word recitations leading to his impending doom: a wreck in progress, with no way to stop it.

Readings continued in the second row with Donnie, who unfurled his sweaty scrap of paper and slowly mumbled his verse. When he finished, he glanced to his left to signal that Jerry's turn was next, and then shot a sniggering gotcha grin at Mark.

Jerry's verse was short. He sped through it, and turned to Bradley.

Bradley raised his eyebrows artfully, smiled broadly, turned red, and stammered through his verse. Each word pounded in Mark's tortured heart.

Bradley turned to his left, his wretched face beaming with all the innocence of an angel—a despicable fallen angel!—with absolutely no compassion for the nasty fate about to descend onto his friend.

Right before Christmas. In front of God and the whole congregation. And Grandma.

The moment had come, and Mark had no choice but to meet adversity head-on. Without pretending to look down at some imaginary piece of paper, he declared with as much certainty as he could muster: "And the wise men rode camels across the desert."

That was it. He was done.

The pageant's narrator had been watching the whole scene unfold. Something like that happened almost every year, so she added the missing details from the Christmas story, thanked the second-graders, and invited them to return to their classroom.

The girls led the way out of the sanctuary. The boys followed, and Mark saw his white slip of paper lying on the red carpet. He decided to ignore it; maybe no one else would pay attention either.

"You were the only one we could hear," Icky told him after the service. "The other boys looked down while they read from some little slip of paper. But not you. You looked out to the entire congregation, and enunciated clearly enough that we all heard . . . every . . . word."

Chucklehead move, Mark realized.

"What happened to your verse?" Millie asked, exposing the ugly truth that they knew he made up the words.

"I don't know," he said.

"Part of your message seemed to be missing," she suggested.

"The paper slipped out of my hand and landed between some girl's feet," he defended.

"At least you read your verse a couple of times, so you were well prepared," she allowed.

"Uh-huh."

"Which was good because Grandma and Grandpa waited through the whole Christmas pageant to hear one boy: their own grandson, who was the very last one to speak," Icky pressed. "What a fond memory that will be for them to hold onto right before Christmas."

"Yup."

"And I'm the Sunday School superintendent."

Mark was sure he was on Santa's "naughty" list now.

"It's also a good thing that you know the Christmas story well enough to finish strong," his mother defended. She refused to make the kid suffer. "That's what's most important."

"Yup," he said again. He'd rely on his mom's version of the pageant.

32

Now the Heat's On

"We got a problem," George reported.

"What kind?" Icky asked.

"Oven," he said. "I ran the usual temperature checks, and we got uneven heating."

"How uneven?"

"A few degrees. Gauges and connections are fine, so I'm thinking it's the insulation."

"Yeah, that would be my guess, too," Icky agreed.

"I pulled product numbers from the back panel," George continued. "The closest supplier is up in Buffalo. They can get some in by Friday if we order today."

"Tell Marion," Icky said. "I'd like to get it installed that evening so we can run tests on Saturday."

When they tore out the old fiberglass, they both saw how dark and worn it was, especially in the corners.

"Maybe I should have been opening the back of the oven to check this every so often," George pulled out a thin blanket of the stuff.

"No, temperature checks are the test," Icky said. "And we've been running full tilt."

"We'll get it laid in good this time," George insisted.

At midnight, Icky finally announced, "Done!" and stood up. "C'mon in the house for a few minutes before you leave."

Millie was still awake.

"That didn't take as long as you thought!" she said they slid into kitchen chairs. She set a beer in front of each of them.

"These ovens aren't as large as the ones at Bolles," Icky remembered. "Replacing insulation in that equipment took a whole day."

"Thanks for helping," George absentmindedly rubbed his forearm. "It would have been a bear to do alone."

"Glad to do it," Icky said. "Tomorrow I'll be testing a new recipe. If it bakes up right, we're done with this job."

"And if the temperatures are off, call me," George offered, "and I'll come back."

The next day, Icky measured the heat in all the corners of the oven. The problem was solved, but he called George anyway.

"I know you're thinking about this, so I'm just letting you know," he said. "We're good to go for production on Monday."

#

Monday was Millie's laundry day, and as soon as she changed the bedsheets and washed the linens, she moved on to the family's laundry. She'd be finished with the ironing by mid-day, take a break to fold towels and underwear, and then put everything away. She left the children's clothes on the chests in their rooms. Mary Lou always organized her bureau immediately. Mark just grabbed whatever was on top of his stack each morning. But a couple of days later, he complained that his clothes felt rough.

"I was scratching all afternoon," he said. "And some of the guys said I was walking like I have ants in my pants."

"Mine feel scratchy, too," Mary Lou said. "Prickly is more like it."

"You probably just have dry skin," Millie responded.

"Huh-uh," Mary Lou objected. "I think it's my underwear."

"Mine, too," Icky said. "Did you change laundry detergent?"

"No," Millie answered, thoughtfully. A moment later she asked, "But tell me this: When you finished replacing the oven insulation Friday night, did you toss the shirt and trousers you wore down the clothes chute?"

"Of course," he answered without thinking.

"Aw, Icky!" Millie protested. "The whole week's laundry is probably full of fiberglass filaments."

"Sorry," he said easily, as if it were no big deal. "I guess we'll just wash them all again."

"And how are *we* going to figure out which items were contaminated?" she challenged.

He didn't answer.

"Exactly which shirt and pants did you wear?" she clarified. "And what about the kids? Their clean underwear is already mixed up in the drawers."

"Not mine," Mark boasted. "I leave mine out so I can grab it quick."

"Not that I appreciate that," Millie noted, "but yours will be easier to identify."

"Can't it all just be run through the machine again?" Icky asked.

"That won't remove fiberglass," she continued. "I'd have to use tweezers and a magnifying glass."

No one said anything.

"And I'm not doing that!" she asserted, her patience dissolving faster than detergent in hot water, and ready to bubble up as exasperation.

"I didn't say you should," Icky began to feel the weight of causing a problem for the entire family. "But we can't just buy all new under clothes."

"We might need to!" she insisted. Initially, she was thinking about towels and sheets, too, but then realized she'd carried them down the stairs instead stuffing them down the chute, and laundered them before the fiberglass contaminated her washer, so they were safe.

"We probably ought to run the machine a few times with old rags or something we don't wear," Icky said, "just to be sure all the insulation is rinsed out."

"Yes, *we* should," Millie repeated. Looking straight at him, she decreed, "So, here's what's going to happen. I'm going downtown to buy one week's worth of new underwear for each of you. While I'm gone, each of you sort through your drawers and toss the bad stuff out. If that solves the problem, we're done with it!"

They all nodded silently.

"And one more thing: since I'll be out, it might be nice if somebody put the dinner dishes in the dishwasher and cleaned up the kitchen," she added, looking at both Icky and Mary Lou. She didn't care which one of them jumped to the opportunity.

33

Biscuit and Cracker Baker

"I NEED TO MAKE sales calls next week," Icky told Millie over breakfast coffee.

"I suspected a business trip might be coming now that spring is almost here," she said. She'd already sent Icky's suit to the cleaners; she'd starch and press his shirts herself.

"How long will you be gone this time?"

"Monday to Friday," he said.

"All week?"

"We need to quickly generate some extra cash to purchase the Quality Cash grocery store that shares the other half of the building with our Salamanca bakery. They're looking to sell."

"Says who?"

"Sam," he answered. "They asked if we'd be interested in buying them out."

"Why would we want to do that!" She wasn't asking as much as expressing alarm. "I thought we needed to build the bank account back up." Their savings had taken a hit to meet payroll through the winter when cutters weren't meeting production standards—some of which was due to late arrival times.

"Another sixteen hundred square feet will let us install a bigger oven so we can bake more product—once everyone's production numbers are consistent. Like you said, that'll grow our bank account."

"That old 'spend money to make money' idea, huh?" Millie quoted. "Seems to me that we're doing a lot of the former."

"Got to. Olean production can't go any higher than five thousand dozen a day. And since the vat room is over here, all of our fruit cookies have to come out of this location."

"Salamanca could put out seven thousand packages with its two shifts if we push them," he continued. "By increasing our space, we'd double that."

"Seven thousand packages is eighty-four *thousand* cookies," she computed quickly.

"Per day," Icky said.

"Can you sell that much?" she asked.

"And more! The new distributors we added in Ohio, Pennsylvania, and West Virginia already want to increase their orders," he said.

Millie sighed.

"Remember when we built that lean-to bakeshop onto the Quonset hut so we'd have room for the Blodgette?" he reminded her. "That oven was larger than we needed at the time, but eventually we ran it at full tilt."

"Eventually," she repeated.

"Right. We'll figure it out as we go."

"You're the boss."

#

Icky pulled over to fill the gas tank and stretch his legs. His trip was only half over, but already he felt the stress of too many miles, too many diner meals, and too much time away from family. Plus, Marion seemed determined to complicate his schedule. Everyone, she told him, needed him to phone in more often.

"It's really busy around here, and you're not around to answer questions," she complained. "If you don't call, I can't keep up!"

"With what?" He couldn't understand how her job could be more demanding if he was out of town.

"Well, now that I think of it, this mess is because of you!" she said with exasperation. "You meet with accounts, and they ring in with new orders, which means I've got to revise production schedules for two bakeries—not just one!—and follow up with both Derby and Harry. Then they realize they're going to run short of inventory, so they call me back, and I've got to reach Pillsbury, Fleischmann's, and all the rest of them, not to mention shortages of other supplies, like shipping boxes. Oh, no! I almost forgot boxes!"

She paused to write a note: order shipping boxes for Salamanca. "You're making a whole lot of work!" she continued, "so that's 'with what.'"

"Oh," he said, thinking she sounded unusually irritable.

"I hope that when our customers call in, we aren't making them feel like increasing their orders is a hassle," Icky cautioned.

"No, I use my happy voice with them," she said. "I save straight talk for you."

"I guess I should be grateful," he said dryly.

He heard her sigh.

"So, Mr. Haut, *Sir*, how else may I assist you?" she faked niceness so he'd know she wasn't rude to anyone . . . else.

"I know you're busy, so I'll just check in again later," he decided.

"No! Wait!" she stopped him. "You got more messages!"

She read a stack of call-ins, wrote his answers to a half dozen questions, and ended with, "Now get back to work!" Then she quickly added, "Oh, no! Sorry, I meant me. I need to get back to work."

"'Bye, Marion," Icky said as he hung up.

#

"What's the good news?" Icky finally phoned his office again at the end of the day. He decided to be cheerful since he hadn't rung in since noon.

"A reporter called," Marion answered. "I don't know if that's good news or not, since in between everything else going on around here, this guy wanted me to track down an employee he could interview."

"What reporter?" Icky asked, suddenly alert.

"Some trade publication guy at, ah, *Biscuit and Cracker Baker*," she reached over an exploded pile of paperwork to retrieve a pink phone message from her spiral desk organizer.

"He's writing about personnel problems in bakeries, and . . ."

"We don't have personnel problems!" Icky almost shouted.

"I know that," Marion said evenly, wondering if the growing stacks on her desk might qualify. "Anyway, Sam was the best choice, so I sent the call over to him."

Icky scowled over learning that his office administrator was deciding who talked to the press.

"Actually, I asked Millie who'd be best since I hadn't heard from you," she added.

"Oh," Icky restrained himself. "Did Sam tell you what he said to 'this guy'?" He half expected she found a way to listen in on the conversation. Part of her job, she always believed, was paying attention to what was going on so she could keep Icky apprised.

"I haven't had time to check," she said. "I can let him know you asked."

"Do that," Icky insisted. "Tell him I'll ring him up at the end of his shift."

After dinner, Icky settled into an armchair in his hotel room, lit a cigarette, and stared at the minute hand on his watch. Salamanca's second shift ended at eight o'clock, and he prayed he wasn't going to regret anything the reporter was able to squeeze out of Sam.

"Hey, Icky," Sam said as soon as he accepted the collect phone call. "Wish you'd been here to tell me what our line is, but I think I handled the questions okay. I know this reporter from when we were Tasty bakery. He's a straight up guy."

Thank goodness for that, Icky thought to himself. Maybe Sam was the best person to take the call.

"What's he working on?" Icky tried to sound unconcerned.

"Some bakeries over in Detroit and Cleveland are having labor problems, and unions are getting in," Sam revealed. "He wanted to know if our people are happy."

"And?"

"And we are—happy, I mean," Sam said.

"Oka-ay," Icky allowed, slowly.

"I said this is a great bakery, and then I told him about the balloons the girls put up when you took over. I also gave him some insider dope about December's Christmas party."

"Anything else?"

"I said there are a couple of other things to add, but he'd have to get them from you—if you were available. Marion already told him you're out of town."

"Other things like what?"

"Well, I was thinking of the bonus program," Sam said. "But if you want to keep that close to the vest, maybe you can talk about how the bakery supports local sports. Neighborhood guys play on our baseball team, and lots of our employees' kids play on the Icky's Cookies midget football team. Both build employee morale—you know what I mean."

Sam's a good man, Icky thought to himself.

"You didn't discuss the bonuses then, I take it."

"No, I just said 'other things,' and figured that you could make that whatever you want."

"Okay," Icky said. "But it sounds like his angle is that union infiltration."

"Well, I'm not writing it, so I have no way of knowing," Sam admitted. "But trade magazines like *Biscuit* make their money selling ads to the big players, so they write stories that make them feel like they're getting an inside scoop on organizations."

"Well, we're not a big player, and we're not buying ads," Icky said.

"I meant corporations with deep pockets. *Biscuit* gives them news the dailies aren't interested in covering. I guess it makes them relevant in the narrow markets they serve."

"How did they even hear about us?"

"I'm not sure. All I can guess is that we're doing well, and we're not facing the same challenges as bakeries in Michigan and Ohio. That's heavy union territory: UAW, AFL, CIO, Teamsters, all of those guys—and for all I know, maybe the Bakery and Confectionery Union operates there, too."

"Okay. I get it," Icky said.

"I made a list of some of the questions he'll have," Sam said.

"He told you?"

"I asked," Sam said. "I said you're really busy, but if he could give me something, I'd see what I could do."

"You did great," Icky assured him. The hotel room had darkened with the end of the day, and he noticed the tip of his cigarette glowing as he raised it for one final drag before ending the call.

#

Icky was back in his office when the *Biscuit* reporter called back. He tried to sound both laidback and professional—to create the impression that yes, he was the guy in charge, but also easy to talk to. The truth was, though, that he was hoping the guy wouldn't ask about anything he didn't want to share.

"How did it go?" Marion asked when she saw the light go out on his phone line. She'd been in a better mood since Icky was back in town and handling his own calls.

"We'll find out when it's published," he said.

When *Biscuit and Cracker Baker* arrived in the mail a week later, Marion scanned its pages, paperclipped the story mentioning the bakery, and ran up the steps and across the driveway to deliver it to Icky in the bakery.

"See here," she said, breathless from hurrying. "It quotes Sam where he touts us for 'good personnel relations,' and 'high employee morale due to enlightened management.'

"You're quoted, too," she added.

Icky stepped away from the mixing station to scan the story.

> 'We initiated a bonus program last year, and the employees have responded positively to it,' President Haut explained.... 'I live in dairy country and I buy milk directly from our farmers because it's easier and cheaper to use than trucking in the solids,' Haut says. He believes fresh cream makes his cookies richer, too....
> 'I couldn't have gotten anywhere without my wife, Millie. She pushed me on. When I wanted to quit, she wouldn't let me.'
> 'I told him I'd leave him if he quit,' she added.

"Call Sam," Icky directed Marion. "Let him know how it turned out, and tell him to call at the end of the shift."

"We got a copy of *Biscuit* over here, too," Sam said. "And the article looks good to me."

"I still wonder how they decided to interview us," Icky said.

"I bet that guy at Pillsbury said something," Sam indicated remarks further down in the story. "He's quoted liberally."

"Hm," Icky noted. "I'll ask Hubbell."

"That's what I'd do," Sam agreed. "The guy is probably in marketing."

"One of those big players who buys ads," Icky made the connection.

"Right. Look through the magazine for advertisements on Pillsbury products. That'll be a clue," Sam agreed.

#

Over dinner, Icky showed the article to Millie.

"I never spoke to that reporter!" she protested over the quote attributed to her.

"Oh, I told him you said that—and it's true; you did say it."

"Well, yes," she admitted, "but in jest! This sounds like I'd walk out on you for real!"

"And you wouldn't," he confirmed.

"Not with two kids!" she exclaimed in horror. "I'd have to be nuts to do that!"

He looked at her squarely.

"Good thing we got them, then," he said.

"Some days I wonder," she said. Then nodding at the magazine, she suggested, "You ought to show this to Ma. She always enjoys seeing articles on the bakery."

But more to the point, her mother-in-law would be as surprised as she was to see the comment about her walking out on Icky. It wasn't so funny in print, and she could count on Ma to tell her son what he ought not repeat to reporters.

34

Breaking the Law

Marion ran up the steps and across the driveway to the bakery to find Icky, who was working production to cover a staff shortage again. She wished he'd hire another baker so she didn't have to chase him down all the time.

"Going up and down stairs twenty times a day isn't in my job description," she grumbled at the top step. "Tomorrow I'm wearing my old sneakers."

She found him hefting a bag of flour to the mixer.

"You've got a call from the advertising agency," she yelled over whirring beaters. "They're waiting on 'hold' to talk with you."

"Too busy," he shouted.

"But they said 'now,'" she persisted.

"I'll call 'em back at the end of the day," he refused to budge. When the morning shift ended, he planned to grab a shower and head downtown for a meeting with the Amateur Baseball League. The season was only a month off, and he was eager to get a team lined up in Icky's Cookies shirts. That was the kind of advertising he was interested in.

"But they said there's some problem with the name of one of the cookies," she persisted.

"Which one?" he stepped back from the noise.

"Sour cream."

"It's not going into production 'til next week. It can wait."

"If you say so," she returned to the office.

#

Millie gathered her cleaning materials so she could drive out to the cottage to wash windows and scrub the kitchen and bathroom. *I know everybody wants to get together at the lake this summer*, she said to herself, *but this is no vacation for me.*

"C'mon Mark," she called. He shoved his Pez dispenser into his pocket and dropped his rod and reel onto the back seat. As soon as they arrived, he yanked back on the car door handle and sped down the path leading to the water's edge where he flipped off his shoes and tiptoed onto the dock to look into the lake's cool shadows.

"Oh! Wow! A bass!" he whispered, his mouth gaping open and shut in unison with the fish. He slithered backward on the dock until he reached grass again, and then ran to the car to retrieve his rod and bait.

"There's a bass under the dock!" he yelled. "Where are my worms?"

Millie found the precious tin can in the corner of the trunk.

"Thanks," he shouted over his shoulder. When he got back to the lake, he dropped onto the grass, tied a hook onto the end of a piece of line, threaded a super-sized worm onto it, and then tied the other end of the line onto his finger. He decided not to use his rod since the fish was right below the dock. This time, he'd lower the bait straight down and let it slip gently into the water.

He crawled stealthily onto the dock, peeking through spaces between the boards until he found the exact right spot where he thought he saw the fish.

It was still there!

Slowly, slowly, he stretched his arm over the dock's edge, and slid the wriggling worm into the water. *Let the bass see it*, his Grandpa Huff's instructions echoed in his ears.

The fish took it! Swallowed the worm and hook in one gulp!

Immediately, he yanked up his arm, and in what felt like a single move, rose to his feet to pull his catch to the surface of the water. Then he hauled up his line, arm over arm, drawing the bass from the lake.

"I got him! I got him!" he shouted. A large green prize with dark markings spun and twisted, snapping its jaws. Mark quickly grabbed hold of its gills and inspected its bright white underside. The fish felt heavy: the biggest one he ever caught! Ever! And he did it all himself!

But where was everybody? Somebody ought to be around to see this!

The bass continued to fight, slapping back and forth, spraying water onto his face.

"Mom!" he ran to the cottage. When he reached the porch, he grabbed the gray metal fishing pail always kept on the porch, and gently settled the bass into it.

"Mo-o-om!" he yelled again as carried the pail into the house and slid it under the faucet in the kitchen sink so he could fill it with water.

"I'm right here," she came down the stairs.

"Look! I got him!"

She expected to see a six- or eight-inch catch—but this lunker curved all the way around the bottom of the bucket. Its nose pointed into its tail.

"What a beauty!" she exclaimed. "He must be at least two and a half pounds!"

"Wait 'til Dad sees this! He won't believe it!"

"You can show him when we get home," she encouraged.

"Let's call and tell him right now!" Mark insisted.

"The phone isn't hooked up yet this season," she said. "I'll be done with chores soon enough."

But the look on his face convinced her to indulge the kid's need to show off his catch while it was still moving.

"I'm gonna' find Dad!" he announced the moment the car pulled into the driveway. An instant later he shoved open the bakery door, and strode into the packaging and shipping department as if he owned the place. Icky had just returned from his meeting with the ABL, and thought he'd take a minute to see how Mary Lou was doing on her new job. She'd been hired to wrap and pack cookies, and worked afternoons after school to get an early start on the summer season.

"I got a fish!" Mark interrupted, and without stopping, brought the pail around to show off his trophy. "I didn't even use my rod!"

Mary Lou twisted her left shoulder toward her ear in a shrug. Another fish, big deal, she thought to herself.

But Icky bent down to peer into the bucket.

"Wow! That's huge!" he said. "Where did you catch it?"

"He was waiting for me under the dock," Mark reported. He then shared all the details about how he put a worm on the hook, slid the line into the water, and then yanked the fish right out!

"Grandpa and Grandma are going to be so proud of you!" Icky walked Mark away from packaging cookies. As soon as they were outside, he said, "That's one beautiful fish."

"Yup!" he answered.

Then, trying not to squelch his son's enthusiasm, Icky added, "But bass season doesn't open until the middle of June."

"Okay," said Mark, oblivious to his father's point.

"If it's not bass season, bass aren't supposed to be fished out of the lake," he continued. "What I'm saying is that you better take this beauty someplace where people don't see it. You don't want to end up in jail."

"Oh," Mark eyed the fish. Was this a problem to be weighed by his young conscience? Or was Dad adding to the thrill of his adventure?

"Okay, 'bye!" he said brightly, deciding on the second option. Then, spreading his fingers widely over the top of the pail, he raced next door to his grandparents' house. He'd get to tell the whole story all over again, and this time, he'd add the part about how the bass was an illegal fish.

#

"What did you think about Mark's catch?" Millie asked at the end of the day.

"It was a bass," Icky said.

"I know, but I couldn't tell him to throw it back," she admitted. "Not this time."

"He still needs to learn the rules."

"You're right," Millie agreed. "Fishing rules are best coming from you, though."

"Or your father," Icky suggested.

"Even better. I'll ask him talk to Mark."

"The bakery almost got me into trouble today, too," he changed the subject.

"What kind of trouble?"

"We had to change the name of the new 'sour cream drop cookie,'" he began.

"I'm not responsible for that name. Somebody in the bakery decided on it when taste tests were run with the crew!"

"I know. This isn't about parsing blame."

"Then what's wrong with 'sour cream drop cookie'?"

"The recipe doesn't contain sour cream—which I should have noticed when I asked Marion to type ingredients for the labels. Rookie mistake on my part," he admitted. "Fortunately, the ad agency called."

"What would have happened if they hadn't caught the error?"

"They said a lawsuit could have been filed for false advertising. More likely, we'd be fined by some governmental authority."

"But it's okay now?"

"Renamed it."

"You?" she challenged. Icky never named anything.

"The agency needed to finish the artwork and send layouts to the printer. Otherwise, they couldn't finish printing labels by next week—which would have meant we couldn't move the cookie into production on time."

"And Marion would have to rework all the schedules," Millie added. "She'd have a fit."

"Tell me about it," Icky concurred.

"So, what's the cookie named now?"

"Old Dutch," he said.

"Good name!" Millie complimented him.

"Ma came up with it," he admitted. "She agreed to suggest something since she didn't have enough money hidden in the bottom of her cookie jar to bail out both Mark and me."

"Both of you?"

"Illegal fish, illegal cookie label," Icky explained. "She said we're both criminals."

#

While Mark liked thinking of his fish as being against the law, he found out that his crime was not a sin against God. Grandpa Huff said so. The reason for fishing seasons, he explained, was because bad guys in the government had their noses in the little guy's business. Since Mark was a little guy—even littler than Grandpa—that meant the government was bullying a kid.

"They should know better than to pick on somebody who isn't even their own size," Mark jutted out his lower jaw, just like Grandpa Huff.

As for sinning, Mark could count on Mary Lou to tell him when he was in trouble with God. She knew all about it, too, because she was the third-grade Sunday School teacher, and unfortunately for Mark, she was *his* Sunday School teacher that year.

He hated being in his sister's class. She not only could boss him at home, but now she made him listen to church lessons, too. He also thought Mary Lou seemed to have some sort of special "in" with God that he didn't have—as if the Lord would now automatically take her side if he did something wrong. He already knew about the Ten Commandments, even if he didn't know what each of them meant. Some had words he never heard before, so he decided he probably hadn't broken them. Like "adultery," which obviously was just something adults needed to worry about, so the teachers always just skipped over it.

He didn't know what "covet" was either, but it looked like "cover" so he thought that maybe it was spelled wrong. The rest of the Commandments could be boiled down to bite-sized rules, such as don't kill anybody, don't steal their lunch money, don't lie, and don't embarrass your parents. The way he saw it, as long as no one yelled at him, he probably was in the clear with God. Even if he wasn't okay in the eyes of his big sister.

Of course, from Mary Lou's perspective, the very least her brother could do was behave. Whenever they read a bible story, Miss Haut, whose perfect posture, folded hands, and heedful rectitude made her the very image of a teacher—but whom Mark would argue was really only Mary Lou—could call on him if no one else volunteered to answer her questions. Like the time she asked the class what the word "sin" meant, and everyone looked at him. Mary Lou looked at him then, too.

"I don't know!" he frowned.

"You do, too!" she insisted. He had amassed all sorts of blotches on his soul, no doubt about it, and now she was pressing him to lay out examples from his whole eight-year-old sordid past, right there in the church basement with everyone in the class looking on. Donny and Jerry and Bradley—the three stooges who goofed off during the Christmas pageant—sat next to him. He was sure that any one of them could have offered examples.

But of course, they wouldn't.

"What happened to the rule that 'children ought to be seen and not heard'?" Mark demanded. He'd be happy to be neither seen nor heard!

But, wait a minute, he chewed his lip. How much trouble was a kid really in if his older sister was watching his every move? Answer: Not much.

This was both good: God would not be too angry; and bad: how would he ever have fun if eyes were on him all the time? Wasn't there something between good and bad? Some of his Catholic friends said their priest told them that they could get stuck in some in-between place called Purgatory. It wouldn't happen until they were dead, which would be a long time after they had fun. That sounded a whole lot better than having an older sister who'd use any excuse she could think of to trap a kid!

Mark pressed his shoulders against the back of his chair and refused to answer any more questions until he got to the fourth grade. Then, Mary Lou would be off to college and he'd have a different teacher. For now, Sunday School might have him stuck in the death of despair, but he would walk through some dark alley full of shadows and scary stuff, and come out on the other side just fine.

35

Moose Men or Cookie Men?

"I'll move a few more bottles of beer into the bakery cooler," Millie said as Icky grabbed his baseball cap. "Win or lose, you'll still want to celebrate the end of the season with your team."

"I didn't think we'd even be in the playoffs," he said, "so just getting to play is a win for the Icky's Cookies team."

A crowd already was forming across the street at Marcus Park. As Icky walked over, he could hear the game's announcer over the loud speaker.

"The final game in tonight's ABL playoff series faces off teams sponsored by the Moose Lodge and Icky's Cookies," he said. "The Moose have been hot all summer with a full roster of solid players. The Icky's Cookies men inched ahead steadily, finally sliding into third place.

"The two teams are now tied going into the final game," he continued, "but *The Olean Times-Herald* is projecting that league champions Moose Lodge with their season-long wins are likely to take home the trophy.

"Who do you think has a better chance?" he asked the crowd as the stands began to fill. "Moose men or Cookie men? Heh, heh, heh, heh."

WHDL radio's two sportscasters moved their equipment in to announce the game and provide color commentary for listeners at home. Cars were parked up and down Sullivan Street along the first base line, and their drivers turned up their radios to hear the play-by-play while they watched the game from the sidewalk.

"This is the third and final game in the best-of-three series," the first WHDL sportscaster began. "Moose took the first game on Monday, 4–3, but dropped the second to Icky's Cookies, 8–1. Tonight is a winner-takes-all game."

"I'm guessing we already got about six hundred fans roaming around the edge of Marcus Park," observed the second sportscaster.

"It's crowded out here, that's for sure! And it's a hot one, too."

"Long lines are forming alongside a couple of beverage trucks located across Sullivan Street."

"Cold beer is gonna' taste really good in this heat!" the first one agreed.

"The concession stands are doing a lot of business, too. Anybody want a hot dog?"

"Nothing's more American than hot dogs at a baseball game. And the buns for those hot dogs are baked right here in Olean at Bolles Bakery."

"Okay, let's all stand for the playing of the national anthem," his partner said as the game announcer in the booth turned up the loud speaker's recording of "The Star Spangled Banner." The entire crowd halted in place, faced the American flag, and placed right hands over their hearts until the final strains concluded, "and the home . . . of the . . . brave."

"Play ball!" the umpire-in-chief commanded.

"Okay, here we go," the first WHDL sportscaster started the play-by-play. "Right-handed pitcher Ray Coss for the Moose is taking the mound, and Icky's Cookies is in the batter's box."

"There's the windup and the pitch!" his partner reported. "Ball one."

Between plays, they entertained listeners with New York baseball trivia. "So how many of you know where major league baseball bats come from? I'll tell you where: right here in Cattaraugus County!"

"You don't say!"

"I do say! For years, the wood that's made into Louisville Sluggers used by Ty Cobb, Babe Ruth, Lou Gehrig, Joe DiMaggio, Mickey Mantle, and lots of the other baseball greats has been harvested from trees grown in western New York state!"

"What kind of trees?"

"Northern white ash. Most of the billets are shipped off to Kentucky for finishing. But the promotional bats given away on 'bat day' at Major League games are made just up the road in Ellicottville."

"All right! Next up to bat is Jim Padlo for Icky's Cookies," the two sportscasters returned to announce play-by-play. "There's the windup and the pitch . . ."

Crack!

"A line drive down the center as Padlo races for a single. Moose grabs the ball, and shoots it to first base. Padlo slides in, a-a-and he's safe."

"That was a long ball! Padlo must have been using one of those Louisville sluggers!"

"Could be," the first sportscaster said.

The inning ended as Coss fanned in a couple of plays and Padlo made it around the bases to earn one run for Icky's Cookies.

"You know what else comes from western New York state? Baseball caps."

"That's right! New Era Caps is located just north of here—up toward Buffalo. More than 30 million caps come out of that factory every year!"

"That's a lot of heads!"

"Word has it they supply sixteen of the big league teams!"

Pitcher Jim Snyder took to the mound for the Cookies, and turned out to be too much for the Moose hitters. He gave up one hit to a fly out, and struck the other two out.

"Okay, Coss is back on the mound for the Moose, and Icky's Cookies is the batter's box again," the radio play-by-play continued. "The score is Moose, 0; Icky's Cookies, 1. And it looks like the Cookies is sending Lou Nicol to the plate."

"A swing and a miss," his partner announced a minute later.

"The catcher tosses the ball back to the mound. Coss spins it around in his fingers a couple of times to check it out, then reaches back, and . . ." *Crack!* "Another long one. and Nicol heads to first. He's . . . safe."

A couple of Moose defense errors let Nicol jog to home plate.

"The Cookies are having a sweet night at the old ball park."

"They sure are!"

"And the score at the top of the sixth inning is now Moose, zip, and Cookies, 2."

"I see Icky Haut sitting up in the stands. He's got to be feeling pretty good about the Cookies' performance this evening."

"He's been out here with his team all season long," his partner noted.

"Haut's Cookie Shoppe is right across the street from Marcus Park at N. Fourteenth and Sullivan," the first sportscaster pointed out.

"Folks around here say that anytime a kid shows up at the bakery's back door to ask if they have any broken cookies, Icky makes sure to find one or two," his partner added.

"Lots of kids are at the game tonight, too. Bikes are being dropped on front lawns all along Sullivan Street as boys run up to the fence or duck in and out of the crowd."

"Boys and baseball: that means Little League."

"Yes, Little League is big in Olean. Of course, Williamsport, P.A. claims to be the home of Little League baseball—and they're just two hours or so southeast of here."

"You know, if we wanted to, we could make a whole list of reasons why this part of the country is the heart of America's favorite game!"

"I bet we could!"

"Okay, here we go again," they returned to the play-by-play. "Ray Haberly is heading to the plate for Icky's Cookies."

"Haberly has a hot bat."

"Here's the wind up, a-a-and the pitch." *Crack!* "Haberly knocks the ball way out, and makes it easily to first base."

Before the inning ended, they added, "Haberly is heading in to home, and the Cookies put three runs on the board!"

"Wow! What a game for the Cookies!"

"Okay, this is it," the first sportscaster set up what might be the last play of the game for radio listeners. "Bottom of the ninth, and Snyder's already sent two hitters to the dugout."

"Right. If the big left-hander strikes out one more, it's all over for the Moose."

Guys who'd been tending to grills and kegs at the edge of the outfield near the railroad tracks stopped flipping burgers and leaned in. Old-timers who arrived early to take a prime spot behind home plate lifted themselves out of their lawn chairs, and tipped down the brims of their ball caps to shade their eyes from the setting sun. Icky's Cookies fans inhaled a singular deep breath and held it.

Snyder looked around the park as if to record the moment. Then, he drew back his left arm, twisted to his right, and shot the ball forward. It discharged from his fingertips like a bullet.

And way out, at the furthest end of the park, Moose outfielders heard it slap into the catcher's mitt.

"Out!" the umpire yelled.

"Cookies eat the Moose!" the WHDL radio sportscasters screamed. "Cookies eat the Moose!"

The crowd roared! Car horns blasted. Kids ran onto the field. Half of the old-timers slapped one another's shoulders.

The other half picked up their lawn chairs, and dragged themselves home with a loss.

"What's all that noise?" Millie demanded as Icky led ten sweaty men across the street and onto the bakery's loading dock.

"Snyder took the series!" he yelled. "We won!"

"You *won*?" she repeated.

"We blanked the Moose!" he repeated, as he reached into the cooler for the cold beers.

"We shut 'em out!" shouted Jim Padlo. "0 and 3!"

"Where's Snyder?" Icky demanded.

"Jim? Some reporter grabbed him."

"Save him a beer! And listen up!" Icky raised a bottle as he named each guy who played for the bakery's team. "Snyder, Padlo, Nicol, and Haberly with John Kreydt, Fran Oliva, Pete Weis, Craig Buck, and John Eaton: Here's to the best team in the league!"

"To Icky's Cookies!" they all shouted.

Thirty minutes later, Millie collected empty beer bottles, and Icky got busy sanitizing the packaging area next to shipping. The bakery's first shift would start in six hours.

"What a surprise!" she said when he came into the house for the night. "You've got to be feeling great."

"No words for it," Icky said. "It was just . . . the best game ever."

#

With a playoff series win under his belt, Icky marched into the post-season roundup, and pitched a challenge to the ABL Board of Directors. In the preceding year, sponsorships had slipped from eight teams to only six—which suggested that local corporations were withdrawing support. That situation needed to be turned around.

"You're just sitting in the bull pen!" he challenged the Board. "There's no excuse for losing two sponsors. That's 25 percent of our support!"

"It's not our fault! Big bucks companies aren't putting money into neighborhood ball anymore," one of them defended.

"They don't even show up to watch their own employees play!" said another.

In point of fact, decision-makers had moved into the country club set, with corporate dollars redirected toward the sorts of events they were personally interested in.

"You're one of them now," another board member pointed out. "You go talk to 'em!"

"Haut's Cookie Shoppe isn't some huge corporation," Icky refused to acquiesce. "Just pick up the blasted phone!"

"Who do you think you're kidding?" another disputed. After all, they'd known Icky all their lives. "They're not taking our calls!"

"Right!" another added. "We're just rank and file. But you're a head honcho now. They'll listen to you."

"Unless you think you're too good to step up to the plate," the first guy accused.

Of course not, Icky thought to himself. But if he were honest, he'd admit that when he joined the Bartlett Country Club, he felt resistance from a few long-standing members. And if that were true, maybe they thought ABL board members weren't important enough to listen to either.

"All right," he finally gave in, "I'll make a couple of calls."

"Then I nominate you as President of the Amateur Baseball League for the 1955 season," one of the members announced.

"I second that motion," said another before Icky could object. "All in favor?"

"Just you wait a minute!" Icky thrust out his palm. He wanted neither the title nor the responsibility.

"No, you're our guy!" they all demanded at once.

"Stop!" Icky ordered.

But the Board was just as intransigent.

"All right," he crossed his arms in front of his chest, stipulating, "but when we get our two new sponsors, you guys will recruit two more teams to play next season. Got it?"

They'd have to play ball his way.

#

"New York Fruit Imports is on line one," Marion leaned into Icky's office, adding, "Talal Kirallah."

"I'll take it," Icky grabbed the receiver. He could use a distraction from the morning's ABL meeting.

"Mr. Kirallah!" he greeted the agent. New York Fruit Imports represented Middle East growers of specialty fruits and nuts to commercial bakeries, and called whenever harvests of figs, dates, apricots, almonds, or walnuts were abundant enough to ship to the United States. "It's good to hear from you again this year!"

"Thank you for taking my call, Mr. Haut," he replied with impeccable diction. "How is your business today?"

"We're continuing to expand," Icky said. "Are you calling with something good to offer?"

Americans always get to the point, Mr. Kirallah thought to himself. It would be better to spend a few minutes building a relationship—to decide first whether or not we trust one another enough to do business together. Ah, well. The United States is a new country, not even two hundred years old. Like a wise great grandparent, we will make allowances for the natural immaturity that drives their singular pursuit of the bottom line.

"We are doing well, and we are happy to share our good fortune with you," Mr. Kirallah consented. "The Medjool date harvest is very strong this year."

"Dates," Icky repeated. Immediately he began to imagine a fruit cookie Neiler could formulate. "Tell me about Medjool dates."

"These are the finest dates available, and they are enjoyed for their natural sweetness. They are larger, darker, and more caramel-flavored than other varieties, such as the Deglet Noor. They will be very good in your cookies, Mr. Haut," he continued, "and because the harvest is plentiful, we can offer you a very good price."

"I might be interested," Icky reserved a commitment so that Mr. Kirallah would have to divulge what he meant by a "very good price."

"When will these plentiful dates arrive? And how many does your customer need to sell?" Icky asked. He'd learned to position an agent's desire to make a sale as a stronger need than his own interest in making a purchase. Plus, he assumed—incorrectly—that the dates would need to be moved to buyers as soon as they cleared customs at the New York City port.

"Your bakery is a very good customer, Mr. Haut," the polite conversation continued, for Mr. Kirallah was an imperturbable negotiator. Besides, he knew that dates continue to mature for over six months, so he had time to find his buyers. "We can make arrangements to ship them to you as soon as you need them," he continued. "You may recall that we gave to you a very good price on the figs that you enjoyed so much last year. We trust that we may find a mutually beneficial price this year as well."

"The price on the figs was good," Icky allowed, reinforcing, "and we also appreciate your offer of a good price this time."

No one would accuse Icky of being patient.

"Of course, Mr. Haut. This is why I called you before contacting other bakeries who will want these fine dates. You are a very important customer to New York Fruit Imports."

Icky leaned back in his chair to consider what he wanted to do. Just as Michigan cherries were a harbinger of summer, and New York grapes announced autumn, Middle Eastern dates heralded winter. Adding date-filled cookies to the product line certainly would sweeten the holiday season. Depending on cost and volume, he'd offer them to John Heinz and his east coast distributors first. If he could negotiate a price on a larger shipment, maybe he'd offer a limited run to distributors in his growing Midwest market.

Still, though he'd *like* to develop a cookie with dates, he didn't *need* them.

"Perhaps," Mr. Kirallah suggested, "you would like to also consider purchasing some very fine walnuts we are expecting at about the same time? The dates and the walnuts baked together would be a very nice product for your bakery to offer."

"Perhaps," Icky allowed. "Again, this would depend on your 'very good price.'"

Now the real dickering begins, Icky told himself. He'd keep his answers short, and repeat the same refrain: a "very good price." But not for long. After a couple of rounds of bargaining, he was done haggling.

"And," Icky said with finality, "these are, of course, pitted dates. You would not contact commercial bakeries unless you were offering very fine ready-to-use *pitted* dates and *shelled* walnuts."

Mr. Kirallah did not immediately respond to this contingency.

"Selling *pitted* dates would break my back unless your bakery is willing to order a very large amount," he finally said, and leaning in to accommodate American business customs, he added, "and at our 'very best price', we would need to ship two tons of dates and two tons of walnuts."

"For a very short time, Icky's Cookies would be willing to work many extra hours in developing a new recipe featuring your very fine and plentiful ready-to-use *pitted* Medjool dates and very fine *shelled* walnuts," Icky countered. "This new product will require us to update our sales materials and adjust our production schedules, of course, but we are willing to absorb these expenses in order to purchase two tons of your pitted dates, and *one* ton of shelled walnuts, both at your 'very best price.'"

"Not *two* tons of walnuts also?" Mr. Kirallah repeated his offer.

"Two tons of your very fine and plentiful ready-to-use pitted Medjool dates and *one* ton of your very fine shelled walnuts," Icky repeated, adding, "at your 'very best price.'"

"I will need to discuss this opportunity with the owner of New York Fruit Imports," Mr. Kirallah advised. His attitude was not a sign of intransigence, but rather, the polite way to show respect for the hierarchy of the agency employing him. "I will advise his decision very soon."

"I always enjoy hearing from you, Mr. Kirallah. And I'm counting on you to let me know the owner's answer within two days," Icky closed the negotiations and ended the call.

"I'm going out to the bakery," he told Marion. He wanted to ask Neiler about his experience with date fillings. They'd need to develop a recipe quickly. Distributors were going to be really happy with a specialty cookie.

#

"You look extra tired this evening," Millie said after dinner.

"I'm upset with myself," Icky admitted.

"What for?"

"Oh . . . I let the ABL name me president for the next year."

"You didn't."

"I did."

"How did you get dragged into that?"

"I complained that they lost two sponsorships last season," he said.

"And the guy who complains about a problem is the one who cares the most about solving it," she noted, "so it's now yours." She'd heard her brothers banter over that claim often enough.

He ran his fingernails over his scalp in exasperation. "The last thing I need is another project."

"I also thought you didn't like politics," she finally said.

"Playing ball isn't politics," he stoutly defended, even though he agreed with her.

"No? How'd you get this new title then?"

"I'm probably the only one who knows the corporate decision-makers well enough that they'll take my calls, that's all."

"It seems to me that you're trying to keep one foot on the base while the other one is racing around the diamond," she pointed out, adding, "just like you do at the bakery."

He inhaled harshly. "All I really want to do is bake."

But by the next morning he'd decided how he'd do what he promised.

"Here's a list of the guys I play golf with," he handed a sheet of paper to Marion. "Get me appointments with each of them."

"Don't you need to set up tee times first?" She wondered if he was going to start telling her to manage his personal calendar next.

"No, I want to meet in their offices," he said.

"And what should I say these meetings are about?"

"Just tell their secretaries that I want about ten minutes," he said. "That's all they need to know." He'd show up with the ABL championship trophy, and report how his bakery's involvement in local baseball was building employee morale. Maybe their companies would like to show off that prize next year.

36

Stopgap

"Remember when we bought Tasty Bakery?" Icky asked.

"Of course," Millie answered. "It was way back before Roy and Herta left for Florida."

"Right—not great timing, but we finally got moving again."

"What I most remember was how we faced a larger risk than we expected."

"What do you mean?" he asked.

"We paid cash, depleted our reserves, and doubled the payroll, all at the same time. And no one knew how to do their jobs."

"Well, we're way past that now—and that's what we need to talk about."

"Oka-ay," she studied his face.

"We bought Tasty because Olean couldn't keep up with increasing orders," he pressed.

"And?"

"It was a stopgap measure," he continued.

"Stopgap," Millie said in a flat tone of voice.

"Temporary," Icky asserted.

"Temporary until what?" she prodded.

"Until we build."

"Build what?" she demanded.

"I'm just facing reality," Icky insisted.

"Which reality are we talking about here?"

"The reality of the baked goods market. It's still expanding, Millie, so if we want to keep up with demand..."

"Wait a minute," she challenged. "We converted that bakery from bread to cookies—and expanded into extra space. And now you want to chuck it?"

"Not chuck it," Icky insisted. "We'd consolidate operations and build one large operation."

"Where?"

"With twenty-seven employees in Olean, and fifty-five in Salamanca, like it or not, it makes sense to build in Salamanca."

"Ha! That'll make their mayor happy," she acknowledged sardonically. She knew Icky didn't trust the guy since he scooped the Tasty purchase to the local press, and ginned up the bakery's employees in the process.

"Yeah, well, making him happy would be an unintended by-product," he said. "Even so, I may have found a property that could work for us if the town installs sewers."

"They'd do that?"

"The mayor is asking the city engineer to survey the lot. That's the next step."

"So you've decided already," she noted.

"I'm just talking."

"But do we really *want* to build way over there?" Millie imagined Icky commuting to Salamanca because with a new building, the bakery's offices probably would relocate there. And, since he also still worked production, he'd sometimes be on the road at three-thirty in the morning for the first shift. How could he even consider an eighteen-mile drive at that hour? Answer: He wouldn't—not for long, so then they'd start talking about leaving Olean—which would mean that Mark would change schools. Her apprehensions expanded like a pan of popcorn set on a hot burner.

"I stopped by the bank yesterday to ask what the loan rates are . . ." he continued.

"Loan?" she repeated.

"Just checking," he explained, "and they asked the same question you did: 'Why would you build in Salamanca?'"

"What did you say?" Millie hoped they took her side.

"I said I was just exploring options," he answered, "which I was."

"Was," she repeated, firmly.

"Am," he corrected. "Look, Millie, if we don't do something, we're stuck."

"Is that so bad?"

He shook his head in disbelief.

"Aren't we 'stuck' in a good place?" she insisted.

His brain conjured up an image of being trapped in a traffic jam, instead of sitting behind the wheel of a race car and speeding down the highway.

"I'd rather be growing," he insisted.

"What about the dream of growing into a *Mittlestand*?" she countered.

"We've got two *Mittlestands*—and they're half an hour apart!" he pointed out.

She didn't respond. When they started their bakery, Icky had no job, and they were almost out on the street. Now he not only had a job; the job had him—or so it seemed.

"Are you really saying that you're 'called' to this?" she finally challenged.

"No," he answered. "I'm called to be a baker."

"And you think building again is baking?"

He paused.

"I don't know. Maybe."

"Okay," she paused. "How's this going to work?"

"The lot isn't far from our Salamanca bakery, and it's big enough to let us consolidate both operations into one. It looks like we'd have direct access to a railroad line, too," he continued to press.

"We'd ship product by railroad?"

"No, we'd get inventory by rail," Icky explained. "Remember when Tom Hubbell said that one day Pillsbury would be delivering railcars of flour to us?"

"You're kidding," she said cynically, recalling that prediction.

"I'm not. Every week, Salamanca uses twenty-five thousand pounds of flour—in addition to Olean's inventory, which adds another 40 percent to the total," he said.

"That can't be right," Millie challenged.

Icky raised an eyebrow in disagreement.

"Plus ten thousand pounds of sugar, seven thousand pounds of shortening, and six hundred gallons of fresh milk," he reinforced. "The milk is sourced locally, but rail can be used for the rest. And it's more cost effective than trucking."

"I remember Pillsbury covering our delivery cost when we started," she said.

"But we've been paying for shipping ever since we bought Tasty, and absorbing it out of our profits."

"Is it a lot?" she asked, "the shipping cost, I mean."

"It's enough," Icky said. "We need to either reduce that expense or start passing it on."

"Increase the cost of our cookies?" she wanted to clarify.

"I don't like that either," he said. "That's why I've been talking to Tom about rail delivery. He says Pillsbury could load our order onto a boxcar at the mill, and when it arrives, we'd detach the car from the train, and pull it onto a rail siding."

"What's a rail siding?"

"It's like a spur: a short run of track that goes directly from a main line to a business," he explained. "Our guys would unload bags of flour onto pallets and then move the boxcar back up the rail siding. When the train comes back through, they'd pick it up."

"And we'd use enough to fill an entire boxcar?"

"Every week—eventually."

"How do you know all this?" she pressed.

"Like I said, I asked Tom," Icky said.

"When?"

"When he was here the last time," Icky answered.

She didn't recall that conversation at all.

"We were sitting right here at the kitchen table while you finished making dinner," he reminded her. "He also said Pillsbury was the source on that *Biscuit and Cracker Baker* story."

"That part I remember. The reporter was interviewing Tom's boss, and he mentioned Icky's Cookies as an example of a bakery that's doing things right."

"And then we talked about shipping by rail, and Tom said the flour would be delivered right to our loading dock," Icky concluded.

"You've thought through all the details," Millie tried to reconcile his determination.

"I hope so."

"But we'd need to take out a business loan?" Millie cautioned.

"We might," Icky insisted. "We've grown enough to be seen as a solid member of the business community now, so we've earned the right to expect a good bank rate."

Millie exhaled, and shook her head: short, little quivers to shake off the idea of going into debt again.

"Are our two existing bakeries really busting at the seams?" she challenged one last time.

"If we don't fix this, we're going to be turning down orders," he said. "And if we do that, distributors will go elsewhere to fill their shelves. Once an opportunity is lost, we might not be able to get it back."

She knew he was right.

"Here we go again," she said, half-heartedly.

37

Getting Trashed

Icky twisted the *Salamanca Republican Press* in his fist and flung it forcefully into the wastebasket behind his desk. "This guy plays dirty."

"Who?" Millie asked as she slipped unexpectedly into his office.

"Sorry," he said, self-conscious over exercising a tantrum. "I didn't see you there."

"Who?" she repeated.

"That mayor." Only a month earlier, the guy leaked a story on how his administration was bending over backward to help Haut's Cookie Shoppe find a property for its expansion. Icky had asked him not to announce those talks publicly since nothing was finalized—which the mayor agreed was prudent. But then an article came out—which he claimed was leaked by someone in his office without his okay.

"Another story on the expansion," Icky nodded at the wastebasket. "This time he's trying to cover his tracks—which he wouldn't have had to do if he'd kept his mouth shut in the first place."

"He's trying to explain why the negotiations failed then?" Millie guessed.

"And the way he sees it, somebody has to be blamed."

"Us," she surmised.

"And the Seneca nation."

"The Seneca nation? What do they have to do with this?"

"The whole town of Salamanca is located on the Allegany Indian Reservation of the Seneca Nation," Icky said.

"Everybody knows that."

"Well, not everybody knows that the Seneca people also own right-of-way access to the railroad. Without that access, the property we were interested in wouldn't get a rail siding. And as it's turned out, we were one of several applicants looking to lease that access."

He paused. "Somebody outbid us—by a huge amount," he finally revealed.

"Is that why the mayor's office was pushing other properties on you, too?" she asked.

"Yeah, but none of those lots have rail access," he said, "and I told him weeks ago that that would be a deal breaker. I guess he saw our decision not to build there as a threat."

"Because he's worried that we'll close our Salamanca operation when we consolidate somewhere else?"

"Right," Icky said.

"But that's probably true," Millie pointed out, "isn't it?"

"Of course. But now he's tipped off our employees—again."

"Can't we just tell them what's going on?"

"A business has a right to negotiate its deals in private," he insisted.

"Well, it's out in the open now!"

"And more talk will just drive up more speculation."

"So, you're upset because the mayor is shooting off his mouth," she confirmed.

"And I should have expected it," he admonished himself.

"You can't know what another person is going to do," she said.

He raised an eyebrow.

"Well, if Salamanca is no longer an option," she moved ahead, "what do you plan to do?"

"What about that five-acre site just on the other side of Marcus Park?" he revealed.

"It's probably zoned Residential."

"I thought so, too, and it is—technically. But Frank Charles says that since it's on the far side of the park and next to other businesses, it should have been zoned as Industrial years ago."

"You already met with the architect?"

"No, I just rang him up to ask a couple of questions. He drove over there, and said that lot would be fine for a bakery."

Icky paused with a twinkle in his eye.

"So, we made an offer on it," he said.

"We did?"

"I thought I'd wait to tell you until I knew the seller's response."

"Don't you need my signature?" Millie looked sideways at him, her Irish blood rising.

"When we close—if they accept our offer," he agreed.

"You're sure about this lot?" she asked. "It's got railroad access and everything else?"

"Everything," Icky said. "And it's only two blocks away. I can walk to work."

"If you're ever in town!" she pointed out.

"Okay, when I'm not on the road," he allowed. He gave her a moment to consider what he'd done. "You're not saying anything."

"It's just that every time I think about this expansion idea, I feel like we're going to be drowning in debt—again," she said. "And that last *Republican Press* article said the new bakery will cost a hundred fifty thousand dollars."

"That came from the mayor—not me," Icky said.

"So, it won't?" Millie asked.

"I would never share a number with the public," Icky evaded.

"How much will it be then?" Millie insisted.

"The current estimate—which is based on the price of the lot, architectural drawings, construction, new equipment, and a 20 percent cushion for who-knows-what—is about a half a million dollars," Icky said, and then added, "more."

"More?" she exclaimed. "That's six hundred fifty thousand!"

"We'll be baking a lot of cookies," he confirmed.

#

The next morning, Icky and Millie walked across the street and cut through Marcus Park to see the five-acre site he'd selected. He wanted her to visualize how their new bakery might be situated.

"We'd put the building here, facing this way," Icky swept his arm over the tract next to N. Fifteenth Street."

She turned to picture it.

"And over there would be a parking lot," he continued. "And land for a siding line is there, right next to the railroad tracks."

Millie stepped away and walked around the five acres by herself so she could soak in the enormity of Icky's decision.

"This lot meets all your criteria," she said as she returned to him.

"So you agree?"

"Don't I always?" But the truth was that her role in the business had changed. It had been years since she worked shoulder-to-shoulder with him in the bakery, so new employees saw her not as a part-owner or even a former member of the crew, but merely as the boss's wife. Magazines lining grocery check-out aisles told her to step back, too, with articles on the evolving role of corporate wives: "The woman who wants to rise up in the world will support the man who takes her there."

She didn't know if she agreed with all that. Still, the expansion plans were all his.

"Who will you hire to build this time?" she asked as they walked home.

"Charles will recommend someone," he answered. "We've got to get this right."

"Now you sound like your father," Millie noted, adding, "How long will it take?"

"I'm guessing it could be a year. In the meantime, . . ."

"I know," she added, "we've still got orders to fill!"

38

Fumes

"Haut's Cookie Shoppe. How may we help..."

"Has he seen today's newspaper?" The caller didn't even say "hello"—but he didn't need to. Everybody in town knew that crusty voice.

"One moment, please, Mr. Shane. I'll put you through to his office." Marion hit the hold button and scurried out to retrieve *The Olean Times-Herald*, all the while bellowing over her shoulder, "Icky! Sid Shane is on line one! He wants to know if you've read today's paper."

Icky frowned. If his attorney called, it couldn't be good. "What's the poison?" he said as he picked up the call; he didn't bother with "hello" either.

"Baseless editorial," Shane spat an accusatory fragment. "They're challenging that petition we filed, and grilling you—publicly and personally—for rushing it through Common Council."

The newspaper landed on Icky's desk with a thud as Marion returned to her desk to attack the last of her paperwork for the day. She needed to leave on time for a change. Her daughter was in a school program that evening, and she didn't want to be late.

"Rush? We've been working toward this expansion for months," Icky countered as he thumbed through the pages—even though he could guess what they'd uncovered. He'd messed up, and then called Shane to fix it—fast.

"Apparently, they don't see it that way," Shane countered.

Icky found the article and gave it a quick glance while the attorney kept talking.

"So far, none of their objections—noxious fumes, noise, vibrations—have any merit," he continued.

"Noxious fumes?" Icky repeated skeptically. "A bakery puts out fumes?"

"They're pointing to environmental hazards—like another Donora." A half day's drive south, near Pittsburgh, Donora was the site of one of the worst pollution disasters in the nation's history.

"Donora and *industrial fumes*," Shane continued the guilt-by-association threat, adding, "and you're looking to rezone that five acres from Residential to *Industrial*."

"We filed under 'Industrial' because that's the category required for commercial bakeries," Icky argued. "And Donora was a decade ago!"

"And air pollution is big news now. Even Winchell called Donora's fumes a 'killer fog' and 'an act of God,'" Shane cautioned. "It's been repeated in the news all week. A ten-year anniversary can do that."

Icky remembered the Donora stories—especially the one that ran in the sports section. The whole town had turned out for a football match between local rivals, but the smog was so thick that nobody could see the pigskin. The game was still in the first quarter when the stadium's public address system blasted an emergency message telling the school's star tight end to "Go home! Go home now!" Fans booed because they thought it was a prank. The kid took it seriously, though, and ran, uphill all the way. Unfortunately, when he pushed through his parents' front door, he was too late. His father was dead.

"They called it acid rain," Icky remembered. More than twenty people died—and Walter Winchell's broadcast made it national news. "But that was a zinc factory spewing gasses up into fog . . ."

"—and trapping it in the Monongahela Valley," Shane interrupted.

"And your point is . . . ?"

"Olean is in a valley, too," he said. "The editorial also points out your neighbors' rights." He wasn't going to be put off.

"Listen," he expanded, "it's all speculation and innuendo, but even so, it could cause a problem if residents in the west end get riled up."

"What . . . ," Icky dragged each word through a slow cadence to suggest he was remaining calm, which he wasn't, "is . . . behind . . . this?"

"I'm . . . not sure," Shane mimicked the full weight of a lawyerly pause. "On slow news days, reporters sometimes dig into rezoning applications."

"But this article isn't in the *news* section," Icky contended.

"No, it's an editorial: somebody's opinion—like they think you're hiding something."

"Hiding what? We already operate a bakery right here, in the same neighborhood."

"Maybe they think home owners ought to worry about their properties being devalued if a factory elbows its way in. Fear can be a terrible motivator."

"It's not going to be a 'factory', not like this suggests," he refused to yield. "And baking cookies doesn't cause air pollution!"

"I know that. You know that. Maybe this writer even knows it," Shane allowed. "Or maybe he thinks residents haven't considered all the ramifications."

"What ramifications? You said it's a bunch of speculation," Icky returned.

"And it is. But the property you want rezoned is a full block from your current operation—and it abuts Marcus Park."

Shane thought he could hear Icky's blood percolating. He knew he'd been up to his neck with business complications before, but this situation was different. He could lose everything.

"Maybe your proposed expansion isn't real to your neighbors . . . until it is," Shane added. "I'm just considering every angle—because we *don't* know what's behind this piece."

"The last thing I need is somebody else criticizing how I run my business," Icky said. He was still burning over Salamanca's mayor's remarks blaming the bakery for tax revenue losses his town should expect if Haut's Cookie Shoppe moved out. Now it looked like the Olean press was cooking up trouble, too. "Just tell me this: How can they put out unsubstantiated drivel?"

Shane wouldn't comment on what newspapers could and couldn't print. He'd had enough experience with knife-edge political ambiguity to know how an editorial could affect a ballot box or sway a town council decision.

"We'd never get into a business that hurts people or devalues somebody's home," Icky continued. "We live in the west end, too."

"That little detail didn't make it into this article," Shane noted.

"What's the bottom line then?" he finally asked. "Are you concerned that the application will be denied?"

"Like I said, I didn't think so when we filed, but that was before this thing hit the streets."

Icky pinched the bridge of his nose to keep his head from exploding.

"I could intervene on your behalf when Common Council takes up your application, but it would be better, I think, for *you* to attend the meeting. And maybe," Shane paused to formulate a strategy, "maybe you can use this editorial to your advantage."

"How's that?" Icky asked.

"Pollution stories are hot these days, but business expansion news still leads the front page, so . . . ," he was thinking out loud, "have your communications guy skip *The Olean Times-Herald*, and pitch one of those new television stations up in Buffalo. Use the slant that your new bakery will create jobs.

"Then, tell them you're appearing before Common Council—both to support your petition, and to contest that editorial," he continued. "Television news is in competition with the press, so the broadcast producer might see your personal involvement as an inside scoop. If they go for it, a segment on your bakery's rapid growth could air on the evening news before the next newspaper lands on doorsteps."

Icky hesitated, gritting his teeth.

"I don't know if . . . ," he despised under-the-table gamesmanship and arm-twisting. And he sure didn't want to be interviewed on television.

"Even though you've got a good chance of getting the votes you need, Council members will protect their own skins first—which means that if public opinion goes against you, they could delay a decision. Or maybe even . . ."

"Or deny it?" Icky finished the sentence.

"Yes, or deny it," the attorney suggested. "Look, you don't have a lot of time to waste. But on the positive side, if the vote does go your way, that editorial page writer will think twice before he puts out another piece that gets bigtime Buffalo egg on his face."

Icky knew Shane was right: the situation needed to be dealt with. He hated politics, though.

"I'll deal with Council," Icky finally agreed. "And I'll think about calling the agency."

"I think that's the best plan," Shane ended the call. "You'll do fine."

"Right," Icky acknowledged flatly. "Thanks for tipping me off."

He locked his desk's belly drawer, grabbed the newspaper, and almost made it out the door before the phone rang again. He glanced toward his secretary's desk: line two, so it was an internal call, probably from one of the guys in the bakery out in Salamanca.

"Blast," he said under his breath as he returned to his desk and grabbed the line.

39

From Every Direction at Once

"Yeah? Now what?" Icky demanded as soon as he answered the line.

"Icky! Have you seen the Olean newspaper yet?" Harry asked.

"That editorial? What about it?" he fell back into his chair.

"One of the second shift girls is passing it around, and she's got everyone stirred up. They want to know if you're closing down operations in Salamanca, and if they're gonna' lose their jobs."

Icky inhaled roughly through his nostrils just as Millie peeked in to let him know dinner was almost ready. She took a chair opposite his desk while he finished the call; he slid *The Olean Times-Herald* toward her, and tapped on the editorial at the top of the page.

"No one is losing . . . !" he stopped short of making promises he might not be able to keep. "We filed a rezoning application. It's a good thing, not a bad thing."

"That's what I said, but I think they need you to tell them, face-to-face."

Icky glanced at Millie. She was scanning the article to see what was going on.

"Normally, I could handle this myself," Harry continued. "But remember how the mayor was spouting off in the *Salamanca Republican Press* about how much he's done for the bakery, and how he's not to blame if we don't build here? Well, that started everyone wondering. Now, this rezoning piece in the *Olean* newspaper has the girls really heated up. It's a mess over here."

"Okay, I get it. I'll head over and catch them at the end of their shift," Icky finished the call.

"You're driving out to Salamanca?" Millie asked. "You haven't even had dinner yet."

"Yeah, I know," he paused, considering whether or not he really needed to go. "Harry says one of the cutters brought the Olean newspaper into work, and she's spinning wrongheaded ideas on what that editorial means. I need to put a stop to it."

"What's this thing about?' she nodded at the newspaper.

"Our rezoning application," he answered. "One of our cutters is using it to cook up rumors about people losing jobs."

"But the article doesn't even make sense," she insisted. "First, it says we're pressuring Common Council to approve a rezoning application. Then it criticizes us for contaminating the neighborhood with cookie fumes. Fumes?"

"Yeah, well," he paused, "some of it's true, but they've twisted the facts." Millie didn't know he'd gone to Shane for help. He'd have to come clean. "Remember when the architect said our new lot would need to be rezoned from Residential to Industrial before we build?"

"Ye-es," she recalled, slowly.

"I thought he meant that he'd be responsible for that," Icky admitted. "He's not."

"Who is?" She could almost guess.

Icky aimed his thumb at his chest. "I should have contacted the attorney weeks ago—before we finalized the purchase of the lot."

"But the article says . . ." she began.

" . . . that Shane filed the rezoning paperwork yesterday," he interrupted. "And since it's being fast-tracked, the newspaper is asking why."

"But since it's filed . . . ," Millie began.

"It's filed, but not approved," Icky explained. "Common Council has to act on it, and if they turn it down, we're stuck with a five-acre parcel that has no value to us—not to mention the money we've got tied up in drawings. And we've already leveled the lot."

Millie nodded, finally putting the pieces together.

"But pollution?" she asked.

"Shane thinks the newspaper might be trying to connect our rezoning request to the kinds of industrial pollution that Donora had ten years ago," he continued.

"That's ridiculous," Millie objected. "Olean doesn't have heavy metals plants." But then she remembered a syndicated piece that ran the week before on how Pennsylvania was dealing with the aftermath of that disaster. "I guess the death rate in Donora is still higher than in surrounding communities."

"Maybe that's why reporters are looking for a pollution angle here," Icky speculated. "They're wrong about targeting a bakery, though."

"The article also makes it sound like we'll be infringing on our neighbors' rights," Millie pointed out. "And like it says, our new operation will be right down the street."

"Shane picked up on that, too," Icky said.

Millie sighed. "When does Common Council meet?"

"Next week," Icky said. "And Shane thinks I should defend the petition myself."

"*You?*" she exclaimed. She knew Icky didn't like to speak in public or be quoted in the press. Appearing before Council would make him vulnerable to both.

"He thinks a personal appeal in addition to our legal standing could help. Right now," he said wearily as he stood, "I need to get over to Salamanca." Before he got out the door, though, he saw Ma coming across the lawn with *The Olean Times-Herald* rolled up in her fist.

"Idkä!" she called him to attention as she came into the house. "In the newspaper is a bad story about your bakery!"

"So I hear, Ma," he said as he invited her up the steps and into the kitchen.

"They say that to the neighborhood your new building will be a danger! And the people have moral and legal rights to keep it out!" On the words "moral" and "legal" she slapped the kitchen counter with the paper.

"I've only glanced at it so far, Ma," he defended.

"Well, that's what it says!" she asserted. "What you going to do about it?"

"I'm going to study the article, beginning to end," he said in a measured voice. "Then I'm going to discuss it with my employees."

"One of the workers in Salamanca saw the newspaper," Millie tried to calm the air. "The bakery manager just telephoned to say they're concerned."

"Why is Salamanca worried about the pollution in Olean?" Ma probed.

"I don't know," he started.

But Ma lifted her chin in disbelief. She expected an answer!

"Remember a while back when Salamanca's mayor gave the *Republican Press* some self-serving pap because we decided not to expand there?"

She nodded, slowly.

"Well, now there's this opinion piece in *The Olean Times-Herald*, and . . ."

"*Jawohl!*" Ma's accent revealed she was firing up her position again. "First, Salamanca writes bad things about the bakery, and now it's Olean!"

"It's nothing to worry about, Ma. I just . . ." he considered careful phrasing. "I just need to clarify what's going on."

She contemplated his response.

"This you will fix then?" she intended to force a commitment.

"I was leaving to talk to the Salamanca crew when you came in the door," Icky said.

"And when you finish with them, you call this reporter, and tell him to take back his words!" she held up her newspaper.

"Do you want to make the call?" he offered. In the background, he heard the phone ringing in the offices downstairs. He'd let the answering machine pick it up this time.

"No, of course not," she declined quickly. She'd never interfere with his bakery. She would, however, speak her piece when it came to friends and neighbors!

"You fix this, and you do it now, before everyone starts to come outside and fuss, or talk about us on the telephone." Party line gossip would roll into a full boil in no time. "We need to tell them it's all okay."

"Thanks, Ma," he patted her arm. "I'll do it as soon as I finish reading the article."

"And when you do, you will see that about this I am right!" she insisted.

He wouldn't argue. Not with Ma.

The kitchen phone rang, and Icky immediately thought it could be the caller he ignored when the office telephone rang.

"I'm not here," he told Millie as he kissed her goodbye, and stepped out the back door before she answered the phone. He slid into the car, jammed the key into the ignition, twisted it with his fist, and revved the engine. The Coupe snapped to attention, but the air conditioning system rebelled by blowing frigid air up his suit's pantlegs.

"Blast!" he aimed an index finger at the fan lever and slid it to the left, roughly. Then, cracking the window, he allowed that maybe he ought to cool down before pulling out onto the street. He kept the car in Park, and spread the newspaper out on the steering wheel.

"Let me look at this thing," he grumbled as he thumbed through the pages.

40

Stoked

When Icky finally read the entire editorial, beginning to end, he was both relieved and irritated: relieved because the piece had no merit, so any objections the Common Council might throw at him probably could be overcome; and irritated because getting embroiled in politics stole precious time away from his business.

Still, he was grateful Shane had let him know about the piece before he heard it from his bakery staff.

As he pulled the Coupe onto Sullivan Street, he hoped that the editorial was all he had to worry about. The timing of Shane's call, as soon as the newspaper came out, made him wonder whether or not something else was also going on. The attorney's background as Chairman of the Democratic party in Cattaraugus County and his wide client list provided an insider's perspective on all sorts of political arm-twisting and under-the-table deals. And since he'd referred to the story as "speculation and innuendo," he might know more than he was saying.

Or maybe Shane was just making sure I saw it, he allowed.

He exhaled, trying to expel self-doubt. This problem isn't like Mace Bolles firing me. Back then, my whole career exploded into smithereens, the way a tiny pinprick destroys a balloon. He frowned as he remembered their confrontation—not out of regret, but perhaps as a reminder of his own obstinacy. Or tenacity. Yes, that's how he'd define it. But I refused to give in, and we started our own bakery. As it's turned out, we made the right move at the right time—not that we planned it so well. The larger truth is the one Millie always holds on to: we had no options, or at least none we could think of. We had kids to feed.

His thoughts wandered as he turned the corner at West State Street. I hope I'm not as oblivious to employee discord as the people in Donora were to pollution. For years, they ignored the smelly air they were breathing in. And nobody—not the plant superintendent or the health department director or even the county coroner—ever connected the zinc emissions to rising health problems. Even when that fog rolled in and workers started dropping, local officials didn't figure it out.

Or maybe they knew and the cost of solving it was higher than they were willing to pay. Some folks just want easy answers to problems so they don't have to think too hard.

And they want somebody else to fix them.

He turned right onto Route 17 and headed west through Allegany. His thoughts shifted to the coming football season. Almost thirty boys are wearing our midget football uniforms this fall, starting with a game at the St. Bonaventure stadium this weekend. But our kids won't have any trouble seeing the ball. He shuddered at recalling the story about the Donora football player running home in poison air.

He redirected his thoughts to the reason he was heading to Salamanca. Now, one of my own bakery employees is stinking up the air with rumors and idle talk. What next?

#

"I don't know what my family will do if the bakery shuts down," one of the cutters said. "My kids need new winter coats this year, and . . ."

"Forget new coats," a second one interrupted. "I'm just glad to earn enough money to put food on the table."

"Our car needs tires," said a third.

"People working the line are always last to get clued in to what's going on," the first continued to complain. Her husband worked at Clark Brothers, building equipment to fulfill U.S. military contracts.

"We don't work an assembly line!" contended the girl next to her.

"What do you call this!" the first stood her ground.

"It just isn't right!" the second cutter interjected.

"Hush! I'm falling behind," the third protested.

"They can just keep their production standards!" the first menaced, defiantly.

After a moment, the second cutter said, "I hope you're wrong about this."

"Uh-oh," noticed the third cutter. "Look who just walked into Truman's office."

They all turned toward Harry's door as Icky arrived.

"The boss probably drove that Cadillac over here," the first accused as she jabbed her chin toward the parking lot. "You can't afford tires, and he's driving a fancy car."

"He's the boss," the second disagreed.

"And we're the ones doing all the work that puts money into his pocket," the first snarled.

#

"Fill me in before we meet with them," Icky stepped into Harry's office. The pace of his words suggested that if he had to drive out to Salamanca to handle an employee issue, he was going to be sure it got straightened out right. "I want to know more about these rumors."

"Sam will be here in a few minutes," Harry said. "I phoned your house to let you know that I called him, but Millie said you'd already left. Anyway, I thought it would be good for the crew to have their old boss with us when you tell them what's going on."

"Now, why would I do that?" Icky challenged.

"Tell them what's going on?" Harry repeated his assumption as a question. "I thought that's why you drove over."

"I'm here to deal with the trouble-makers you called about," Icky corrected.

"All they want to know is how that editorial is gonna' affect them," Harry clarified.

"And they'll find out when it's time for them to know," Icky's irritation began to rise. "Until then, it's nobody's business!"

After a brief pause, Harry continued, "Okay, but maybe you also want to say something to calm them down. Because if you don't, production numbers are going to be off."

"They're threatening a slow down?" Icky asked abruptly.

"No, that's just a fact. When the girls get upset, they can lose their focus. You know how it is . . ."

"Sorry I'm late," Sam arrived. "Josie tracked me down at the ball park. The boys had a game this evening."

"We were just talking about how upset everybody is," Harry cleared his throat.

"I haven't seen the Olean newspaper," Sam admitted. "How bad is it?"

"It's not a news story; it's just an editorial—and a bunch of hooey," Icky answered, "but Harry says one of the girls is getting everybody fired up over it."

"Who?" Sam asked, though he could guess.

"One of the cutters," Harry reported. "You know."

Sam nodded.

"Rumors were floating around when you bought Tasty, too," Sam advised Icky. "Same kind: Was I closing? Selling out? Were they losing their jobs?"

"I didn't know that," Icky said.

"I didn't think you needed to know," Sam defended. "And I handled it."

"Handled it how?"

"I told them not to worry, and that I'd give them more information in a few days—which I did. We closed the sale pretty fast, and you came in with all this new business. Remember?"

"Something like that," Icky said. What he recalled was that the crew was slow to make the switch from baking bread to producing cookies. Maybe Millie was right. Maybe he did need to tell them about the bakery's expansion. Not all the details, she suggested, but maybe just enough to get everybody back on track.

But, no. He still believed they had no right to evaluate how he was doing his job! And even if they did question him, he couldn't respond until after the Common Council meeting—because if the rezoning application wasn't approved, the bakery's future wasn't going to be the one he'd hoped for, and there wouldn't be anything to announce.

"What I'm worried about is that if you don't give them some straight dope, there's going to be a feeding frenzy over any little leak that comes their way," Harry insisted.

"And what would be the source of that leak next time?" Icky challenged.

"I don't know," Harry said protectively. Then, rattling the paper, he added, "I didn't expect this thing in today's newspaper, but here it is."

Icky nodded. At first he thought Harry was suggesting some other outside source was hovering. Like the article in *Biscuit*. Or like the employee in Salamanca's City Hall who tipped off the mayor when he bought Tasty. Or later, when the mayor scooped him in the local press. Somebody somewhere always seemed to be nosing into what he was doing.

"Worry breeds distrust," Harry continued.

"And in today's strong-armed union environment, an us-versus-them attitude can promote paranoia," Sam hinted at the trouble in Detroit and Cleveland that led to the *Biscuit* story.

"I hope that's not how it is around here," Icky insisted, adding, "but I hear you. Even if the crew isn't entitled to know what I'm working on, I can confirm that we're continuing to grow. But they better hear another message, too, loud and strong. They have their jobs to do, and I have mine. And I don't like being cornered!"

#

"Before you leave this evening, we want to address an editorial that appeared in today's Olean newspaper," Sam said to the employees gathered in the break room.

The new cutter who brought the newspaper into work sneered an I-told-you-so look toward her team members.

"Harry and I know that some of you may be concerned about what it means—just the way you were worried when Tasty was purchased by Haut's Cookie Shoppe," Sam continued.

"No one knew this piece was going to show up," Harry defended. "If the reporter had said something ahead of time, well, things might have gone different."

"Thanks, Sam, Harry," Icky stepped in. "A while back, Salamanca's mayor took us to task in the *Republican Press* for not purchasing a piece of property that the town wanted to sell. If you saw that story, you probably figured out that we're working on a plan to grow the bakery again."

Heads nodded throughout the staff.

"Now, in the years since you joined the Haut's Cookie Shoppe family, you've seen a lot of growth," Icky continued. "We added second and third shifts to meet increasing orders. We expanded into the building next door. And we built this nice break room that you're all enjoying. Right?"

They nodded again.

"From where I sit, this growth points to a strong, vital company. But then today, I get a telephone call because some of you are passing around this editorial," he held up *The Olean Times-Herald*, "and suggesting that it means that we're planning to shut down. Or that jobs are going to be eliminated, or that your pay is going to be reduced.

"Where's the logic in that nonsense?" he crossed his arms in front of his chest.

Employees' eyes shifted, avoiding association with the production crew who had been stirring up trouble.

"I drove over this evening to tell all of you that spreading rumors doesn't cut it around here," Icky said forcefully. "When we have something to report, you'll hear it—from me! Not from some newspaper! And definitely not from gossip! Any questions?"

No one said anything.

"Good, because if you want to be part of this bakery's future, you need to be on board with its growth. That means keeping up production standards, every day, without wasting time on opinion pieces—especially when they're coming from some guy who refers to the scent of freshly baked cookies as 'fumes'!

"You'll hear more about our plans when the time comes," Icky continued. "Until then, I expect your best work to continue."

He marched out.

"Thanks for staying," Harry said to the employees as he followed Icky to the door.

"We appreciate it," Sam concurred, lingering behind. He'd hired some of the original crew who moved from Tasty to Haut's Cookie Shoppe, and he knew they needed to see that he was on their side.

41

Nobody's Leaving and Nobody's Getting Fired

MILLIE SET A BOTTLE of Southern Comfort on the counter and moved two martini glasses into the refrigerator to chill. She'd keep watch for the Coupe's headlights to flash in the kitchen window as she made a couple of deviled eggs. Icky missed dinner before going to Salamanca, and while she knew he wouldn't want much to eat at night, he couldn't drink on an empty stomach either. Maybe he'd like cheese and crackers, too.

A few minutes later he pulled in, and saw Millie in the kitchen. He knew she'd still be up, waiting. She always was.

"Two of these with stems?" she lifted the bottle of maraschino cherries as he came through the door.

"Mind-reader," he eyed the plate of cheese and crackers. "Thanks."

"You're welcome," she set deviled eggs on the table, too. "You didn't have dinner."

He shrugged.

"How's Salamanca?"

"Okay—for now. I just told 'em they'd know more soon, and until then, they ought to mind their own business."

"I bet that went over well," she hinted.

"The drive home gave me time to think about this rezoning application," he continued, missing her sarcasm.

"So you're definitely representing the bakery yourself before Common Council," she repeated her earlier concern.

"Yeah," he wouldn't elaborate. "The editorial also said something like 'people have rights, moral and legal!' Remember Ma slapping the newspaper against the counter with those words?"

"I do," Millie answered.

"Well, I'm going to meet adversity face-to-face," he said. "I'm going door-to-door to ask our neighbors what questions they might have about our plan to build. If they're okay with it, Common Council won't have any reason to deny our request."

"But," Millie cautioned, "the members of the Council are politicians."

"So?"

"Sometimes their decisions are less about facts, and more about perceptions."

Shane made the same observation.

Icky lifted his martini glass and wearily proclaimed, "*Dienst ist Dienst und Schnaps ist Schnaps.*" Looking over its rim at Millie, he said, "Pa says it sometimes: 'Work is work and liquor is liquor.' Today felt like all work, no liquor—until this," he nodded at the glass.

Millie nodded.

"When you talk with the neighbors, you could ask them to sign a paper showing their support. You know: one of those forms with a question at the top, like, 'Do you approve of Icky's Cookies building a new bakery next to the park?' Then you'll have proof that Council can't ignore when you get to the meeting."

When he didn't respond, she said, "It's just an idea."

"It's a good one," he finally agreed. "Politicians like to see signatures on a page; it's how some of them got their names on the ballot."

"And if the neighbors sign, you could let them know when the Council meeting is being held. Maybe they'll show up."

Icky doubted anybody would want to sit through a boring Common Council meeting, especially when the most exciting item on the docket would be a rezoning application.

"I don't think anyone would go to that," he disagreed. "I wouldn't."

"Just mention it," she pressed.

#

"Are you going to talk with Marion about creating that signature form?" Millie asked Icky the next morning as she poured him a second cup of coffee.

"Yeah," he said. "If she can get it done quick, I can walk around the neighborhood with a clipboard on Saturday."

"Good plan," she agreed before posing a second issue she'd been pondering. "Did you ever think about how many things Marion does that aren't really her job?"

"Huh? What are you talking about?"

"She does a lot of extra things," Millie prodded. "Like that form. It's for the bakery, but it's extra."

"No, this is part of her job," Icky contended.

"What about setting up appointments with executives you wanted to talk to in support of the Amateur Baseball League. That was an ABL project."

"But we sponsor a men's team, so that was bakery work," Icky insisted. "What's your point with all this?"

Millie sat up straight, and said, "I heard her complain to herself as she came up the stairs to go out to the bakery to find you. She tracks you down like that all day long, and it interrupts her other work. I just wonder whether or not it might be time to add a second person to the office staff."

Icky didn't say anything.

"She was hired to support you like Jean did. But now we're a whole lot bigger, and she's helping not only you, but Derby and Harry, too," she said. "Something's got to give."

"What are you suggesting?"

"Talk with her," Millie said. "Ask which tasks she'd like to unload onto someone else, and then hire a second person who'd be good at doing those other things.

"And while she's writing an ad for that person," Millie continued, "she can run one for a salesman."

Icky set his coffee cup on the table and looked straight at his wife.

"Because if we're building, you can't be on the road all the time," she insisted. "You need to be here, making decisions."

He knew she was referring to how he missed filing that rezoning application.

"Aha! That's what you're really getting at!"

"I'm an equal-opportunity mediator," she admitted. "I take everybody's side."

"I think you mean equal-opportunity 'meddler,'" he said off-handedly.

"Nope," she disagreed. "An outsider is a meddler. I'm still a part owner, so I'm a mediator." She'd stand her ground this time.

#

"Marion, come here," Icky called from his office. "I need you to make up a form."

She rolled her eyes, grabbed a notepad and pen, and stood in front of his desk.

"When does it need to be done?" she asked, "because we've got a lot going on today."

"Friday noon," he ordered as he pushed a handwritten page toward her. "After I okay the draft, I'm going to need copies, so you'll have to either type out a few pages, or ask the ad agency to mimeograph something. You know what I mean."

"What's this for?" she read the question at the top. "And what are all these lines?"

"They're for signatures. I'm going door-to-door on Saturday to ask the neighbors if they have a problem with us building our new bakery down the block. Then I'm delivering their signatures to Common Council."

"Is this about that stupid opinion thing in yesterday's *Times-Herald*?" she asked, "'cause nobody with half a brain is gonna' pay any attention to that! . . . Er, wait a minute," she changed her mind. "You said this is for Common Council. That's a whole group of half-brainers. I see your point."

"Regardless," Icky ignored her critique, "just move typing this form to the top of your to-do list."

He caught himself giving orders.

"Another thing," he commanded since he was on a roll. "You better sit down for this one."

"If you say so," she pulled over a chair. This must be a doozey if he wants me to sit, she thought to herself.

"We need an employment ad," he began. "Figure out what you like to do least, and write a job description. Then, run an ad in Sunday's paper, interview candidates, and recommend somebody."

She stared at him.

"You . . . you're firing me?" she snapped.

"Of. Course. Not!" Icky enunciated each word abruptly. "We're adding another person, and since you pretty much run this office, you get to decide what work you want to hand off. Just be sure the new girl likes doing that sort of thing—whatever it is."

"Oh!" she said with surprise in her voice. She didn't think he noticed how busy she was. "Okay, then," she continued, "if it's up to me, I'd get rid of the daily production schedules and the weekly inventory restocking, which is actually twice a week with both bakeries, plus all the other stuff that goes with operations.

"I'm better at keeping you in line," she added without thinking.

He closed his eyes, and shook his head. Marion thought she heard marbles rolling around.

"You know what I mean: handling your calls, typing your letters, making multiple copies of your recipe cards every time you formulate a new cookie, dealing with the ad agency and holding off magazine reporters, and soon there's gonna' be a lot of calls about this new bakery you're putting up. And also stuff like this form," she shook the paper. "I think this is called a survey, by the way. My point is that somebody else can support Derby and Harry."

"That sounds like a good division of labor," Icky allowed, though he wasn't sure he agreed with how much managing she thought he needed. Then again, maybe he did need someone to handle details. And paperwork. He had, after all, misunderstood the architect's comments with regard to filing that rezoning application.

"While you're at it," he continued, "draft up an ad for a new salesman, too. But hold on to that one for now. If this rezoning application is approved, you can run it."

"Now *you're* quitting?" she blurted.

She's 0-and-2, he thought to himself.

"I might," he set his jaw with obvious intentionality. "Or I might just need to hang around here and bother you while the new bakery is under construction."

"That makes more sense," Marion nodded. "Anything else?"

"That's enough for today."

"No kidding!" she agreed as she returned to her desk.

#

Marion was almost finished typing the newspaper ad for the new office girl when she decided to add one more qualification: "Reports to the boss, so employee must be able to work under extreme pressure. Cream puffs need not apply."

She placed that version on Icky's desk for his approval when she left for the day. He could use a little levity.

42

Getting Grilled

"You've got a call on Line One," Marion yelled into Icky's office. "It's the ad agency."

"I hope you have something good to tell me," he grabbed the call. He'd decided against Shane's idea about contacting the Buffalo television station to refute Olean's editorial. More to the point, he really didn't want to be interviewed.

"We've written a short piece for *The Olean Times-Herald* in support of your rezoning application," the exec said. "We'll send it over to your office by courier so you can approve it."

"Just tell me what it says," Icky snapped as papers rustled in the background.

"Okay, here it is. Ah, first the headline says the bakery is expanding and is expected to bake a quarter million packages every week," he said. "Then the copy announces the Common Council meeting, and ends with some good quotes from that interview you did with *Biscuit and Cracker Baker*."

"Okay, it's fine," Icky expected to finish the call.

"Good job with that trade magazine article, by the way," the exec added. "We can get you more of those industry stories if you like that sort of thing."

And then we'd have to pay you for designing ads and placing them, Icky thought to himself.

"Let's just see what happens with this Common Council situation," Icky said. "That's what we need to focus on right now."

"Do you want me to send over a copy of the press release?"

"Not necessary. Just go with what you've got," Icky decided.

"Right," the exec confirmed, "first thing Monday morning."

#

ICKY'S COOKIES TO BAKE 225,000 DOZEN COOKIES EVERY WEEK

A hearing to review a rezoning petition that would allow Haut's Cookie Shoppe to build a new forty-two thousand square-foot building in the west end will be reviewed by Common Council this week. Rezoning would require the city to grade and extend N. Fifteenth Street to the plant site. Leveling of the site by bulldozer was in progress last week.

A recent article in *Biscuit and Cracker Baker* magazine noted the Olean bakery's "good personnel relations," and referred to "high employee morale due to enlightened management."

Haut's Cookie Shoppe sells product under the Icky's Cookies® label. If rezoning is approved, the bakery expects to increase production to almost a quarter of a million packages of cookies each week. Common Council will consider the petition at its Tuesday, Oct. 9 meeting.

#

"Icky!" Ma called out when she saw him pull in. "Did you see today's newspaper? They wrote about your bakery again!"

She waved *The Olean Times-Herald* in the air as she paced briskly across their abutting yards.

"I know about it," he answered.

"A million packages of cookies every month: this your bakery will do?" she asked, surprised by the production estimates.

"That's what it says. Can you believe that?"

"Just because they write it does not mean you got to do it—even if they put it in the newspaper!" she insisted. "You tell them to fix that!"

"Okay," he agreed. "You go with me this time."

"Who ever heard such a thing!" she repeated.

"What's going on?" Millie joined them.

"This story!" Ma said. "The newspaper says Icky will bake a million packages of cookies every month!"

"Right!" Millie said. "They also mentioned the bulldozer. I thought it was a good indication that somebody downtown expects the rezoning request to be approved."

"I think we need to be prepared for either outcome," Icky cautioned.

"You talk to the newspaper this afternoon?" Ma asked again, still focused on the claim about the number of cookies coming out of the new bakery.

Icky shifted his attention to her concern.

"Maybe we ought to ramp up production first," he said. He had a bit of his father's jokester personality. Using his most serious face, he added, "To do that, we might need to use Millie's kitchen for a while again. And yours, too, Ma—like the morning when our first oven went kaput in the old Quonset hut bakeshop. Remember how we carried trays of raw dough over to your house to bake? Could you help again?"

Stunned by the revelation that the article might be correct, she stiffened her resolve. Of course, she'd never refuse to help her children when they needed her, but this request was . . . ludicrous!

Then she noticed Icky's face.

"Those eyes of yours are like your father's: Your lie is in them!" she said, relieved that her kitchen wouldn't be taken over by the bakery.

"The newspaper is right, Ma," he admitted. "We are projecting those numbers for the new location."

"*Ja?*" she asked with surprise in her voice again. "You grow your bakery that fast?"

"I think so!" he said. "And it isn't just our bakery. It's the whole economy. Times are good, so if we want to increase our business, we need to build again—and soon."

"My *Weihnachtsplätzchen* you won't need anymore," she said wistfully. She could tease, too, once in a while.

"We always need your Christmas cookies, Ma," Icky reassured her. "Our cookies are great, but nothing is as wonderful as the ones that come from your hands."

"Right," Millie agreed. "Yours are the originals, and as far as we're concerned, they're the only true *home*-baked cookies."

Ma smiled at her daughter-in-law, and then gave Icky a little shove in his shoulder. He deserved it for leading her on.

#

"How do I look?" Icky asked for Millie's approval before he left the house to attend the Common Council meeting. At forty-two years old, he wore a suit well—probably because carrying hundred-pound sacks of flour on his shoulders gave him stature and presence. This evening, he'd find out if he could rely on his guts to carry the future of his bakery.

"You look fine," she straightened his tie. "And you'll do fine. Just tell them how everybody in the west end supports the expansion."

"I think I've got everything," he said mechanically as he thumbed through his briefcase. He'd already stuffed in the clipboard with the signature pages. "Almost a hundred neighbors signed the petition, both husbands and wives, so we got twice as many as expected."

"And Ma said a few people plan to attend the meeting. She promised you'd bring cookies—which are boxed and packed in the car."

"The press will be there, too," he said, wishing they wouldn't show.

"They always cover Common Council meetings," Millie said. "This is nothing special to them."

"Okay, I'm leaving," he announced. "Wish us luck."

"Good luck!" she mustered a good measure of enthusiasm. But as the car pulled out of the driveway, the Irish in her fretted over the possibility that the application could be rejected. And if that happens, she said to herself, we're in deep trouble.

Icky parked near the Municipal Building, slid his briefcase over the top of the carton of cookies, and headed into the meeting. He didn't know what to expect, and immediately wished Sid Shane was representing the bakery.

"What was I thinking?" he chided himself as he grabbed a seat at the end of a row in the middle of the room, and set the cookies in the aisle. As he tried to calm himself, he noticed a couple people who signed his petition come through the door and take seats in the back. They must be the neighbors Ma encouraged to show up.

A minute later, two more people came in. Then a few more. Half of the chairs in the room were taken, right up to the row where Icky was sitting. He felt like they had his back.

A ritual of gavel-banging, calling to order, and announcement reading preceded the usual committee reports. Finally, the Council President, who was seated in the center of a long table at the front of the room, asked the Council Secretary to read the meeting docket.

"At the top of the agenda is a petition to rezone a property at N. Fifteenth and Sullivan Streets," he announced.

"The Council will now hear from representatives of the business community who have standing on this matter and any citizens who wish to speak," the President invited.

"You got cookies in that box?" one of the west end residents leaned forward and whispered in Icky's ear.

He nodded.

"We'll pass 'em out," she offered as she opened the flaps.

Icky stood, introduced himself, and laid out his case for rezoning the lot.

"Why is this application important?" one of the Councilmen asked. "Don't you already have a bakery in the west end?"

Icky heard plastic wrappers being torn open behind him. A moment later, one of his neighbors quietly slipped past him and walked to the Councilmen's table up front.

"You fellows shouldn't be left out," she said as she passed down several packages of cookies.

"Sorry, Icky," she said quietly as she returned to her seat. "I didn't mean to interrupt."

He smiled weakly at her.

"Your voice carried over that microphone!" her husband admonished when she sat down.

"Oh! Sorry!" she said loudly enough for Icky to hear.

The Council President had been studying the rezoning application throughout Icky's remarks, so when a package of cookies was placed in front of him, he simply unwrapped it without taking notice of where it came from. Other Councilmen followed his lead and opened theirs, too.

"As supermarket chains purchased or replaced independently owned grocery stores, the demand for cookies increased," Icky continued to explain. "For almost nine years, we've been meeting local needs, pursuing regional opportunities, and growing into a strong supplier in the nation's baked goods market.

"Now is the time to expand to a new building that will accommodate larger ovens and consolidate our operations," he continued. "We could build in Salamanca; we operate a larger facility there. The mayor in that city has gone on the record with how diligently he's worked to broker a deal for us—and it's no secret that we've considered that. But our hometown is Olean. This is where we live and where we started our business. So we'd like to hear what you have to say."

Just like when negotiating the price of imported fruits, he handed over to the Council the burden of trying to keep the bakery in Olean.

The Councilmen knew Icky's claims were true. When Haut's Cookie Shoppe purchased Tasty Bakery, Salamanca's mayor had mouthed off about how his town was taking business from Olean. That deal was an acquisition by an Olean-based business, of course. But since then, Icky had been active in both cities' business communities.

"What was that story in the *Republican Press* about some dinner recognizing your bakery over in Salamanca?" one of the Councilmen asked.

"Yes," Icky wondered where this line of questioning was going. "The Board of Trade honored us last month."

The Councilmen shared looks among one another, and mumbling started to build in the back half of the room.

"Haut's Cookie Shoppe is leaving?" he heard west end neighbors ask one another.

"I did not attend that event," Icky continued, "as I already had out-of-town appointments scheduled."

"They held a dinner for you, and you didn't go?" the Councilman asked, dubiously.

"The Reverend Frank Bauer attended on our behalf," Icky answered. "Since you're aware of that article, you no doubt also read his comments about our planned expansion. We've been working toward this for some time."

"What's the benefit to Olean?" another Councilman challenged.

"Jobs and tax revenue," Icky answered easily. "We employ nearly eighty people, more than half of them in Salamanca. As a result, most of the tax revenue we pay currently goes there, too. Once we build, we'll hire again," he continued.

"What kind of jobs? Baking? Clerical? Union?"

"Bakers, mixers, dough cutters, packagers—but no union," Icky said firmly. "With the new facility, we expect to quadruple capacity."

"That's . . . ," the Councilman paused to consider the numbers.

"Twelve million packages a year," Icky interrupted.

"Who eats all those cookies?" asked another.

"Everybody!" Icky said easily. "Don't you?"

The Councilmen were still munching, and Icky saw a photographer from *The Olean Times-Herald* swing around to take a few shots of them.

That'll be in tomorrow's newspaper—I'd bet on it, Icky told himself.

"So, you're now seeking Common Council's approval on this rezoning application, right?" the President redirected the discussion.

"Yes," Icky affirmed. "It's a five-acre parcel at Sullivan and N. Fifteenth Streets."

"*The Olean Times-Herald* reported yesterday that you've already started leveling the site," one of the Councilmen pointed out, "as if you expect approval from us."

"I own that property," Icky said. "If I want to level it, I am within my rights to do that. And there's already another business nearby."

"What kind?"

"Toppers. It's a beer distributorship," Icky moved the conversation away from an accusation disguised as an observation. The only legitimate objection to his expansion was truck traffic—but since Toppers was just down the block, that argument couldn't be held up as a reason against rezoning.

"What about families in the neighborhood? They might not like a bakery nearby."

"Why not?" Icky refused to accept vague assertions.

"Pollution," one of the Councilmen pressed.

"Such as?" Icky pressed again.

"The sort that drips over the edge of smokestacks—the way that coffee drips from the lip of a mug," another interjected as he lifted a cup with his company's logo on it. He thought his comment would make a good quote—and if the newspaper photographer took a picture, maybe it would earn him a few votes in the next election.

That Councilman's political theatricality is grating, Icky thought to himself, and hoped that no one else in the room seemed impressed.

"Vibrations also come to mind," another Councilman competed with self-important authority. "Marcus Park's playground is also nearby. I care about those children."

"First of all, Icky's Cookies is a bakery, not a manufacturing plant. Bakeries don't pound metal, so no children or neighbors will have to worry about noise or vibrations.

"As to pollution odors," he continued, "bakeries don't have dripping smokestacks. And as far as I know, a few whiffs of cookies coming out of our ovens have never offended anyone."

The Councilman who made the dripping-lip remark carefully slid paperwork over his coffee mug.

"I surveyed residents along Sullivan Street from N. Thirteenth Street to N. Fifteenth Street, and all along in between; they're closest to the site on our rezoning application. And I asked whether or not they'd approve a bakery being built on this property," Icky delivered his final blow as he handed over the clipboard. "Every one of them signed these papers in support of our expansion.

"Haut's Cookie Shoppe is a good neighbor," he concluded. "People in the west end like us. They like having us around. And they support our growth—on that lot, right next to Marcus Park."

"My signature is on that petition!" Jim Fleming spontaneously stood and raised his hand, which happened to have a half-eaten cookie in it. "Just thought I'd say so in case you need an in-person endorsement."

Council members passed the clipboard quickly across the front table, and then returned it to the President in the center. He glanced left and right, looking for remaining questions.

"Shall we call for a vote?" he finally asked.

"So moved," one said immediately.

"Seconded," said another.

"All in favor of rezoning the property at the corner of N. Fifteenth and Sullivan Streets from Residential to Industrial so as to accommodate a commercial bakery, raise your hand."

Icky remained standing as if he were a defendant in a trial, and held his breath.

The petition passed unanimously.

Everyone in the room stood and applauded! Icky, however, felt he'd just swallowed a full mouthful of how Olean politics and the press could interfere with his business. And even though his petition passed, the tenuous nature of the process tasted bitter. He picked up his briefcase and headed out the door, the unexpected crowd of neighbors at his heels as the photographer snapped up the action for the next day's newspaper.

A couple of the Councilmen rushed in to appear in the middle of the photos.

"After all," one of them said loudly enough for the press to hear, "we were the ones who approved that rezoning application. Somebody ought to quote us!"

They ignored him.

#

"We got it!" Icky announced as he came through the back door.

"Congratulations!" Millie greeted him with joy and relief. But Icky didn't look as happy as she expected. "Aren't you glad? Didn't you get everything you wanted?"

"We did, but first they raised a lot of objections."

"Like what?" She tried to imagine the Council's interrogation.

"The same nonsense that was in the editorial—like whether or not we'd be polluting the air."

"What did you say?"

"They were eating our cookies," his face finally relaxed, "so I suggested they take a whiff."

"What would you have asked if you were a Councilman?" she wondered.

"That's never going to happen!"

"But if it were up to you, what would you want to know?"

"I'd say we need to eliminate the whole process!" he answered gruffly. Then, in a more considered tone, he added, "Or maybe, since the town probably needs some sort of planning, Common Council could try to help businesses. They could ask themselves, 'How do we all make this work?' instead of, 'Who's going to get mad at us if we okay this application?'"

"Well, now that you know how they think, you're prepared if you ever have to deal with them again," Millie said.

"Let's hope we don't," Icky tossed his tie onto the bedroom dresser.

As they settled in for the night, she said, "You missed one of your favorite movies this evening."

"Which one?"

"*The Long Gray Line*."

"Yeah, one of my favorites," Icky agreed.

"I can see why," she continued. "The main character starts his career as a dishwasher, and by the end of the film, he's a non-commissioned officer."

"At West Point!" Icky added.

"And you started as a bakery laborer, and now you run your own business," she made an analogy.

"Are you saying that I remind you of Tyrone Power?" he suggested.

"He played an Irish immigrant in this film, right?" she continued, a smile in her voice. "I'm half Irish, so I guess it's natural for me to be attracted to that scrappy sort of fella."

"I thought he usually played romantic leads," Icky snuggled close.

"That's right," she agreed.

He paused for a moment.

"You know," he hesitated, "each kiss in a guy's life is a calculated risk."

"Oh? How's that?" she asked, coyly.

"The girl can always turn her face away."

"Well, you've had pretty good luck so far," she encouraged.

43

Hitting the Roof

For nearly a year, Icky watched his bank account slowly drain to cover the new bakery's construction costs. Soon he'd have to shell out payment for the roof, and his savings were scraping bottom. The time had come to seek financing, so he made an appointment to see a loan officer at the First National Bank at State and Union Streets.

Clerks who handled the bakery's accounts knew the reputation of Haut's Cookie Shoppe, and always greeted Marion or Millie when one of them came in to make deposits. But in the ten years since the bakery had been in business, Icky had established no borrowing history. No mortgage. No car loans. Nothing to indicate whether or not he'd be a good credit risk, except that all of his profits had been funneled into a bulging account.

"How much money do you need?" the loan officer finally asked.

"I think one hundred twenty-five thousand dollars should finish the job," Icky answered, matter-of-factly.

"That's a hefty sum," he noted, a noncommittal look on his face. He had just spent a year on the road, getting to know the bank's customers—an entry-level job to help new bankers meet the business community. In Olean, most were in the manufacturing sector. Some had long histories that smelled of money—and not copper pennies, but much-handled grimy bills passed around in under-the-table deals. Since that sort of financing wasn't unusual in the more mountainous parts of western New York state, he decided to dig into the baker's situation.

Pulling a form from his top right desk drawer and unscrewing the cap from his new Parker fountain pen, he prepared to take notes. "And what is the collateral?"

"The new building as far as it's up already ought to be enough," Icky said. "I got over four hundred thousand dollars in it so far."

"And who financed that?"

"I paid cash."

"And where did that come from?" the officer raised an eyebrow.

"My savings in this bank," Icky grew agitated. Didn't this guy look up Haut's Cookie Shoppe accounts before this meeting? He'd had a week's notice of this appointment, so it wasn't like he didn't have time to prepare. "Here's a summary from the architect."

The loan officer pushed back on the bridge of his glasses as he flipped open the folder and studied the documents. Drawings showed a large work floor, laboratories, fruit filling vat room, inventory and refrigeration areas, cafeteria, locker rooms and lounge areas for employees, and packaging and shipping.

"Frank Charles, Architect," he read out loud. An architect suggested quality that the bank could count on. "What's this laboratories line item? In a bakery?"

"When the government updates food regulations, they can require us to change our flour blend to meet the nation's nutrition needs. We've got to follow their requirements, but we don't just alter our recipes without testing an additive. You never know if it might change a product's flavor. Or its texture."

"Folic acid was the last one," he added casually.

"Acid?" the officer repeated, with just a pinch of alarm. "In cookies? How often does that happen?"

"It's just Vitamin B," Icky clarified, adding, "Or maybe the nation's grape harvest is bad one year, so raisins are expensive. But a good supply of dates is available, so we adapt our fruit cookie recipe to accommodate them."

"Is that such a big deal?" the banker made conversation. It was better not to reveal to a customer any concerns regarding financial risk. The possible shortage of an important ingredient wasn't a good sign.

"We process up to three tons of fillings each season," Icky clarified, "so yes, inventory flexibility is important. And we know what we're doing."

"I had no idea," the banker continued investigating. "How many different varieties of cookies do you produce."

"Fourteen, so far."

"And what about these mixers, ovens, cooling systems? How will you pay for them?"

"Already covered—and when the equipment is installed, that'll be another hundred and fifty grand in collateral."

"Oh!" the loan officer said, surprised. Maybe this loan opportunity was worth more attention than he initially thought. "We'll require a couple of days to look at your accounts."

He hadn't dedicated any of his valuable time to research them yet. Why would he, until he knew what the customer needed? That's how he saw it, anyway.

"You do that," Icky said, suspecting that the loan process was about to become boggled in forms, probably in triplicate, and passed upstairs for overpaid executives to sign. "But here's what you're going to find. We've been in business for over nine years, and we've paid all of our bills on time. We're making money, too, so if you've been paying attention to who your long-standing good customers are, you've seen us grow.

"But if all of that isn't good enough . . . ," he continued with understated authority.

"Well, uh . . . !" the banker tried to change his tone.

"I don't ask for help 'til I need it," Icky informed him. "But when I do ask, I don't expect to waste my day while all of you sit around some fancy table talking about it."

"What's the time frame you had in mind?"

"We're putting the roof on today, so . . . now," his jaw locked in place.

"Now?" the banker repeated with surprise.

"Yeah."

Icky thought one-word answers might help the guy see how this loan process needed to proceed if the bank wanted his business.

"Well, uh, you'll need to complete the application and sign some documents."

Icky hated paperwork.

"Like I said, there's no sense in me taking *my* time to fill out a bunch of forms when *you* got all the information you need in *your records*. Look it up."

The loan officer hesitated as he contemplated how simple rules of decorum ought to suggest the importance of showing deference when a man requests a large loan. Didn't this fellow know he ought to approach a lender with humility?

But Icky wasn't offering up any false subservience.

"It will take some time to move that much money from one account to another," the loan officer gently protested.

"And the roofers need to be paid as soon as their work is finished," Icky refuted as he stood. Pointing to the desk, he said. "I see you got some record-checking to do to fill out all those documents you mentioned, so I won't keep you any longer. You can bring 'em by for my signature if you decide to go ahead with this deal.

"I'll be at the bakery all day," he continued toward the door, "because that's where we do the work that brings in all the money we've been keeping in this bank over the past decade."

His message was clear: he was done explaining. If this loan officer wanted his business, all the bank needed to do was move numbers from a little column on one page to a little column on another page.

He, on the other hand, was going to get back to actually earning it.

"Thank you for your business, Sir," said the loan officer, realizing that this customer wasn't a hoop jumper. "I'll bring the paperwork by this afternoon."

"You got the address on my account," Icky nodded as he left.

#

"What did they say?" Millie asked when Icky came in the back door.

"The loan officer was some new guy who expected me to fill out a bunch of forms," Icky answered with a measure of disgust, "but I think he finally figured out how to get it done himself. If so, he'll bring 'em around for our signatures. I told him we need the money to be transferred by tomorrow."

"Good!" she approved.

"He knows they aren't the only bank in town," Icky said.

"You always say that about buying a car, too," Millie noted.

"And I always go back to the same guys at O'Laughlin's, don't I?" he smiled.

"Well, that's because they know how to treat people," she said.

"Goes both ways," he pointed out. "We earn their trust. They can earn ours, too."

44

Toasted

The headline on September 24, 1957 edition of *The Olean Times-Herald* business section announced, "Haut's Cookie Shoppe to Have Open House." The big news, the article asserted, is that "the bakery's two fifty-foot Werner recirculating heat ovens make Icky's Cookies a leader in the commercial food production industry.

"They give back all the flavor we put in," Ma read her son's words out loud to herself. "Even with the several varieties of hand-cut cookies, which can vary considerably, we get just the color we want every time, too."

That sounds very good, she decided. Didn't she look for the same quality in her own cookies? She did!

"We can let these ovens run empty right through the lunch hour without any danger of scorching the first batch when we start up again," the article continued quoting Icky. "In short, we count on them to give us the texture, color, and flavor Icky's Cookies is known for."

"How large is Icky's new bakery?" Ma asked Pa as he opened the back door. "Other bakeries: they are this big?"

"Are you ready?" he ignored her question as he guided her out so they could walk to the new bakery.

"We ask him how large when we get to the party," Pa decided. As they passed Icky and Millie's brick ranch house, he asked, "Remember when they put up that old Quonset hut?"

"*Ja*," Ma remembered. "Mary Lou was eleven, and Mark was a toddler."

"And then they got some accounts, and build their first little bakery," Pa pointed to the brick building across the driveway from the ranch. "Of course, that was just a couple of years after he almost blew up the hut by lighting a match to fix the first gas stove!"

"Don't remind Millie of that," she cautioned.

"A happy day for her: that one was not," Pa agreed.

"The two of them have done well—and good it is for our little family to succeed in this country," Ma reflected.

They crossed the street and cut through Marcus Park.

"We were young ourselves when to the United States we came," Pa said. "The children, they don't know the trouble Germany was in back then. No jobs. I had to leave."

"Same with my sister and me: we had to leave," Ma allowed without delving further into her own history. "Then I met you."

"And you shared with me some German cookies that you baked," he recalled.

"You liked them: this I remember," she said.

"*Ja,* so I got to marry you to get more of those cookies!"

She shoved his shoulder gently, even as they walked.

"Icky gets his first recipes from you," Pa pointed out.

"And I get them from my mother, before she was gone," Ma recalled.

"You remember, all these years?" Pa asked.

"*Ja.* Also, I add some imagination."

Pa nodded. He also knew her secret ingredient: love. Both Icky and she added it. It was what made their cookies special.

"He tells the newspaper he will bake almost a million packages of cookies every month now," she continued.

"No," Pa challenged. That couldn't be right.

"You do the numbers," she insisted.

He glanced at her in disbelief.

"*Ja!*" she held firm.

"I didn't charge Icky enough for that corner lot he put the first brick bakery on!" Pa decided. "I got to go back and fix that deal."

"I don't think you can do that," she said, her voice low.

"This is Olean," he argued. "We got lots of people who can strong-arm him."

"Your own son!" she said. "Don't say such a thing!"

"Okay," Pa said, "as long as he gives to us the cookies for free, we leave it."

"There you are," she said. He glanced at her with a husband's devotion. Ma was like an old stove pot: maybe a little dinged up from life's injustices, but still shiny on the inside where it mattered most. He thought it was the best compliment a woman could ever get.

He stepped aside for her to enter the new bakery first, and noticed how the door's hydraulic hinge sucked in air to keep it from slamming. Icky put quality into every part of this building, he thought to himself.

Immediately inside the little lobby was an easel featuring a double-page centerfold that ran in *The Olean Times-Herald*. It invited everyone in town to attend the Grand Opening.

"Look here," Pa said. "Photographs they show of people who work for Icky."

Ma read each of the names carefully: Carrol North, plant manager; Leo Derby, plant manager; William Johnson, supervisor, hand-cut cookies; Stanley Batesky, supervisor; Francis Hart, supervisor; Frank Neiler, supervisor; Frank Palmer, sales manager.

She gave thanks for everyone who helped make her son's bakery successful.

"Also, they show the office girls: Kathryn Gillespie, Orpha Start, Marion Simpson, and Mary Lou Haut!" Ma pointed out.

"Mary Lou has her name as an employee!" Pa said with pride.

"*Ja*, always in the summer the girl works."

"And Mark's photograph is here, too, with Icky and Millie," she added. No one in their little family was left out.

"We go in now, and see the rest," Pa insisted.

Balloons were tied to all the equipment, just as they were when the Salamanca plant transitioned from bread to cookies.

"Flowers in the bakery!" Ma exclaimed, pointing to the abundance of roses, lilies, carnations, daisies, and chrysanthemums, all of them arranged in lovely vases or large baskets, and tied with satin bows.

"Aren't they beautiful!" Millie greeted her in-laws. "More than two dozen bouquets! Everyone we've ever done business with sent them!"

"They thank you for the good work you do together!" Ma approved. Slowly, she removed cards and examined names of all the companies who wanted to help her son celebrate his success: Crosby Dairy, Durkee Famous Foods, Continental Can Co., Inc., Henry H. Ottens Mfg. Co., Armour & Co., Phil H. Knobloch Associates, Fairmount Food Co., A.C. Beverage, LCS Plumbing & Heating, The Exchange National Bank, Upstate Sales Co., Hardesty & Stineman, W. Shisler Trucking, Standard

Brands, Inc., McCourt Label Cabinet Co., Lever Bros. Co., A.E. Staley Mfg. Co., First National Bank of Olean, and Fischer Bakery of Ocala, Florida!

"Look here! Flowers from Roy and Herta!" Ma exclaimed.

"We sent flowers to them when they opened their new bakery in Ocala," Millie recalled. "These were delivered to the house, but since the two of them worked shoulder-to-shoulder with the crew, it seemed right to move their bouquet to the bakery."

"The first vase near the door is from Crosby Dairy," Ma noted. "This is where Icky buys milk for his recipes?"

"It certainly is," Millie said. "A couple of dairies provide other ingredients, but Crosby is his primary milk supplier."

"Interesting," Ma reflected.

"You know your son," Millie confirmed then, realizing that her mother-in-law had made the connection. Miss Crosby was Mace Bolles's niece.

"Our Icky is a good man," Ma said.

"Very," Millie agreed. "He knows he wouldn't be running his own bakery if Mr. Bolles hadn't given him an apprenticeship."

As for her, she'd been frosted when that old man fired her husband and put their family at risk—and with a one-year-old, no less! Once Icky found his way, though, she was determined to leave those feelings behind. Mostly, anyway.

"*Ja*, he never holds a grudge," Ma said. But she, too, had found it difficult to give up her anger toward Mace Bolles for turning on Icky. What sort of person would do such a thing to a man with a family! But now, in looking back, she could see the Lord's hand, for hadn't God been with them through all of their trials?

"From way over on the other side of the room, I see you smile, Ma," Pa said as he returned.

"All the flowers," she said. "Even from First National Bank. Remember when Buko made such a commotion, sneaking in their front door and climbing up the stairs to their roof?"

"All that barking!" Pa recalled the boxer that was Mark's devoted shadow.

"He was a good pal, though," Icky joined them. "We miss him."

"Taste-tested every cookie recipe you baked, the dog did," Pa agreed.

"Unless Mark grabbed it first," Millie reminded him. "That was only fair, though. Mark also took a bite out of Buko's biscuits before he handed them over to the dog."

"Look who's here!" Icky welcomed John and Bertie Heinz with their son, also called John. "Here's our bakery's future: cookie eaters and midget football players of tomorrow!"

"Congratulations on the expansion!" John said.

"Thanks," Icky responded. "How's business?"

"Keeps on growing, right alongside you," John said.

"Just like this little guy," Bertie nodded toward their boy.

"That's how we like it," Icky said.

"Can we offer you some cookies?" he said as one of the employees came over with a tray of samples. After the Heinz family was served, Pa chose one molasses cookie—and then changed his mind and selected a second: "Old Dutch, like me!"

Ma chose spice bites. It was one of her favorites, and she always liked to compare the bakery's cookies against her own.

"The people want you to succeed, I think," Pa noted.

"How's that?" Icky asked.

"*Was lange währt, wird endlich gut,*" Pa answered.

"Which means?" Icky pressed.

"What goes on for a long time eventually ends good," Pa instructed. "You work on this bakery for ten years, and today you arrive with cookies in both of your hands—which is good!"

"I didn't do it alone," Icky acknowledged.

"*Ja,* we see the Good Lord with you all the way," Pa agreed.

"I'll have a sugar cookie," Icky thanked the employee who was serving cookies. "It's still my favorite."

"Did you ever try heating them in the toaster?" asked a neighbor who saw the grand opening invitation in the newspaper and moseyed over to tour the new bakery. "My daughter Michele really likes them that way for breakfast."

Icky's shoulders straightened as he inclined his head with interest.

"Tell me more about that!" he smiled as he guided her toward the samples.

THE END

Author's Note

THIS STORY IS BASED on the early career of Edward A. ("Icky") Haut, who apprenticed as a bread baker, and later, with his wife, Millie, founded Haut's Cookie Shoppe, a home-based bakery in Olean, New York. In the 1950s, the business was trademarked *Icky's Cookies*, and expanded to serve grocery chains throughout the northeast quadrant of the U.S. While pseudonyms were used where it seemed prudent, and liberties were taken with regard to conversations and the actual timing of events, the narrative nonetheless represents the family's resilience and hope-filled spirit born out of their trust in God who always is with us in our struggles.

www.ingramcontent.com/pod-product-compliance
Lightning Source LLC
Chambersburg PA
CBHW062006220426
43662CB00010B/1243